D0975178

CALL SIGN: LIGHTNING

Inside the Rowdy World and Risky Missions of the Marines' Elite ANGLICOs

SCOTT MESSMORE

STACKPOLE
BOOKS
Guilford, CT

Published by Stackpole Books
An imprint of Globe Pequot

Distributed by NATIONAL BOOK NETWORK
800-462-6420

British Library Cataloguing in Publication Information available

Library of Congress Cataloging-in-Publication Data Available

ISBN 978-0-8117-1585-0 (hardcover)
ISBN 978-0-8117-6374-5 (e-book)

∞™ The paper used in this publication meets the minimum requirements of American National Standard for Information Sciences—Permanence of Paper for Printed Library Materials, ANSI/ NISO Z39.48-1992.

Printed in the United States of America

For Jeffrey Eugene Messmore,
a big brother lost too soon

For years I tried.

Countless times I wasted my breath explaining my Marine Corps service.

"I was Marine ANGLICO. It's a small Special Ops unit I jumped with," I'd say.

"Special Ops! You were in Special Forces?" they'd ask breathlessly.

"No. That's the Army's Green Berets. Did I say SF?" I'd counter. "Plus we were all paratroopers."

"Airborne? Were you Recon?"

"NO! Did I say Recon? I said ANG-LI-CO," I'd reply in vain. "Like Ang Lee, the movie director!"

"He made a movie about you guys?"

"NO! Oh, forget it. Just tell your friends I drove a truck," I'd say in conclusion.

It never worked.

Sixty years and America doesn't know us. Until now.

Contents

INTRODUCTION

WHEN A LIEUTENANT COMMANDER IN THE U.S. NAVY OFFICE OF PUBlic Information has never heard of your Marine Corps unit, it's time to start writing.

Twelve years in uniform and no one knows what the hell I did. U.S. Marine ANGLICO is an acronym that stands for Air/Naval Gunfire Liaison Company. Our stated mission from the Pentagon is to provide naval gunfire from U.S. Navy destroyers and battleships or close air support (CAS) attacks from fighter-bombers for the U.S. Army or friendly foreign troops. A large part of an ANGLICO's service isn't even with the Marines at all.

The American public has never heard of a Marine Air/Naval Gunfire Liaison Company. With naval gunfire origins dating to the Korean War, ANGLICO units have fought in nearly every war, conflict, police action, or "other" for the last half century. With the continuing fight against global terrorism, "Anglicans" will be fighting for a long time.

Even with the expansion of American Special Operations capabilities after September 11th, there are only five ANGLICO units worldwide with probably fewer than twenty-five hundred Marines and sailors. Over the years, I've even met quite a few Marines who weren't positive of the ANGLICO mission themselves, to say nothing, for example, of the U.S. Army infantry units who, busy preparing for field operations, usually weren't told by higher commands we were going with them until the last minute. Most weren't happy and didn't know why we were there or who we were.

"ANGLICO? Why are you here? Is that your name?" asked a very confused and impatient U.S. Army first sergeant.

"No, First Sergeant. I'm not Italian, it's my job title," I answered.

Every time I was attached to the Army, I went through this little exercise. Frustrated, I sat down one day after returning from another peacetime exercise and figured out how to get the Army to understand what ANGLICO could do for them.

A few years before the UPS "What can Brown do for you?" campaign, I decided to create a sales pitch. I'm not a sales kind of guy. In my bar, a pint of beer costs three dollars. Either you want it or not, and if you argue, you'll just get kicked out as I call the cops. However, this was different. It was public service and needed to be solved. Master salesman Zig Ziglar advocated speaking to different groups in their own language. I always resisted this as I thought of it as catering to others' conceit and laziness, but I was still doing all the talking and not getting through to the soldiers we were there to help.

I was always amazed to learn the Army had simply no idea what their country's naval ships could do. I don't drive tanks for a living, but I know it's huge, loud, and has a giant cannon that can blow apart small buildings with one shot from 3 kilometers away. Marines call that being a professional: If you might encounter a weapon on the battlefield, then learn its capabilities. Marine corporals and sergeants routinely quiz their teams on aircraft types, weapons capabilities, or combat first aid. It's called "hip-pocket" training and it's done while you wait around for trucks or helicopters to arrive.

I wrote down a quick summary of naval gunfire: A 5-inch shell fired from a destroyer can fly 17,500 meters and creates a blast pattern (crater) roughly 50 meters wide and 150 meters long. That's more or less the size of a football field.

Furthermore, they were a bit lost on the lethality of a 5-inch round. I converted 5 inches to millimeters and it equates to around 127 millimeters, which is much larger than the Army's 105mm cannons. But Wait! There's More! Since destroyers had automatic loaders, they could fire twenty rounds per minute until the ammunition ran out. Now I had them, and you could see it in their face.

"Each round might take out a football field, it's bigger than our own 105s, and five minutes of firing brings in a hundred rounds? Glad to have you ANGLICO! Or whatever the hell your name is!"

Mission accomplished.

While this little anecdote is funny—and true by the way—naval gunfire is brutal. When I was in Naval Gunfire School in Coronado, California, an incoming round skipped off the ground and detonated 400 meters from our position. We were shooting at a target 2,300 meters away and 400 meters lower in elevation. Since ships obviously fire at sea level, the trajectory is like a Peyton Manning pass: flat as a laser beam and haulin' ass. I tell my friends this and they're astounded. The target area was so flat the round ricocheted 1.5 miles and detonated almost 400 meters up the mountainside we were stationed upon.

Marine ANGLICO's abilities with naval gunfire are in addition to CAS missions that guide jet attack aircraft or Cobra helicopter gunships for strikes near friendly troops, and artillery missions from regular Army or Marine batteries. To date, ANGLICO is the only unit in the Department of Defense that combines all three. This book focuses on Marine ANGLICO's unique role within the Department of Defense.

If you take an Army artillery forward observer, an Air Force forward air controller (FAC), a Navy gunfire spotter, a field radio operator, mix them all together, pin gold jump wings on his chest and lace up his jungle boots, well, that's an ANGLICO Marine.

While I was with 4th ANGLICO, I served with communications and the line platoons for twelve years. I attended:

Platoon Honor Man, Recruit Training, Parris Island, South Carolina

Airborne School, Fort Benning, Georgia

Scout/Forward Observer School, Fort Sill, Oklahoma

Naval Gunfire School, Coronado, California

Long-Range Maritime Navigation School, Coronado, California

Mountain Warfare School, Pickel Meadows, California

Air-Load Planners Course, West Palm Beach, Florida

Embarkation/Logistics School, Little Creek, Virginia

I trained at the Joint Readiness Training Center (JRTC) with the Army three times and deployed to Norway twice on Operation Battle Griffin '96 and '99. I'm very proud to have slept on the ground nearly 150 miles inside the Arctic Circle. I also spent countless weekend exercises locally, within Florida, or jumping into Camp Lejeune to call in air strikes or fire artillery missions during live-fire training. Plenty of times, in one weekend we would fly to Fort Benning, Georgia, jump in, train in land navigation, throw live hand grenades, stay up half the night on simulated communications exercises, run CAS missions, and then suit up for another jump back into Florida. It was hard and busy, but fun and productive.

Despite my lifelong experiences with selling ANGLICO, I was surprised when present 4th ANGLICO inspector/instructor Lt. Col. Andrew Kelley told me when I first met him that as a young officer his commanding officer had warned him not to join ANGLICO if he was serious about an artillery career in the Marine Corps. A tall artillery officer sporting nearly five rows of ribbons after eighteen years in the Corps, including his most recent fifteen months in Afghanistan, Kelley told me that as a young second lieutenant he had wanted to join the infantry and "run through the jungle with his M-16." However, the Marine Corps decided his skills would better serve the artillery community, so that was that.

"I was at graduate school at the University of Wisconsin, and when I finally came to the Marine Corps, I didn't know anything about it. I just wanted to do something different, get out of Wisconsin and serve my country for a little while," he said. After hours during his initial basic training as a Marine officer, Kelley would prepare for the next training day and listen to prior-enlisted lieutenants talk about the different job assignments throughout the Corps. Most Americans have heard of Recon and the red-coated musicians of the President's Own band that plays at the White House, and quite a few have seen the Silent Drill Team. But ANGLICO? Kelley was in the same position. As artillery is fully one-third of the combat mission support that ANGLICO provides to the Army and foreign units, Kelley would be a prime candidate. Marine officers that had been prior enlisted did not share his CO's opinion, and they encouraged him to take his newfound artillery skills to ANGLICO after he finished his first tour. Being the first member of his family to join the Marines, Kelley didn't know much of the internal culture of the Corps, but like most new lieutenants, he knew a rockin' good time when he heard one.

"I remember then, when guys were telling me about some of the cool things that were out there. One of the first things they explained was ANGLICO," he remembered eighteen years later. "'Oh, you should go to ANGLICO,'" they said. As it turned out it wasn't that easy."

In late 1997 young Second Lieutenant Kelley reported for artillery duty with the 10th Marine Regiment at Camp Lejeune, North Carolina, and lo and behold, 2nd ANGLICO was right down the street. Kelley noticed the independent streak of your typical ANGLICO Marine, a trait that kept me in West Palm Beach for twelve straight years.

"They always had a little bit of swagger, attitude, and different appearance that appealed to a motivated young lieutenant. So it was something I wanted to do early on," Kelley said.

After two to three years as a battery officer, the equivalent of a platoon leader in the infantry, Kelley was looking for another assignment. Consulting with senior officers in the 10th Marines, including his own battalion commander, Kelley faced a unified and harsh response. Do what you want, young lieutenant, but playing with the ANGLICO "cowboys" will come with a price.

"I was very clearly told if you go to ANGLICO right now, you're going to be blackballed from the artillery community. You're not going to be welcomed back," Kelley starkly remembered. "If that's what you want to do, if you want to be 'high speed,' do cool stuff, get it out of your system and move on with the rest of your life, but if you want to stay in the Marine Corps, don't go there."

When I heard Lieutenant Colonel Kelley's remarks, it was the first time I had heard such organized opposition to what we did, and did so well. Blackballed? Really? I haven't used that word since my fraternity days at the University of Florida. Where were all of these blackballing officers when 4th ANGLICO was detailed on a foreign operation such as Norway's Battle Griffin? We'd end up 150 miles inside the Arctic Circle and I needed to turn an admin clerk into a radio operator or give a newly joined aviator a crash course on artillery call for fire (CFF). What help were all the doubters, complainers, and whiners then?

"The perception was there that junior officers went there [ANGLICO] and were 'ruined' because they became the proverbial cowboys and independent, that wasn't really in line with the rest of the Marine Corps," Kelley continued. "It was very similar to a lot of infantry guys that would go to Recon or Force Recon and never come back on a normal career path with their peers."

In other words you can be high speed and low drag with ANGLICO, Recon, Force Recon, or maybe Radio Battalion, but as an officer, you won't become a general one day if that's your goal.

I have to admit, there is one very valid reason a large portion of the U.S. Marine Corps doesn't like ANGLICO: Sometimes we just didn't follow the rules. Every once in a while, we flat out broke Marine Corps regulations or verged on breaking the law. Other Marines saw us as unprofessional cowboys who only jumped out of planes and swaggered around with our gold jump wings, laced our jungle boots with 550 cords, and couldn't perform proper fire planning. We dressed differently, and we talked differently. Basically we weren't normal Marines. I fit in perfectly. My twelve years in ANGLICO remains the longest crazy, fun, scary love affair of my life.

When the Pentagon sends the U.S. Army to Fort Polk, Louisiana, for training and asks for naval gunfire from Headquarters Marine Corps, HQMC sends us. But Congress only allows enough funding for us to arrive for the battle two days before it starts. So your boots hit the ground with four thousand Army soldiers and forty Marines and Navy corpsmen, soon to be split into four-man teams. In other words: All of the planning we've done for the last year just went out the window. So, we'd just wing it and enjoyed every damn minute of it. Marine ANGLICO are nothing but a bunch of cowboys? Well saddle up buddy boy, because otherwise you ain't gonna make it.

If we wanted to leave Fort Polk and go to a local burger joint, we did. If an off-base surplus store had better prices than the Army's PX, sayonara boys! If we didn't like the barracks the Army assigned us, we left and found another one that suited our needs. And we always cleaned our newly chosen barracks better than the Army did. Always. It pissed off a lot, and I mean a *lot*, of other Marines, but we didn't care about that either. Which of course only pissed them off more.

Don't think I'm lying or exaggerating. The first time I was in Norway in 1996, after the operation was completed, we were stuck with around six hundred other Marines, our tents all set up in a wood line. My platoon commander, a major, thought it sucked and that was the end of that.

"Everyone pack your shit up. We're not staying here packed together with people we don't know," he said. "The regimental commander will be calling for me every twenty minutes and he doesn't even know me."

We all knew that as "outsiders" with any unit, they would force every crappy work detail on us while they stayed warm in their tents. The major and the platoon sergeant left to find new digs and we packed up. Just like that. We were always ready to go in ten minutes anyway, so it wasn't a big deal. We didn't tell anyone and we certainly didn't ask for permission, 'cause we all knew the answer to that question. Major Attitude and Gunny Let's Haul Ass (both of whom shall remain nameless obviously) went off for a drive and found a perfect location: an indoor soccer training facility in the tiny speck of a Norwegian village of Bjerkvik, across the fjord from Narvik. The village is pronounced "B-yeark-vik," but most of us naturally called it "Jerk-vik." We moved in to an empty hall well equipped with gym-sized showers, sauna, and a sound system we quickly jury-rigged to play our 1990s-era radios and Walkmans. At the end of the dirt road, there was a little gas station that sold whole loaves of bread that we would cut up with our K-bars and smear with this weird cheese-in-a-tube with tiny shrimp mixed into it. At first we thought it was gross, but being Marines we learned to love our new Norwegian tube cheese just as much as we loved the locals. It was ANGLICO paradise: on our own, doing our thing, eating whole bread with shrimpy cheese after an operation done well. Plus my new Norge girlfriend was driving me around in her mom's Mercedes.

We instantly fell in with the Bjerkvik locals, and they adopted their new American jarhead cousins with equal vigor and friendship. Mark my words: If any American ever meets a Norwegian citizen anywhere on planet Earth, make them your friend. Ask them if they're OK. Make sure they're not lost or in a bad neighborhood. Get them drunk on crappy beer. Hell, just take them home to Mom and Dad for a home-cooked meal and let them sleep in the basement. Why? Because that's how every Norwegian treats every U.S. Marine and Navy corpsman who travels to their homeland to help defend against the Russians.

Here's a perfect example. After Battle Griffin '96 was complete, we were waiting for a flight home. Of course, being ANGLICO our C-141 kept breaking down and Operations simply forgot to place us on another aircraft. Remember that "we're very small and no one knows what the hell we do" mantra I keep harping on? Well, it's alive and well my friend. The Marine Corps doesn't like to be late. Ever. Careers are ruined over such things in the Big Green Rifle Club. You're always late? Since you can't be counted on in peacetime, then you'll be worthless when the steel starts to fly. In a world where you get your ass chewed for not showing up "fifteen minutes prior" to everything, 4th ANGLICO was *days* late going home. It just wasn't our fault.

"How in the world have we managed to get marooned in an industrialized, NATO country?" I asked my buddies, after taking a big bite of tube cheese and dark bread.

We were actually stranded. Back in West Palm Beach, Florida, the Inspector & Instructor staff was calling all of the families every day to keep them informed about when we would come home. To this day, it gives me a good feeling that they showed so much care for the families of their deployed Marines. But, since we weren't going anywhere, it was time to buy presents for family and hit the bars with the locals. Since Bjerkvik is tiny we would end up at a Norge's house drinking the best lager and pilsner I've ever tasted, plus the local moonshine, which no doubt could be used in the gas tank of a jet fighter in an emergency. Crazy as it sounds, to this day, I've had more Norwegian hooch than American 'shine and half of my family is from Kentucky!

Marine ANGLICO has been serving the American public for more than half a century. This is what we do.

CHAPTER ONE

ANGLICO, Huh? Well That Explains It

FOR THE FIRST TIME AS A MARINE, I STARTED TO WONDER IF I WOULD make it.

That doesn't mean making the cut, making the grade, making you happy, or making out with that blonde chick at the bar last night. That means making it out alive in '95.

And I wondered if I would.

It's 32 degrees, 3:00 A.M., and I'm soaking wet. Lying on the ground wrapped in Gore-Tex and a plastic poncho, Captain Byrd and Sgt. William "Gonzo" Gonzalez are taking turns hugging me for warmth as my body goes into spasms. In northern Louisiana the 101st Airborne Division scout team we were supporting had chosen to cross any water obstacles less than chest high, in the month of January. On one of those crossings, I lost my balance and went down in freezing water.

Scouts in any military never carry much, but Marine ANGLICO teams have backpacks the size of a Volkswagen. ANGLICO backpacks are heavy, routinely weighing anywhere from 55 to 70 pounds, and you have to keep up with infantry, paratroopers, Rangers, or foreign troops running around like little kids. We were always loaded to the gills. We always carried the normal combat gear, food and water, plus radios, classified code books, antennas, comm wire, and at least a two-day supply of batteries. The high-frequency (HF) radio in my backpack weighed 25 pounds alone; its two nickel cadmium batteries are *not* the AAA batteries you snap into your television remote control. Picture the fancy new watch your mom and dad bought you for graduation: the box is about 3 by 4 inches and almost 3 inches thick. That's one battery—and if it gets wet, it catches fire and might blow up. In ANGLICO you're loaded with these green monsters. To this day my friends ask why we couldn't just use a cellular phone. We'll discuss this in detail in a later chapter, but here's why: Your cell phone is a glorified retransmission set. That means your voice is sent to the nearest tower and retransmitted between towers across America. You're not talking directly to Aunt Betty in Kentucky; your voice signal is skipping from tower to tower to her living room 1,000 miles away. The HF set I had in my pack performed that in one machine, which is why it weighed so damn much.

When we boarded for parachute jumps, four Marines were always stationed on the rear ramp of a C-130 Hercules or Air Force C-141 Starlifter to haul our butts onto the bird. Think of it: young Marine paratroopers in great shape and they're carrying so much combat gear that they can't step up 18 inches on their own. A skinny eighteen-year-old could easily weigh 300 pounds on a typical jump operation.

For the third time I had volunteered to train in two-week simulated battles run by the U.S. Army's Joint Readiness Training Center in Fort Polk, Louisiana. JRTC, as it's called, is the infantry version of the famous tank fights in the American southwestern deserts. It's basically a giant game of laser tag with electronic sensors on each piece of gear in the fight. Troops wore them, tanks had them, helicopters, jet fighters, C-130 transports—you name it. If you could shoot it, you could damage or kill it.

Nearly every year during the 1990s, 4th ANGLICO sent forty to fifty Marines to JRTC to call in naval gunfire missions from a simulated U.S. Navy destroyer. Obviously, a destroyer wasn't deployed in the woods of northern Louisiana, so 4th ANGLICO officers and enlisted Marines mimicked a ship's fire-direction center. While 4th ANGLICO Marines volunteered to go to JRTC for the simulated combat and become better public servants, we hated it.

Since we were reservists, Congress wouldn't allow enough funds for us to arrive a few days before the "war" started, which meant we were behind the planning cycle before we stepped off the airport buses. As a team chief, I warned my Marines who had never been to JRTC to be ready to step off the bus, grab ammunition and MREs, and move out straight into the field.

Since JRTC is a "force-on-force" free-for-all, it closely simulated the chaotic, ever-changing, what-the-hell-happens-next atmosphere of a real fight. For example, visiting infantry battalions never assigned enough guards on their supply trucks. As we've seen in Iraq, the first thing the bad guys do is blow up the logistics train. Every time I trained at JRTC, I ate one MRE per day for two weeks. That's what JRTC is: fourteen meals equals fourteen days. Keep movin', Marine.

It toughened us, but it was another reason we hated JRTC. Within 4th ANGLICO we had an expression: "Remember—JRTC is a four-letter word!" We were always playing catch-up. The Army units had never heard of us until we showed up and didn't know what the hell to do with us. Time after time I had this conversation:

"Well, who are you?" a grumpy Army company commander or first sergeant would ask.

"We're Marine ANGLICO. Regiment sent us here to call in naval gunfire for you," I'd respond.

"What! I wasn't told about this," he would say in a very irritated manner. "What did you say your name was? ANGLICO?"

"NO! It's not my name, it's my job. No! I'm not in the Navy! Look at my haircut!"

I would then explain the entire Department of Defense mission statement of U.S. Marine Corps ANGLICO "to provide naval gunfire support and close air support missions for the U.S. Army, NATO, and friendly foreign units." That's the idea. It's not the reality. When things heat up, ANGLICO ends up doing it all: artillery; naval gunfire from U.S. Navy destroyers or battleships; mortar missions; and air strikes from jet fighters, helicopter gunships, and even AC-130 Spectre gunships firing 105mm cannons and thousands of machine-gun rounds per minute. Anything less than a B-52 or B-1 bomber, we do it.

Every time I was attached to the Army, I went through this little exercise. Whether we're supporting the U.S. Army or a foreign military unit, ANGLICO Marines learn one thing very fast: You're on your own. This isn't to say that we're not given what we need, be it food, water, or transport. Soldiers and foreign troops just aren't used to having Marines around, so they never plan for it.

Say you've been a platoon sergeant in the 101st Airborne for two years—you lead and care for around thirty soldiers. Counting yourself and your platoon leader, your "magic number" for plans is thirty-two. Gas masks? We need thirty-two. Sleeping bags? Thirty-two again. MREs? Thirty-two multiplied by three per day multiplied by how long you'll be in the field. Add four ANGLICO Marines at the last minute, and it screws up everything.

We learned fast. If you need something, you'll have to ask each time. Or steal it (more on that later).

ANGLICO is a strange, hybrid bird unknown to most of the U.S. military, much less the American public. In West Palm Beach, Florida, we had officers from the artillery, infantry, and naval aviation fields. We had a U.S. Navy lieutenant commander as the in-house naval gunfire expert plus a dozen Navy corpsmen to fix us when we invariably got hurt. In 4th ANGLICO the bulk of Marines in "the teams" were college kids led by local country boys who played in the Everglades, street-tough black guys from Miami, former Recon Marines, and even one refugee from the Army's Green Berets. We had Vietnam veterans with Purple Hearts; guys who saw combat in Beirut, Grenada, Panama, or the Gulf War; one Canadian and an Irishman; and we were all paratroopers. Since 4th ANGLICO is a Reserve unit, we had more cops, firefighters, and paramedics than a small town in Indiana.

We also looked and talked differently than normal Marines. Since we all went to Airborne School, we carried our K-bar combat knives in hard plastic sheaths that were slung low like a six-gun in the Old West. We wore jungle cammies even in colder months because they dry faster and replaced the shoelaces in our jungle boots with parachute cord. Now widely known, 550 cord is always handy for survival, but it just looked so damn cool in our boots. Hardly any of us used the new-style combat vests, because we jumped out of planes so often and the vests couldn't be worn under the heavy 68-pound parachute rig. We spoke a mixed language of Marine Corps ("Grab your deuce gear and let's go!"), supporting fires ("The bubbas want to know the Time on Target for that SEAD mission!"), high-speed radio communications ("I need more slash wire for the HF net to run arty!"), and even started calling our backpacks "rucks" (short for "rucksack" in German), because the Army had served so long in Germany.

One time when I was with 2nd Platoon, we spent fourteen twelve-hour days in a row training at Camp Lejeune, North Carolina. It was an ANGLICO paradise. We called in air strikes with F-18 Hornets, artillery fired 155mm shells in CFF missions, and Cobra helicopter gunships launched rockets at old tank hulks. Our Navy corpsman, Doc Tesnar, had taught us first aid so well, we were sticking each other's arms with saline intravenous injections (IV).

After two weeks we got liberty and hit the local bars. Someone loaned us an old Ford F-150, a Marine volunteered to be the designated driver, and the rest of us piled in the flatbed. To make a long story short regarding what I call "The Great Chigger Massacre of 1998," we had spent a lot of days in the field. In August in the Carolinas, that means chiggers, tiny insects that leave deep, red welts that itch worse than any poison ivy. If you've never had them, you simply don't know what miserable means. A couple of Marines had streaks of red welts all over their abdomens and legs. Riding back to Camp Lejeune through the coastal islands at night, it was beautiful even in our beer-addled state. The chiggers were acting up, and someone insisted that saltwater eases the pain and itching. I thought it was crap. Are we going to drown them? Blind their beady little insect eyeballs with saltwater? But a few guys were ready to try anything. Before you can say "boo," we screeched to a halt and ten Marines took off for the sand dunes without any pants on.

As my buddies were in the surf scrubbing their bodies with saltwater to stop the itching, I stayed with the pickup truck. I was exhausted and had my fill of local beer, but I wasn't the driver, so I stretched out in the truck bed. I was out like a light. Instantly, I was dreaming of distant tropical shores and gentle breezes with Courtney and Jennifer playfully tapping my shoulder.

"Scotty, would you like another beer, sweetie?"

"No that's okay. Just put it on the table next to the bacon and Hostess cupcakes."

Well, it wasn't Courtney and Jennifer.

It was a cop—a good cop on routine patrol through a sleepy Carolina coastal trailer park who came across a lone jarhead spread-eagled in the back of a pickup. I was flat on my back with my right foot up behind the driver's seat window and my left foot dangling out of the truck bed. I must have looked like I was dead.

Remember when you were a kid and your parents woke you up at 4:00 A.M. to hop in the car for a big vacation? You can't see straight, your eyes are bloodshot and watering, and basically you don't know what the hell is going on. That was me. Thankfully the cop was a Marine too. He had done his four years, got out, joined "the force," and even signed on with a local Marine Reserve unit. So he knew how hard real training was and why I was out of it. All the while, I'm peeping over his shoulder terrified that ten of my buddies will come crashing through the sand dunes sans pants. Scotty's not praying, he's *prayin'*.

Please, please, please, please, *please*—someone have some damn sense!

"Are you by yourself? Have you been drinking?" Officer Butkus asks me.

"Yeah, but my buddies and the designated driver are running around in the surf right now," I stammer out.

"Why are they in the water at zero two-fifteen?"

So here I am. All by myself with a good cop explaining two weeks of dawn-to-dusk Marine training, where I'd been that night, parachute jumps, F-18s dropping bombs, artillery firing their cannons, and why my half-naked friends aren't here to help me out.

"Chiggers? Saltwater won't do anything! You know that, you're a sergeant! Who was practicing with an IV on you? When did . . . are you . . . just what unit are you with anyway?" the incredulous officer asked.

"4th ANGLICO. We're up here from West Palm Beach to blow stuff up," I said in my first real moment of clarity.

He pauses for a second.

"ANGLICO, huh? Well that explains it," he said with the tone of a tired parent.

And just like that, it was okay. My fully-clothed, half-soaked buddies returned and verified my story, our stone-cold sober corporal pulled out the truck keys, and all was well. To this day, he's one of the better cops I've dealt with. Luckily, I was dealing with one of the few people in the American military who knew what I did and how weird my job could get.

Here's what happened in 1995. A battalion of the Army's 101st Airborne Division deployed to Fort Polk for their two-week fight, and 4th ANGLICO was there to call in naval gunfire (NGF). My good buddy and former Recon Marine, Gonzo, and I were assigned to a Firepower Control Team (FCT) that would back up the battalion's scouts. On paper an FCT (a "FICT" in ANGLICO slang—yes we had our own language; more on that later) was led by a captain with a sergeant as team chief. Four enlisted Marines who were either 0861 2531scout/forward observers or field radio operators rounded out the team. FCT teams were the Marines on the ground with "eyes on" the target about to be destroyed. As I liked to describe us: small teams with big radios.

Gonzo and I were thrilled. We'd be on our own in front of friendly lines with the scouts. No "suits" to nag us, just running through the bush to locate, fix, and destroy the enemies of American democracy. We felt the scouts would be just like us: a bunch of camouflaged cowboys who jumped out of planes, blew stuff up, drank beer, chased chicks, and always found a way to get in trouble. There was only one problem. They didn't want us. At all.

It was the same old song and dance. The 101st scouts didn't know we were coming. They didn't know what we did ("No! I'm not Italian, it's my job!"). And they wanted us to go away. In less than forty-eight hours, my team was going to exit friendly lines with this crowd on a 12-kilometer night movement to our observation post (OP). After the usual call to Regiment to confirm our story ("The jarheads *are* going with you. Don't call me again!" Click!), the scouts stood firm in one regard: Six extra Marines was too many. So, myself, Gonzo, and our boss, Captain Byrd, would spend the next two weeks carrying the gear and doing the jobs of six Marines. It sucked and we hadn't even started.

During the 1990s I trained with a lot of U.S. Army soldiers. Some were great; some were terrible. One group I never cared for were soldiers who passed Ranger School in Fort Benning, Georgia, but had never been in the Ranger Regiment. That distinction is important. The Rangers are a tough, agile, wild bunch that doesn't really give a shit what the rest of the U.S. Army does or thinks. The Marines of 2nd ANGLICO have trained with Rangers countless times. Those troops are great. Some of the Ranger School–only soldiers, who earned their "Ranger tabs" only (patches worn on the left shoulder of their uniforms), were so hell bent on proving their toughness, they had no common sense or field wisdom. As the old saying goes, a little knowledge is a dangerous thing.

Which brings us to the subject of water crossings during winter. As a young Marine, I was taught that if you have to get wet, then that's the way it goes. However, if you can avoid it, stay dry as long as possible unless it jeopardizes the mission. The mission comes first in the Marine Corps. Always. But a split second later comes the welfare of the troops. A few of the scout leaders had Ranger tabs and were out to prove it. Gonzo and I didn't like what we heard at all.

"They've been here for two weeks and this is the best plan they have?" Gonzo asked me. "Chest high water? It's 34 degrees here at the airport. It'll be below freezing when we get in the bush for sure."

Gonzo was right. We were about to load onto a CH-47 Chinook that would insert us 4 kilometers from the front lines and then we would move on foot 10 to 12 kilometers to the OP. The "no later than" time to be in position was 0600. We wouldn't make it. Gonzo was an old Recon hand with extensive field time in hot climates, including the first Gulf War where he tracked Iraqi movements along the border before we kicked the crap out of them in '91. He specifically came to JRTC to practice his cold-weather skills, but jumping into 32-degree water wasn't part of his plan. We were pissed, but overruled.

Water crossings are always considered a danger zone for troops. By default almost every creek, stream, river, or waterway is an open area, which means the bad guys can see you and deploy heavy machine guns to blow you away. Infantry companies train, train, and train again for proper river crossings. Who goes across first? Where do you emplace your machine guns? Where will the command element be? You're on full alert and either swift-moving or deep water is slowing you down. Slowly and silently, we moved toward the front line walking through two streams before we came upon a small stream around 18 inches deep. It was pitch black, my ruck weighed a ton, and, for the first time in my military career, I just slipped and fell down like a two-year-old at Grandma's house.

It was a huge crash. I'm embarrassed, as I might have just revealed our position to the bad guys, but mainly I was stunned from the freezing water. This was bad. Very bad. After moving another 500 meters, it got worse. We halted into a hasty OP to see if we were being followed, and I started to get hypothermic. If we started moving again, I'd be fine. Gonzo and Captain Byrd helped me get my Gore-Tex pants from my backpack to put on and trap the heat leaving my body.

Here's what's nearly impossible for people to understand. Even during peacetime exercises, ANGLICO Marines carried so much heavy comm gear, we packed the bare minimum. For me that meant if I couldn't shoot it, eat it, drink it (H_2O only), or speak into it (radio), with the exceptions of code books and first aid gear, I didn't take it. For JRTC '95 that meant I didn't have dry clothes to change into. We never did. Also, unless you're in the snow, the truly miraculous fabric Gore-Tex was too hot, and *then* you're a heat casualty.

But there I was: 4 kilometers in front of friendly lines with only two other Marines. Your 60-pound backpack has enough radios and classified gizmos to put you in Fort Leavenworth for eighty-five years if you lose it. Your combat gear weighs another 30 pounds, you can't feel anything below your waist, your upper body is in spasms, and the Army still doesn't know what to do with you. But it's time to move out.

It's crazy. It's hard. It's 32 degrees and three hours til dawn.

ANGLICO, huh? Well that explains it.

Chapter Two

My Time in the Sun

My interest in the U.S. Marine Corps goes so far back I can't even remember when I first decided to join. Many Marines mention late-night John Wayne movies, an epiphany on the Fourth of July, or the March 1945 raising of Old Glory at the peak of Mount Suribachi. Not me. For me it was as old as happy memories from Christmas, St. Patrick's Day parades in small towns from Indiana to Florida, or the annual June family reunion in Kentucky. It was just always there. Since I'd buy a World War II Corsair over some stupid corporate jet if I won the lottery, it probably has something to do with watching *Baa Baa Black Sheep* on TV when I was in middle school. I could see how Americans looked at Marines and what they expected of their behavior even after leaving uniform. To this day I hear it all the time—"You're a Marine!"—regarding actions they don't like, or some positive move I've made to help someone out. I think more than anything I saw the Marine Corps as a group of men and women who were the ones to step up and step in when others weren't up to the task. Firefighters have the same attitude—when there's a fire, or a firefight, they just run to the scene of the trouble and pitch in to solve the problem, consequences be damned. I wanted to be in that line of Marines stretching back across time to 1775 and the foundation of the Republic.

In the spirit of full disclosure, I should also confess that I joined the Marine Reserve in 1987 to take a break from my spectacularly average academic career at my beloved University of Florida. Simply put: I'm a lousy academic. Always have been, always will. I had spent four years in

Navy and Marine ROTC driving my instructors to anger with my crazy attitudes about higher education. But I finished my military studies courses, attended and graduated Officer Candidate School (OCS) in Quantico, Virginia, and, typically me, I had completed all of my political science courses first instead of general requirements such as Geology 101, nicknamed "Rocks for Jocks."

A typical exchange between myself and the marine officer instructor (MOI) concerned my back-against-the-wall refusal to sign up for Economics. A Navy/Marine ROTC MOI is sort of the commandant of midshipmen responsible for military strategy, how you behave as an officer, and even details such as close order drill and physical fitness. However, he was also the unquestioned leader of each student who chose to join the Marine Corps and not the Navy. In other words, he talked and we listened. I listened; I just didn't do what he wanted me to regarding academics, and it pissed off almost everyone.

After four years of this, I was ready for a break and so were my ROTC bosses, terrific officers that they all were. I resigned from ROTC and instantly enlisted with a Gainesville, Florida, recruiter. I figured I would get some field experience, join the West Palm Beach Marine Reserve unit to go to Jump School, and then reapply for a commission as a lieutenant after a couple of years. But something unforeseen happened: I fell in love with the crazy jarheads of 4th ANGLICO.

On August 25, 1987, I reported to boot camp at Parris Island, South Carolina, near the Hilton Head resort area. Since I'd been to college, I was older than the other recruits, most of whom were straight out of high school. I didn't have too many surprises in boot camp as I'd known so many Marines before arriving, and my ROTC classes had given me some preparation. I worked my ass off on Parris Island and was rewarded with my senior drill instructor, Staff Sergeant Snyder, making me the Honor Man for Platoon 2090. We graduated November 19, 1987, and my mom and dad watched as a two-star general shook my hand as I stood at attention in my brand new dress blues. I was off to a roaring start, but little did I know I would end up being one of the dreaded "hard rank" Marines who hardly ever get promoted, even though I outworked almost all of my peers. My own definition of being good was to be in the top

5 percent of everything we did. That meant shooting expert on the rifle range, a first-class score on the annual physical fitness test (PFT), having junior Marines come to you for advice and counsel, and most important of all: When the line platoons were gearing up for a field operation, if I volunteered, they always took me with them. And I mean always. Not one time in twelve years did a platoon commander or platoon sergeant turn me away from an operation.

For me the choice to join 4th ANGLICO was very simple. After going to Parris Island for boot camp, I was sent to the Jacksonville Marine Reserve unit. However, I knew all along I wasn't going to stay. As I checked into the amphibious tractor unit in Jacksonville, the administration chief asked me about my plans, and I said I was going to 4th ANGLICO. He didn't care a whit. In fact, he was happy that he wouldn't have to file a travel claim for me, which every veteran knows to be one of the worst paperwork snafus in the U.S. military. It was complicated, it made no sense, and if you didn't do exactly as someone told you to do, it always came out wrong and you never got your travel pay. It was a great system. I don't think I was there an hour before I left never to look back. I drove home to Delray Beach, Florida, to stay with Mom for a while and hang out with my brother Peter, who had a new apartment in Fort Lauderdale. I graduated Parris Island and was on leave for a couple weeks before I reported to Little Creek, Virginia, for Embarkation and Logistics School. While at my brother's apartment, I called 4th ANGLICO, told the admin chief who I was, and asked when I should come and check in to formally join the unit. He told me I was still under orders to go to my first formal school, and I would be with the 4th as soon as I got back in late December 1987, the start of my twelve-year run with the best, craziest, rowdiest group of U.S. Marines that I've ever known.

Reflecting the hybrid nature of Marine ANGLICO, most of us had multiple military occupational specialties (MOS). I had three and should have had a fourth after working in the communications section (COMM) for six years. HQMC could never make up its mind regarding on-the-job MOS certification, which always pissed me off. After six years in COMM and dozens of field exercises, you're telling me an eighteen-year-old private that attended the formal field radio operator course was a better operator than me? Doubtful. But I never got a fourth MOS.

My first school in Little Creek, Virginia, made me an embarkation/ logistics man. When a unit embarks on ship or aircraft, all the gear and vehicles need to be arranged just perfectly for one very important reason: If it's wrong, the ship will flip over, and we all drown on our way to the bottom of the Atlantic Ocean. Good reason, huh? To this day I can remember that a gallon of water weighs close to eight pounds. It's actually a little less, but we always rounded up. If the combat load is underestimated, the center of gravity of the naval vessel will shoot to the top and capsize.

When I heard that 4th ANGLICO would be sending a detachment of Marines to Mountain Warfare School in California, I did whatever I had to do to get on that gig. Mountain Warfare School is considered one of the premier schools in the Marine Corps because of the high level of expertise provided by the staff instructors and the totality of the experience. During the Korean War, mainly after the horrendous ordeal of the 1st Marine Division being surrounded by tens of thousands of communist Chinese troops after Gen. Douglas MacArthur overextended U.S. troops into North Korea, the Marine Corps knew it had a problem on its hands. After spending the 1930s and '40s fighting in Central America and then across the Pacific Ocean during World War II, the Marine Corps found itself ill-equipped to fight in temperatures that rarely rose above freezing during the daytime winter months. After the 1953 truce was signed and active combat operations ceased, the Marine Corps went looking for a location to train its Marines in extreme cold weather. The site they settled on was near the tiny town of Truckee, California, about an hour and a half west of Reno, Nevada, in the general vicinity of where the infamous Donner Party met its horrible end in the 1800s.

For several months leading up to our December 1994 departure for Mountain Warfare School, 3rd Platoon and all of the Marines who had been attached to the deployment were frequently separated from the rest of the company for specialized physical fitness routines and classes on how to survive in the cold, and we were also issued an avalanche of gear from the Marine Corps' Special Training and Allowance Pool, or STAP, which we called "STAP gear." The physical fitness routine had a strong emphasis on your body's core muscles and primarily your legs in preparation for all the marching, snowshoeing, and cross-country skiing that we would be doing at nearly 10,000 feet in the Golden State's Sierra Nevada. While I was born in the Hoosier state of Indiana, I grew up primarily in South Florida and was worried about living twenty-four hours a day in the snow where the daytime temperature wasn't going to rise above freezing. In fact, that is the Marine Corps' definition of extreme cold weather, when the daytime temperature maxes out at 32 degrees.

The STAP gear was as first-rate as anything you're going to buy on the commercial market. I know that Americans love to believe that everything in the civilian world is vastly superior to what the military is issued, but they couldn't be more wrong in this case. The Marine Corps had spent a lot of time and a lot of money to buy Gore-Tex jackets and pants and what is known as expedition weight polypropylene long johns underwear. To this day the military-issue Gore-Tex jackets are by far my favorite cold-weather jacket I have ever worn, and I wish someone would copy the design for use in the civilian world. It incorporated many of the best aspects of civilian jackets. It was nothing new to have a hood that rolled up and zipped up so it didn't drag on your back. It wasn't new to have a jacket with zippers that would go halfway so you could aerate your body core while exerting yourself. And plenty of civilian jackets have pockets all over the place. Two of the features I loved that were unique to the military-issue jackets were the zippers located underneath each armpit and two large concealed pockets sealed with Velcro strips located on your chest. The zippers were to release the heat generated by troops working in the field or serving in a combat zone. Once we were in the snow of the Sierra Nevadas, it was nothing to be on a ski march with both armpit zippers wide-open, and the front of the jacket held together by the two-way zipper that made it look like you were wearing a one-button suit. All these features were designed to keep you from getting wet. Because if you're wet and it's less than 32 degrees, your core body temperature will start to drop. Another piece of gear that became one of my favorites throughout my entire service with 4th ANGLICO was a thick wool neck gaiter about 2 feet long.

While your armpits retain heat, your head and neck area performs the opposite function, losing much of the body's internal heat. If you took the wool neck gaiter, folded it in half, and wore it around your neck, it would keep you warm all the time because wool, as a natural fabric, retains its heat even when it gets wet. Since it was folded in half, if you got colder you could roll the rest of the gaiter up around your chin and up to the top rear portion of your skull, and then secure it with another wool watch cap or a standard-issue Marine Corps cap. I wore my neck gaiter constantly for nearly three weeks, and it is one of my favorite pieces of field gear to this day.

Being issued this little mountain of extreme cold weather gear took almost an entire day. Since I knew my mom was concerned about me going to Mountain Warfare School, I decided to take all of the gear over to her house to show her the high quality of what the Marine Corps had provided for us. I brought in two or three full bags and a large mountain backpack stuffed with all my new gear and promptly dumped it all on her kitchen floor. She took a seat in one of our dining room chairs, and I proceeded to pick up every single item to tell her what it was, what it was for, put it on for her to see, and then handed it to her so she could examine it herself. When I was done with my instruction, there was a mound of gear almost 4 feet tall on her kitchen floor. Other than classified information I always tried to tell my mom everything I did in the Marine Corps to help allay her fears about the inherent dangers of serving in the military, whether it was peacetime or wartime. Of all the things she worried about with me being so high up in the mountains during December, the last thing she should have concerned herself with was whether the Marine Corps was providing the proper field gear. To receive the same type of training and experience in the civilian world, you would need to go on an adventure vacation costing more than five thousand dollars. Though I grew up mainly in balmy Palm Beach County, after Mountain Warfare School, training in Fort Drum, New York, in January, and two trips to Norway including sleeping on the ground 150 miles inside the Arctic Circle, there isn't a cold climate in the world that I would hesitate to go to. And that includes going back to the Arctic Circle or making the trip down south to Antarctica.

We knew we would be going from 88 degrees in West Palm Beach to living in the snow surrounded by pine trees 8 to 10 feet wide and a couple of hundred years old. But along with our reservations about the dramatic change in climate, we were also geared up to learn what the staff of Mountain Warfare School was going to teach us.

We landed in San Francisco, loaded all our gear onto Greyhound buses, and drove across the Golden Gate Bridge to start our climb into the mountains. We made a quick stop at a McDonald's restaurant that was owned by former Oakland Raider great Jim Otto, the last man to play both sides of the ball in the NFL. While I am a staunch Miami Dolphins fan, it was pretty cool to see a display of Otto's famous 00 jersey fitted with a white horse collar that he wore around his neck during his entire career.

Once we arrived at base camp, a little below 6,000 feet in the Sierra Nevadas, we were issued still more gear for the school, and surprisingly to us we all had to take physicals. Marines with extremely high blood pressure weren't allowed to go "up the mountain" for training, because the lack of air pressure at higher altitudes could lead to a stroke or some type of embolism. I thought it was crazy at first, but during the next three weeks, I saw a couple of dozen Marines repeatedly having nosebleeds, even though they had no history of nosebleeds. In fact some of them had nosebleeds so bad that they had to be removed from training and sent down the mountain, and once you left the mountain, regulations prohibited you from going back up again.

The main new piece of field gear we were issued at Mountain Warfare School was a fiberglass sled that the Marine Corps had learned about from working with the Norwegian military. It looked like a very shallow kayak or canoe with white canvas attached all the way around to contain all of the various cook stoves, tents, temples, 1-gallon metal cans full of white gas, and of course the ever-present 5-gallon jerry cans full of water. The Norwegians called them "ahkios," which we were told was Norwegian for snowplow or snow boat, as it had a bottom like the hull of a boat and it would cut through the snow just like a vessel. It could carry 300 pounds and was designed to be dragged by six Marines with three on each side. Ropes about 10 feet long had leather straps attached to them that formed a loop that you draped over each Marine, kind of like a horse collar. We had all of our combat gear including our individual weapons, whether they were pistols, M-16s, or for the infantry companies even M-60 machine guns, plus our large backpacks stuffed with clothing and food, and now we had to drag around a 300-pound sled with even more crap. It was becoming very obvious that the extreme in the term "extreme cold weather" was turning out to be true.

Three weeks in the snow may not sound like much for veterans who have experienced much worse, and the staff told us they were attempting to cram eight weeks of instruction into around twenty-one days. That being said, the mountain warfare instructors were nothing less than incredible, and some of the most well-qualified Marines I've ever been around. It was amazing the little things that we learned. For example, during a survival situation where the only thing that matters is that you live, the instructors showed us how to make a drink by boiling pine needles. Now I'm not saying that it's the same quality as having high tea with the queen at Buckingham Palace, but if you want to see your family again, these are the types of things you need to do. The instructor also taught us a great trick to remember if you had survived the crash of a civilian plane. He told us to search the crash site for things to set on fire to keep yourself warm. He made the point that just after any crash plenty of things would be on fire, which is obvious, but then again there might be pockets of fuel that hadn't ignited that you could use to survive. He then took a standard in-flight magazine that we've all seen hundreds if not thousands of times in our travels and made a terrific point: If you need wood to burn, roll up the magazine and turn it into a log. It's made out of paper, right? And paper used to be a tree, right? That's the thing about field craft. There're so many little tricks of the trade that seem so obvious after someone teaches them to you.

One of our lead instructors was a Marine named Sergeant Black, who I always referred to as "trusty Sergeant Black" whenever he showed up as an instructor because he was so damn good. It was like listening to the burning bush regarding cold-weather training. He was a strong advocate for each Marine carrying an old-school buttpack on their web gear almost solely to carry survival gear. As your typical Marine ANGLICO is a paratrooper, nearly all of us already had buttpacks, and I had carried mine ever since I joined in 1987. Trusty Sergeant Black was discussing what to carry in a survival kit, large or small, and he came to the subject of what type of food to carry with you in case things really hit the fan. Everyone loves to bring little packets of dried Gatorade, hard candy for a sugar boost, and everybody's favorite go-to item, chocolate candy bars. Well, trusty Sergeant Black rejected all of these items and with good reason. His position was that if we bought all of this great candy or drink powder, when we were sitting around bored waiting for trucks or helicopters to show up to transport us to another training area, very few of us would be able to resist the siren song of our favorite candy bars. I never thought of it that way, and he was 100 percent right. Then he pulled the food out of his own buttpack and taught me a trick that I used for the rest of my career and taught every junior Marine that would listen to me.

Only carry food for your survival kit that you can't stand to eat. Now think about that. Gee, Scott, why in the world would I buy food that I can't stand? Easy. Unless you're about to die, there's no way in hell you will touch that food. For trusty Sergeant Black his choice of meal was the main food packet of the one MRE that I categorically refused to even consider eating after four years of ROTC at the University of Florida and twelve years with 4th ANGLICO: the ham and cheese omelette, or as I referred to it every time I mentioned it, "the disgusting ham and cheese omelette." It violated one of my most basic rules about food and beverage: If I can't stand to look at it, there's no way in hell I'm going to stick it in my mouth. I've eaten thousands of MREs, and every serviceman has their favorite one. However, the disgusting ham and cheese omelette is probably how every civilian envisions military food. It was yellow and slimy with little ham-like particles, and I didn't want the damn thing within 10 feet of me. And trusty Sergeant Black was right: Unless I would die otherwise, there was no way in hell I was going to eat one. After that one little thirty-minute class, I instantly traded some of my own food for three packets of the disgusting ham and cheese omelettes and placed them in my buttpack, where they sat lurking in the dark for the next five years. Fortunately I never had to eat one and I never will.

Consider that lesson the next time you go camping for some type of day hike. Bring your food and water for your normal meals but always, and I mean always, carry a survival kit with some food to sustain you in an emergency. Just make sure you hate it.

All jokes about ham and cheese omelettes aside, Mountain Warfare School was hard on the Marines of 4th ANGLICO. If I remember correctly, we had a 15 percent casualty rate due to injury, problems related to blood pressure and altitude, or Marines who simply couldn't handle the extreme temperature ranges that we were experiencing. As my good friend and old compadre Kenneth McKelton warned each Marine in our detachment, though desert and jungle environments have a reputation for being the harshest locations for training, those Marines who hadn't trained for the Arctic Circle were about to learn the harsh reality. "Cold weather is what separates the men from the boys," McKelton intoned.

He was right. I saw some good Marines thrown in the back of an ambulance to get taken down the mountain for medical treatment even though they were practically throwing punches to keep training with their buddies. This is what Marines are like: We're here to train hard and I want to stay with my friends. I saw several Marines who were very loud and very macho raise their hands and declare that they needed to go down the mountain for treatment. If you don't apply what the mountain instructors are teaching you to keep yourself healthy, then it's almost a guarantee that you're going to get sick, which is why after these alpha dogs were out of our midst I told everyone that I thought some people allow themselves to get sick in order to get off the mountain. When I started I was nervous about the extreme cold weather, but you have to learn and stick it out. This was why we were there.

I had a great excuse to take a hike down the mountain after my good buddy and West Virginia truck-driving redneck friend Jeff Bishop smacked me in the face with one of his cross-country skis. We had just returned from a nighttime ski march, wearing our combat gear and M-16 rifles and skiing in file through the mountains of the Sierra Nevadas at night. Since the Marines of 4th ANGLICO were South Florida residents, you can imagine how hard this was on us.

Bishop's cross-country skis had one metal shoe that was bent and giving him fits during and after ski marches, especially the nighttime movements. Since the metal frame was bent, it left a space underneath one of his boots that quickly filled with snow, which the pressure of cross-country skiing compacted and turned into ice. When we get done Bishop's right boot was locked into the ski, and the only way he could get it off was to lean on another Marine's shoulder while he lifted his right leg straight out in front of him and smacked the tail end of the ski on the hard frozen ground. After one such nighttime ski march, Bishop, who was a lance corporal at the time, asked me if I could help him out. Bishop started to pound away on his ski while I stood there staring up at the nighttime sky, when all of a sudden something smacks me upside the face and my entire vision lit up like a pack of fireworks. I wasn't seeing stars; it was like I was staring over the surface of the sun. While Bishop was busy pounding away, he had lost his balance and the wood and metal ski had angled over and struck me on the brow of my right eye socket.

"JESUS CHRIST BISHOP! WHAT THE HELL DID YOU JUST DO?" I screamed. Actually it was much more profane than this, but hey, my mom has to read this book.

"Oh shit, I'm sorry, Sergeant Messmore! Let me get my flashlight and take a look at it," Bishop stammered.

Bishop took out his flashlight while gently trying to calm me down, realizing that striking one of your sergeants in the face with a 6-foot-long ski is probably not very conducive to a lengthy career in the U.S. Marine Corps. Now keep in mind we had just come off of a two-hour romp through the snow and hills near the 10,000-foot mark, so my blood and adrenaline were moving through my body at a pretty good rate. What I thought was going to be a black eye or a goose egg over my right eye instead was a small cut in my eyebrow that sent a sheet of blood down the entire right side of my face and sent a wave of panic through Lance Corporal Bishop. The way he examined my face I still see as a bit comical. He was treating me with kid gloves because he knew I was mad in addition to being hurt, and he calmly pulled my hand away from my face to take a look. With two clicks of his flashlight and one quick glance at my face, Bishop had his answer.

"CORPSMAN!" he yelled at the top of his lungs.

"Corpsman?" I asked. "How bad is it? What the hell are you trying to do? Get me kicked off the mountain?" I yelled.

It was pitch black at night in the mountains, and it is not like I carried a compact mirror with me, so I couldn't tell how big of a gash Bishop had given me. Our corpsmen showed up in less than a minute to clean me up and give me a quick assessment of the wound. As it turned out, it was almost the exact thickness of my eyebrow and located on the end near my right ear. The corpsman said I should go to the battalion aid station, which was located further up the mountain. I was examined by a Navy doctor. He told me he didn't think it needed stitches, but he couldn't keep me from visiting the medical station down at the base camp. When my heart rate and blood flow had returned to normal after the ski march and Bishop braining the shit out of me, the wound had stopped bleeding and the medical staff quickly cleaned me up. I told the doctor I would stay on the mountain, as I knew I wouldn't be allowed to return if I left. Mountain Warfare School is in fact just that, a school that you graduate from, and it's entered into your service record book for all time. Plus I knew if I didn't make it through the school I would not have a chance of going on the deployment to Norway, one of the highlight trips in a Marine's career. He gave me a handful of pain pills and a pocket full of Band-Aids and sent me on my way like a little kid going back to school. About the only long-term effect of Bishop's ski attack was having everybody stare at me when we went on liberty in Reno, Nevada, as I walked around with a bandage stuck to the side of my face.

After three weeks of joining a new world of field operations in preparation for our deployment to Norway in 1996, we flew home to Palm Beach County, turned in our mountain of mountain warfare gear, and I drove home to Gainesville a much better Marine than when I left. The following year, in January 1995, I would learn the real meaning of the word *cold*.

I was first introduced to a whole different form of cold when we traveled to upstate New York for more cold-weather training as part of our preparation for Norway. We would spend a couple weeks at Fort Drum, New York, which is next to Watertown and about an hour from

Syracuse. One of our fellow Marines, Joe Macantee, hailed from the Syracuse area and had been warning us just how cold it could get in the area during winter.

Fort Drum is a huge U.S. Army base with more than 100,000 acres and is home to the famed 10th Mountain Division that was formed near the present-day city of Vail, Colorado, during World War II. They were organized specifically to fight in mountainous terrain, which is why they started in Colorado. If you visit Vail today, right smack dab in the middle of town is a very large statue of a 10th Mountain soldier in full stride carrying cross-country skis on his shoulder. During their initial World War II training, the soldiers would sit around and dream of future days after the war and what a great location their training ground would be for a ski resort. In fact the soldiers who survived their brutal ground combat in World War II did return to their old stomping grounds and did just that, which led to the founding of the city of Vail. I've been to Vail, and plenty of people talk the city down as too commercial or touristy, but the people of Vail take their heritage and attachment to the 10th Mountain Division very seriously, as demonstrated by the large statue. Now when I say large, I mean large. The bronze casting is 12 feet tall and weighs in at 7,000 pounds. I can assure you the ritzy parts of South Florida (yes I'm talking to you Boca Raton and Palm Beach, Florida) wouldn't dream of placing a 12-foot-tall monster right in the middle of everything. I was surprised at the gear the World War II soldier in the statue was carrying and wearing, as it was so similar to the cross-country gear we were using more than fifty years later.

I'm not sure why the U.S. Army decided to relocate the 10th Mountain Division to upstate New York. I just assumed there would be more mountains than there were in Vail. After all the word *mountain* is obviously prominently displayed when talking about the 10th Mountain Division. So I was very surprised when we flew to Syracuse and were on final approach to the airport only to look down at terrain that was as flat as a pool table. The entire freezing time we spent at Fort Drum I don't think I ever climbed a hill that was more than 30 feet tall, and none of us can figure out why the 10th Mountain is here—but then again we never discovered the hows and whys of all sorts of things the U.S. Army did.

As I wrote previously, the Marine Corps' Mountain Warfare School in California was staffed with excellent instructors. At Fort Drum our instructors consisted entirely of a small unit within the 25th Marine Regiment, a collection of Reserve units situated throughout the New England area. The 25th Marines had an Arctic Warfare Cadre that traveled around the country training Marines in extreme cold weather techniques and tactics. Also attached to the unit were a few exchange NATO soldiers, mainly British Royal Marines and in our case Dutch Royal Marines, who are the oldest corps of Marines in the world, having been founded in 1665 more than a hundred years before the U.S. Marine Corps was founded in 1775. The British Royal Marines officially stood up in 1755, and of course neither organization will waste any time reminding any American Marine that they were around first and not us. It's friendly ribbing and competition, but they are fierce fighters that are always on America's side.

For the millionth time 4th ANGLICO was reorganized to suit the situation we were facing on the ground, and we were divided into ten-man tent teams that would fill Korean War–era canvas tents that the Marine Corps still used. A tent team leader was selected for each ten-man tent who would interact with the Arctic Warfare Cadre staff regarding training or whatever was going to happen that day. While the Marine Corps is deadly serious about rank and issuing proper respect for any senior Marine, it is also very practical when it comes to field operations. In the movies or on television, it's the easiest thing in the world to have some bumbling staff NCO or brand-new second lieutenant placed in charge of a small group of Marines only to screw everything up. I guess it makes good drama, but it's taught generations of Americans that military leadership is frequently incompetent. During multiple cold-weather training deployments and trips to Norway including 150 miles inside the Arctic Circle, whichever Marine had the most experience in extreme cold weather was always the one who would be in charge. My tent team had our platoon commander, Major Fernandez; however, my old friend and comm shack partner Rick Taylor had more experience and was chosen as tent team leader even though he was a staff sergeant and Major Fernandez outranked the crap out of him. Major Fernandez loved it, as he wasn't in charge of the training, wouldn't have to be harassed with a dozen little football huddles each day, and could just sit back and learn like a young Marine who had just joined.

As I was still living in Gainesville, Florida, working in restaurants and starting my writing career, Taylor quickly appointed me as team cook, which in Arctic warfare training is a job with very limited duties. I wouldn't be cooking food for anybody. For the next two to three weeks, I had one job: boil water whenever we had any break in training.

The reason for this is twofold: to fill up the cast aluminum thermal jugs each Marine was required to carry at all times, and to cook the freeze-dried meals and very expensive extreme cold weather rations. Usually for any field operation, a Marine would be issued three MREs for each day in the field. Cold-weather rations look like two fat MREs in white plastic bags stuck together with a large fat rubber band. Even when we were inside the Arctic Circle, you were issued one of these per day. A standard MRE has nearly three thousand calories for three meals, whereas the cold-weather rations had roughly 4,500 calories each. While everybody bitches and moans about the taste and quantity of food in MREs, we actually loved the cold-weather rations. The rice and beans chili mix meal was very popular, and the cold-weather rations were loaded with little packets containing mix to make hot tea, little packets of mixed nuts for protein, little chocolate bars, chocolate cookies, and the ever-present crackers that were included in every MRE I ever ate in the Marine Corps. This double pack of food was designed to be eaten in its entirety in one day, but there was so much of it that I never personally finished one cold-weather ration in a twenty-four-hour period, and I don't know of any other Marine in 4th ANGLICO who finished one off either. It was great. It was one of the rare times in Marine field operations that we had tons of food everywhere we went. We traded food back and forth like Arab traders on the old spice routes from Asia to Europe during the Middle Ages. As cook, it was my job to keep enough hot water boiling all the time to rehydrate all of this food.

The other crucial aspect of me boiling so much water all the time was what we were taught to call a "hot wet." A hot wet is simply, and literally, a cup of hot and steamy liquid to drink multiple times throughout the day to keep you warm. As we learned at Mountain Warfare School, the human body in any cold-weather environment, much less field operations in sub-freezing conditions, needs to work harder to keep itself at the proper core temperature of 98.6 degrees. I learned to think of my abdomen as an old Ben Franklin cast-iron potbelly stove that needed to be stoked with fuel twenty-four hours a day. Obviously the fuel for humans is food and water, hence the massive calorie content of Arctic cold-weather rations and the need for at least one member of each tent team to be designated as a cook. At first I was kind of crapped off that Taylor had made me a cook, as I felt it was a thankless task, but he quickly pointed out to me that with my water-boiling duties I would be exempt from all of the little working parties, resupply runs, and even some guard duty. Our cold-weather rations had plenty of small packets of freeze-dried coffee, powdered chocolate cocoa, and a lemon-flavored tea mix that was my favorite.

Attending the Marine Corps' Long-Range Maritime Navigation School in 1995 was a fun fluke for me. We covered absolutely every aspect of oceanic navigation in only ten business days. Only one topic was left out, which was how to use a sextant to make a "star shot" to establish our position. Since we were using 10-foot Zodiac boats for offshore raids, we wouldn't have a stable enough platform to get a proper fix with the sextant. I finished with an 88 percent score and not only was that not a B+ grade, I was actually near the bottom of the class.

Long-Range Maritime Navigation School also had the acronym of OTH, which stood for over the horizon. Modern weaponry had become so advanced by the 1980s that anything that can be seen on the battlefield can be hit, and if it can be hit, it can be killed. Hence the Navy decided to develop a lot of weaponry that can be used from over the horizon, so an enemy force can't take an easy missile shot at one of our ships. It's why U.S. Navy ships operate so far offshore, and it's also why it costs so much money. Even with the 10-foot-long rubber Zodiac boats that we used in navigation school, we trained to be launched from a Navy vessel at night around 26 miles out at sea. For a raiding company this would provide cover of darkness, and the enemy wouldn't see you coming from so far away. Now that sounds simple enough, but when you add in sea currents 26 miles out at sea, whether it's the Atlantic or the Pacific, you can begin to see how complicated these missions could get.

I was very lucky to attend the school. If I remember correctly, in October 1995 HQMC simply had an open seat at the school out in Coronado, California. I happened to be free for about thirty days of active duty, and there was always work around the unit, so when my bosses asked me if I wanted to go to navigation school, after quickly saying yes, I then asked what the hell they were talking about.

"It's rubber boat school. They'll train you to be the lead navigator on a raid company," they told me. "Hey it's two weeks of active duty pay in Coronado and you get another notch in your belt. How bad could it be?"

They were right. Long-Range Maritime Navigation School was fun, though it was demanding, because I don't have a natural technical mind. Old salty boat captains have a couple decades to learn about the small variations of tides, currents that change multiple times each day, the weather, the wildlife, safely competing with other vessels for right-of-way, safe passage, and even the various color patterns of different lighthouses. We did all this in ten training days. One of my favorite memories was performing speed runs in San Diego Bay on board our chase boat, a large Boston whaler equipped with two twin 250-horse-power motors, radar, and "US MARINES" written in very large letters down both sides of the hull. The boat was so fast that when one of our instructors went to full throttle, he would shout "going up on plane" to warn us to hold onto something. Otherwise some hapless Marine would shoot off the back of the boat. Conversely, when he wanted to slow down, he would shout "coming off step," and again we grabbed onto something to hold onto so we would not get launched off the front of the bow. The Navy had placed two markers, 1 mile apart from each other, on the shoreline of San Diego Bay so students could learn how to calculate how fast they were going out in the open ocean. Using a quick little equation of distance equals speed multiplied by time and all of its little variations, if you are missing one piece of the three items of the equation, you can determine the third. It was nicknamed "D-Street" for D=ST and it worked like a charm. For example, the most obvious case would be when the D is your variable and on the other side of the equal sign you have 50 for your speed in miles per hour and 2 for your time in hours. It doesn't take a genius to figure out you will end up traveling 100 miles in whatever vehicle you're in. However, it was new to me and just one of dozens of little calculations needed to be performed in proper mission planning, including the always difficult task of being at sea at night and determining the height of a lighthouse in the distance. I won't bore you with the details of how that's done, especially since I blew it on every single quiz I took. It was a fascinating course even with all the brand-new information that was jamming our brains in only ten business days. If there's one thing I learned about being a competent boater, navigator, or raid company Marine, it is that the sea is completely unforgiving and maritime gear needs to be of the highest quality, as does the post-mission maintenance. It was a great school, but when I went back to 4th ANGLICO, I never used it again. It was back to endless communications exercises, field operations, and jump ops.

By 1998 I was having serious trouble getting promoted to staff sergeant. My Marine Corps experience echoed my life in the world, in that my bosses had no problem giving me the work of two people, but someone else always got the promotion. I've had more than a few jobs where after being burned out and quitting, a former coworker would tell me it took two people to pick up my workload. In the Marines I didn't mind as the work was for my country. As a young man, I took it as a source of pride, but being young and stupid I didn't realize it would dog me into middle age. If I didn't get promoted, under the Marine Corps' up-or-out policy, I would be forced out at twelve years of service. After reorganizing the unit for the millionth time, all of the mismatched MOS Marines were grouped into 2nd Platoon, where we trained in all aspects of the communications MOS and the scout/forward observer MOS, the job I really wanted. We had some great training, even going so far as having one of our great Navy corpsmen teach us how to place IV needles, which we practiced on each other on one hop to Camp Lejeune. We did this in an empty training building we were allotted away from our superiors, as it was a major no-no to be jamming needles into each other. Even with all the training we did, HQMC yet again started to drag its feet and hem and haw regarding when we would be given a new MOS. I was fed up and formally requested to go to Fort Sill, Oklahoma, for Artillery School and Coronado, California, for Naval Gunfire School. Plus, conventional wisdom held that making a career lateral move by attending a formal school would result in me being promoted to staff sergeant.

I thought I hated Jump School, but man, it doesn't have anything on Fort Sill, Oklahoma. Hotter than hell during the day, the next day it would drop to the 40s, dust flew everywhere, and it didn't get fully dark until almost 10:00 P.M. I wondered what kind of hellhole the Marine Corps had finally dropped me into. The only cool thing was the base museum still had the prison cell that housed Geronimo, the hellion Apache war chief. That wily old warrior sure pulled a fast one on the U.S. Army. I was incredulous.

"We fought the Indians for this place? We should have let them keep it. Geronimo is still laughing his ass off over this stunt," I told my classmates.

That being said, the Marine Corps' Scout/Forward Observer School final exam is simply the hardest test I've ever taken, including the University of Florida, boot camp, and whatever the Florida state school system threw at me. We had two instructors, both Gulf War veteran gunnery sergeants with years of experience in artillery and fire direction planning. The first day of training one gave us the heads up.

"I know the final exam is thirty days from now and it seems like a long time. But I'm telling you right now: that test is a motherfucker," he flatly warned us.

Military schools are obviously hard, but most people think it's due to the physical demands. That is true to an extent, but civilians don't know the sheer volume of knowledge imparted in a typical military school on any topic. As one veteran friend observed on the matter: "They'll come right out and tell you what's on the test but then it's: open mouth; insert fire hose; and then turn it on full blast." He's right.

I was warned how hard the final exam would be before leaving South Florida for Fort Sill. Hell, they even let us use our notes, an open book exam in other words, and the allotted time for the bastard was *four hours*. At Florida I never had a final scheduled for more than two hours. Scout/Forward Observer School is great preparation for any ANGLICO Marine as it covers so many subjects: tactical communications (read that as using encrypted radios that "hop" through radio frequencies at around eight channels every few seconds), land navigation, artillery and mortar call for fire, targeting, which rounds to use against which target, patrolling, combat first aid, mission planning, bomb damage assessment, basic logistics for your team, and essentially every conceivable damn thing under the sun. What made the test difficult is instead of having a four- or six-man team to assist in planning a mission over two weeks, you were doing it all by yourself during one exam. I went so far as to buy an old lined-paper composition notebook like the kind I used in middle school to take notes and then attached sticky plastic name holders to each section under artillery, mortars, communications, land navigation, etc. With advance warning, open notes, and even the chance to walk outside and drink a soda or eat a candy bar (yes, the honor system is alive and well in the Marines), it still took me two and a half hours to finish the test with a 90, the highest score in the class. Gunny was right; that test was a motherfucker and we hadn't even done our live-fire testing.

Artillery is very misunderstood by the public, who generally think of shells as giant bullets that fly through the air. In truth, artillery pieces are finely tuned instruments that can wipe a town off the map within hours if properly used. The largest U.S. artillery piece, the 155mm cannon, fires a 95-pound shell 18,000 meters, weighs 15,000 pounds, costs half a million dollars, and can be airlifted by heavy helicopters only minutes after firing a mission. Artillery is classified two ways: indirect fire weapons and area weapons. Indirect fire means just that: You're not firing directly at the target, but one that is far away, hence the need for forward observers to "observe" the target and destroy it. An area weapon means that the impacting shell is designed to explode and send deadly fragments in a radius called the "killing zone," the area where fragments have enough punch to kill enemy troops. The kill radius on a 155mm piece is half a football field. The kill radius on a hand grenade is 15 meters, still quite big for something the size of a baseball. The retired Navy battleships main 16-inch guns fired 2,000-pound shells with a blast radius of 1,000 meters. In the Gulf War sailors were taking out entire grid squares on the map, 1,000 by 1,000 meters, one shot at a time. One of our Navy officers, Lieutenant Caminetti, spotted an Iraqi artillery battery and dusted it off with one mission from the USS *Wisconsin*.

After the heat and dust of Fort Sill, Oklahoma, we flew to the Pacific paradise of San Diego where we would attend Naval Gunfire School at Coronado Amphibious Training Base, made well known as the home turf of the Navy SEALs.

Bored people searching through satellite maps discovered that the main barracks for enlisted troops at Coronado is shaped like a massive Nazi swastika. I stayed in those barracks several times. You can't tell the shape while you're on the ground, but I'm not the genius who stared at a set of plans and signed off on them. Minor goose-stepping problems aside, I loved Coronado just as much as I hated Fort Sill. Granted, it's a Navy and Marine Corps town, but the people are polite, teach their children proper manners, and there's military crap everywhere. Never seen an aircraft carrier before? Take a boat trip around the harbor and you might see three of them docked next to three destroyers and a guided missile cruiser. However, in the post–September 11th environment, if I were you, I'd check in with the harbormaster, or better yet, just set sail on a tourist cruise so you won't get machine-gunned by a nervous sentry from a nearby destroyer.

Sooner or later it's everybody's time to "get out," the near universal expression for separating from the Marine Corps. I don't know the statistics, but it seems that most Marines get out after serving their first four-year enlistment whatever the reason might be. There are a million reasons why Marines get out: missing your family too much, you're starting a family and you're away too much, the Marine Corps isn't what you thought it would be even though you'll always love the Marines you served with. So Marines are forced out, kicked out, some hit service limits as I did, and what is obviously very common these days, some simply tired of one too many deployments and getting shot at by the Taliban. As I stated in the introduction, my twelve years with 4th ANGLICO were like a wild, raging love affair from some Hollywood action adventure romance. Looking back at my time in West Palm Beach, I realize my love and affection had started to fade right around the tenth year of my service. Getting out never occurred to me, as I thought I would always be in uniform until the Marine Corps kicked me out due to old age.

The first time I noticed there was a problem was just after I had traveled to the Kennedy Space Center in Cape Canaveral, Florida, to cover John Glenn's return to space. Glenn was a sitting U.S. senator and a retired Marine Corps fighter pilot with a near legendary status in the aviation community. I spent four days prior to the launch following around an old *Life* magazine photographer named Ralph Morse, who took the iconic photograph of John Glenn in his space suit and helmet for the 1963 cover of *Life*. Ralph was a legend in his own right in the photography community, and my coworker Jon Way and I had a great time tagging along with Ralph as he spoke with the likes of astronauts Wally Schirra, Scott Carpenter, Buzz Aldrin, Pete Conrad, and Gordon Cooper, and Morse was interviewed by several news outlets once they discovered who he was.

The following week I returned with Ralph and John to cover Glenn returning from outer space onboard the Space Shuttle as it landed back at Cape Canaveral. The shuttle landed on a Saturday that also coincided with not only the November drill weekend but also the weekend of the Marines' annual celebration of our founding called the Birthday Ball. I would miss that year's celebration, because it's obviously not too often that you get to see a Space Shuttle fly overhead at multiple times the speed of sound and come to a rolling stop only a quarter mile away. 4th ANGLICO knew that I was covering the Glenn space mission, and I was excused for that Saturday of the November 1998 drill weekend. After concluding our news coverage, I hopped back in my Ford Ranger and drove back to South Florida. Sunday morning I got up, put on my older camouflage utility uniform that made me look like an "old salt" or a Marine that had been around the block and seen a lot, pinned on my sergeant stripes and gold jump wings, pulled on my well-worn jungle boots that were laced with 550 cord of course, and stood in front of the mirror to check myself out. And then it happened.

For the first time since I graduated Parris Island on November 19, 1987, instead of feeling like a warrior suited up for battle, I felt like I was wearing clothes. I actually said "Uh-oh" out loud. I wasn't supposed to be feeling like this while I was in uniform. Any image you conjure up in your head about why you're serving your country—whether it's a knight in shining armor, cowboy in the saddle, being a Rough Rider with Teddy Roosevelt charging up San Juan Hill, wearing old World War II–style dungarees as you climb up Mount Suribachi to help plant Old Glory on top—you weren't supposed to be feeling like you're wearing clothes just to go work out in the front yard. Almost exactly twelve months later I was out.

My contracts with the Marine Corps had been extended several times, and I was years past my initial obligations to the U.S. government. I was serving because I love it, and later on as a sergeant, it actually paid for my monthly ticket on my little Ford Ranger. I was in the pipeline for another trip to Norway in spring of 1999, which I did deploy on, but I could see that my own standards and performance were starting to slip. And believe you me I bitched and moaned about it to both friends and family.

One Friday night at my favorite pub, Power's Lounge, in my hometown of Delray Beach, Florida, I was in full-on complaint mode with a friend of mine who had served in the Navy during the Vietnam War. Like any good combat veteran, he was just sitting there listening to me prattle on, waiting for me to shut up so he could actually get something in the conversation. Typically he was straight to the point.

"Look. You're done, okay? You're done. What do you Marines always say: If you're not going to wear the uniform correctly, then be a real Marine. Hang your suit up in the closet and go on with your life," he told me flatly. "You had a great run. You got to do some really cool things that most Marines will never do, you got to stay in the same unit for twelve years with all of your friends, you got to go to Norway twice, and even though you volunteered for combat two or three times, you never had to go in so you won't have any nightmares the rest your life. What's the confusion?"

He was right. His stern admonition came just a little while after my own mom had simply asked me if I had ever considered getting out. I hadn't considered it. As usual, Mom's laser-like observations were right on target.

Still I struggled on through the summer and fall of 1999, but finally faced the music in October: It was time to move on. The affair was over. I did have a great run with a great group of Marines who were (and are) always on my side no matter what. Would you like to know one of the great things about the Marine Corps? Sometimes "being on your side" entails setting you straight, handing you the worst cussin' out you've ever heard (but always behind closed doors and away from the troops), and insisting you had to be better prepared than all of the junior Marines combined. As one sergeant major of the Marine Corps once stated: "We don't expect you to be perfect. We expect you to try." I decided to tell the career planner and old friend Kyp Hallmark that I would reenlist and to shift me to the Inactive Ready Reserve (IRR) "just in case of a national emergency." Little did Kyp and I know the terrible events that would transpire in the Big Apple and inside the Beltway in less than two years.

I went about my business "checking out" of 4th ANGLICO, a day I never thought would come until I had all-white hair like Santa Claus. I walked into each section tying up loose ends and turning in equipment. The medical staff ensured that, in fact, I was still alive and fully qualified to be released from the U.S. military, but mainly I shocked the hell out of a lot of Marines and sailors when they discovered I was "getting out." I had several Marines of all ranks come looking for me to say, "I just heard you were checking out? Is that true?" It was true, and it still makes me feel good to this day that I was considered "one of the good ones" who was supposed to stay in any good unit. Hallmark came and found me and said we needed to go talk to the colonel. I assumed it was the standard pre-reenlistment pep talk and mini-rehearsal. ("Don't knock over my new plant, my wife bought me that." "Aye, aye sir.") Instead, we met with Lt. Col. Tom Byron, an officer who had written me several fitness reports that I would describe as "walking on water" reviews of my performance and always wrote "ready for promotion, now." He walked from behind his desk as Hallmark closed the door as he left.

"Here, let's have a seat here," Byron said as he motioned me over to the leather couch in his office.

I was confused as he had such a sad look on his face. In the only case of the Marine Corps letting me down in twelve straight years of service,

Byron was the one who got stuck telling one of his favorite Marines that he had been passed over three times for promotion to staff sergeant and I was out at the end of my contract. Even more harsh my ECC, or end of current contract, was in about ninety-six hours. To be clear, to get promoted to the staff NCO ranks, Marines are required to assemble a "package" that includes a photograph and your entire record for submission to the promotion boards. If you are passed over three times, you're out. My problem was that I hadn't submitted a third application. I knew I was cutting it close, but I didn't want to be a staff NCO at 4th ANGLICO as there were too many. I saw brand-new staff sergeants walking around performing tasks I would assign to a lance corporal. Not me. I was trying to be made a warrant officer and serve out my time as a cranky expert in a particular field, such as one chief warrant officer who was an Arctic Warfare instructor when I trained at Fort Drum, New York. He wore a Korean War–era pile cap on his head and had a huge Jim Bowie knife strapped to his hip that hadn't been within any military regulations since the two-week battle for the Alamo in 1836. His hair was all white, and since he knew his job so well and had so much experience, he dressed and worked as he saw fit. I wanted to be just like him. However, I could never get any help in my quest to be a warrant officer and simply ran out of time. But it was time, anyway.

However, the beef I had with HQMC was that the promotion board didn't even get a package from me. This means they opened my permanent record, said "No," and passed me over. Here's the problem: They didn't tell anyone. They didn't tell my commanding officer. They didn't tell my sergeant major. They didn't tell the career planner Kyp Hallmark, and they sure as hell didn't tell me. If I hadn't decided to check out of 4th ANGLICO and made the snap decision to join the IRR just in case my country needed me in an emergency, we wouldn't have found out until my paychecks suddenly stopped coming after my EOS, or end of service. I can still see the look of sadness and even embarrassment on Hallmark's and Lieutenant Colonel Byron's faces. Hell, I even felt sorry for them. Instead of having a year to prepare for separation, I was gone in less than forty-eight hours.

I had always been a hard luck case for getting promotions, and I was already on my way out of the door, as all of my legal obligations to Uncle Sam had been completed for several years. However, like most people, you always want to move on in this life on your own terms. Most of the time you do, but sometimes you don't.

However, for any Marine reading this book, I can hear you speaking right now. "Well, he didn't attend the Sergeant's Course so of course he got pushed out at twelve years."

Didn't attend, huh? Just when was I offered a slot for this course? I wasn't. In 1998, 4th ANGLICO was offered exactly two Sergeant's Course billets for fifty-four sergeants in the unit. Since I was always involved with embarkation and logistics, I knew exactly how many officers, staff NCOs, NCOs, and enlisted Marines we had at any given time. Looking back, the writing was on the wall in neon spray paint, but that's just life. Two very fine Marine sergeants were more senior to me. Two slots for the school and I was number three. And that was that. Plus I personally knew twelve staff sergeants who didn't attend the course either. Sure I should have gotten out at a flat ten years, but I stayed and managed one more trip to Norway and a bunch of airborne jumps with my buddies.

Ironically, considering how hard I tried to apply to become a warrant officer for the last two years I was in 4th ANGLICO, years later I started asking around about how my buddies were doing. No less than five of my good friends, Marines who were in my little twelve-year club, picked up warrant officer *and* stayed with the unit and led combat teams in Iraq and Afghanistan. It wasn't in the cards I guess, but hell, I never get promoted in the corporate world either, so it's a great thing I taught myself to write. It got me in the Library of Congress after all. If this was the worst that could happen during my time, I had a charmed career with all of the other experiences I had.

The best thing I can do for my old Marine buddies is just tell it like it was for us in the late 1980s and the 1990s. We played hard, partied hard, trained ten times harder, and—courtesy of jet fighters, helicopter gunships, and Navy warships—had a blast the entire time.

CHAPTER THREE

First Wings at Fourth

OF ALL THE PEOPLE WHO HELPED GLENN "TOP" MIZE DECIDE IF HE would join the Marines, George Washington was the most important.

Specifically, it was old George's pony-tailed face on the silver quarter Mize was about to toss into the air in a West Palm Beach office building hallway during his senior year of high school in 1967: heads, Marines; tails, Airborne School with the U.S. Army. The previous year, Mize's two hunting buddies had joined the military and he was following along. One friend joined the Army and served with its storied 173rd Airborne because his dad was a Korean War Army veteran. The other joined the Marine Corps because his dad had fought with the Marine Corps in World War II. Mize had grown up in little Delray Beach, Florida, listening to the combat stories of all the older men and watched dozens of movies with John Wayne blasting the Nazis or planting Old Glory on top of Mount Suribachi. Even with more than 485,000 American troops in Vietnam by 1967, Mize had no hesitation about joining.

"I wanted to make sure I got in on it. You know, in those days, it was the thing to do. If your country was at war, you joined the armed forces," he said.

Which branch to select? Now that was a different matter. Mize actually skipped school one day of his senior year and drove up to an old post office in downtown West Palm Beach and found himself in an office hallway with a big decision on his hands. Army or Marines? As a boy, Mize had heard all the great stories of the Marines in the Pacific War, but also admired the U.S. Army paratroopers and really wanted to go to

Jump School. Even today there aren't many opportunities to go to Jump School in the Marine Corps; in 1967 it was almost a certainty that you wouldn't go to Airborne School if you joined the Corps.

"I went upstairs and the Marine Corps is that way and the Army Airborne is the other and I was going to go one or the other. I pulled out a quarter, flipped it, it came up Marine Corps. I always kind of regretted that I didn't have the opportunity to go to Jump School," he said.

Little did Mize know that five years later he would be the first Marine in a newly formed ANGLICO company to attend Jump School. Mize spent his time in Vietnam with an artillery unit, arriving "in country" just in time for the infamous Tet Offensive, where he would be wounded by friendly fire. It was the only time he was hit during combat.

I knew Top Mize the entire time I was in 4th ANGLICO. I saw him as the calm, no-need-to-yell-unless-I'm-pissed combat veteran that my father had told me about when I was a little boy. Dad was in Vietnam so early that the U.S. government still doesn't acknowledge he was there. Since Dad got out of the U.S. Air Force in 1962, you can figure out on your own just how early that was. In a very Kipling type of moment about keeping your head when others are losing their minds around you, he told me the big mouths were the worst the first time enemy fire came in and the quiet ones got the job done. That's what Top Mize is to this day—a quiet one.

Mize was in the West Palm Beach Reserve unit even before it was an ANGLICO company. While there has been a Reserve unit in West Palm Beach since the early 1950s, 4th ANGLICO's history to 1991 is the same as Mize's and he is an unofficial unit historian of sorts. I had always heard rumors that the West Palm Beach unit had started as a result of Korean War veterans forming a club of sorts and having monthly get-togethers. The meetings became so large and organized, I was told they petitioned HQMC to form a unit, and it was granted. I never fully believed this, but it took on some credibility when Top Mize showed me the unit's history, which showed its founding in April 1954 as the 99th Special Infantry Company, whatever the hell that means. Apparently, it meant at the time that there weren't enough Marines to fully staff a normal infantry company of around 225 men. Five years later the name was changed to the

99th Special Rifle Company. In 1962 the first big change happened when the infantry unit was abandoned in favor of a company of amphibious tractors (Amtraks), which makes perfect sense as the unit is only 2 miles from the Atlantic Ocean.

"We started out as a special rifle company. And then we were Amtraks. Then we were part of Fourth, then we were part of Third, and then we were 4th [ANGLICO]," Mize said.

Foreshadowing the never-ending changing nature of ANGLICO, in 1962 the West Palm Beach Reserves was Company D of the 4th Amphibian Tractor Battalion. In 1965 it changed to Company C, in 1967 to Company C (-), which stands for "minus," meaning it was not up to "TO" strength, the Marine slang for a fully staffed table of organization. It wasn't until 1971, seventeen years after its founding, that West Palm Beach magically turned into an ANGLICO company. As an artilleryman, Mize had served alongside some ANGLICO Marines in Vietnam and was one of the few of the Few and the Proud who actually knew what they did for a living.

As far back as 1944, the Navy and Marine Corps had formed Joint Air Support Companies (JASCO) and staffed them with naval gunfire spotters and aviators who would radio air strike requests to their fellow pilots above. These units provided support for U.S. Marine units, the U.S. Army, and Allied forces such as the British army and the always supportive Australians. It was similar to the U.S. Army and Army Air Corps in the European Theater deploying veteran pilots with ground troops who radioed fighter-bombers to attack the Nazis.

"They'll have a good idea and then they'll stop. And the next war comes along and someone will remember it and they try to put it together again," retired MGySgt. Glenn Mize said. "Just like snipers, you know? They use them and then they let them go fallow for years until they need them again. Then they scurry and put together another program."

Promptly following World War II, the JASCO units were disbanded, only to be reformed by the newly named ANGLICO companies in the late 1940s. As Mize remarked in his Delray Beach, Florida, home nearly sixty years later, ANGLICO was born by being reborn, a never-ending process for ANGLICO Marines that you'll learn by reading this book. Two ANGLICO companies were formed under the banner of the 1st Signals Battalion, with one located at Camp Lejeune, North Carolina, and the second with the 1st Marine Division in California, while another was created at Pearl Harbor in 1951. ANGLICO Marines served throughout the Korean War in the Korean peninsula, supporting everyone from the Marine Corps and Army to Allied units, primarily the infantry and armored units of the South Korean army that had been so badly mauled during the initial days of the war.

With the huge increase in the number of American troops arriving in South Vietnam in 1965, 1st ANGLICO of the Fleet Marine Force Pacific established Sub Unit One, which would serve as a base of operations for the next eight years. While fewer than two thousand Marines served in Sub Unit One during this time, a remarkably low number to me for how much combat they saw, the unit did its normal job of providing everything from Tactical Air Control Parties (TACP), to Naval Gunfire Spotter teams and calling in countless artillery missions, some of which were no doubt fired by our own Master Gunny Mize. Sub Unit One worked with Aussies, Kiwis, Koreans, South Vietnamese, and American soldiers and was the only U.S. Marine Corps unit to report directly to Gen. William Westmoreland's Military Assistance Command, Vietnam in Saigon. Another author named Thomas Petri, who served with Sub Unit One with the Korean 2nd Brigade, has written a memoir of his time using the ANGLICO motto "Lightning From the Sky, Thunder From the Sea" as his title. It's received good reviews, but focuses on Sub Unit One's fine record, while I'm trying to teach the American public about a highly trained yet unknown asset that might get more "bang for the buck" than any other military unit the same size—plus our budget is a hell of a lot smaller than all of the other Special Ops units.

After the final death throes of the Vietnam War in 1975, after watching Huey helicopters shoved into the sea from U.S. Navy aircraft carriers with the rest of America, Marine ANGLICO began to look to the future of fire support. Marine leaders serving with 2nd ANGLICO at Camp Lejeune began to warm to the idea of the now accepted norm of what was then called a "universal spotter." Instead of forming a TACP, forward observer team for artillery, or a Naval Gunfire Spotter team, now an FCT team would consist of around six Marines who were effectively trained in each task, plus field communications. As we'll discuss later, FCTs were located at the combat level with U.S. Army and Allied units (even riverine boats sometimes in Iraq) and were controlled at the battalion level by a Supporting Arms Liaison Team or SALT. This format would become the table of organization (TO) for all ANGLICO units to this day and paved the way for the modern Joint Terminal Attack Controller (JTAC) program used by each branch of the U.S. military.

The 1980s were a very busy time for all Marine ANGLICO companies with small teams being sent around the world virtually year-round, including the combat deployments to Beirut, Lebanon, beginning in 1983 plus the invasion of Grenada the same year. In 1989 all ANGLICO units were left behind and did not take part in the overthrowing of Panamanian dictator and drug-dealing shithead Manuel Noriega, which angered nearly everyone in the ANGLICO community. However, in August of 1990, everyone's favorite Middle Eastern idiot (other than Khaddafi or the Ayatollah of Iran) Saddam Hussein provided ample opportunity for each ANGLICO company to jump in the fight with his invasion of Kuwait. In California 1st ANGLICO virtually ran with their gear to awaiting jetliners to fly directly to Saudi Arabia, while 2nd and 4th ANGLICO, my unit, trained even harder and packed out sea bags and gear for the big fight. Everyone knows the outcome of that short and brutal fight, and it is too large of a subject to discuss for an introductory book on ANGLICO, even though 2nd ANGLICO played a central role in the battle of Khafji.

With the end of the Gulf War and the collapse of the Soviet Union, the entire U.S. military establishment underwent the usual budget cutting and soul searching that occurs after every major conflict. In spite of military cutbacks, the Clinton administration wasted little time sending American troops to world hotspots such as Somalia, Bosnia, Kosovo, Liberia, and Serbia. The bulk of my service covered the entire decade of the 1990s, and during this period we had our hands full at 4th ANGLICO with deployments around the country and the rest of the globe. ANGLICO would die out and then be reborn several times over the ensuing years, as detailed in chapter 5. The rest of the book will detail the wild and wonderful world of one of the least known and understood units in the U.S. military. We worked hard, we partied hard, blew shit up, and had a nasty tendency to do things exactly the way we wanted. When you get tossed around the world in very small teams and left to your own devices, you develop a "cowboy" mentality very quickly. Even though he needed the help of a dead president with wooden teeth to join the Marine Corps, MGySgt. Glenn Mize was certain in his choice of service that started with the Tet Offensive in Vietnam and ended in the era of cellular telephones, wheeled NASA rovers making tracks on the Martian surface, and the World Wide Web. Mize had been the first to get his wings from 4th ANGLICO in West Palm Beach and had led Marines on three continents.

"Looking back on it, I wouldn't have done it any other way," Mize said.

CHAPTER FOUR

Marine Speak

IT WAS ONCE OBSERVED THAT THE DEFINITION OF A U.S. MARINE WAS "a soldier that talks like a sailor and couldn't stand either one of them." Funny, but it's also true to an extent. Marines have always cherished and shown off our unique status within the Department of Defense. Love us or hate us, we've been here since 1775, before the Declaration of Independence, and as Secretary of the Navy James Forrestal told Marine legend Gen. Holland "Howlin' Mad" Smith after spotting the American flag during the battle for Iwo Jima, "the raising of that flag of Suribachi means a Marine Corps for the next 500 years." I think old Jim was correct, and also a very good man for being a Cabinet-level secretary who insisted on landing on the beach of that volcanic island while active combat was raging around him. And since the Big Green Rifle Club will be around for several more centuries, you might as well learn some of our lingo.

Take the individual combat gear we wear on our bodies. During Iraq and Afghanistan the military switched to flak jackets that incorporate pouches for ammunition and various other things, while everyone wore the awesome Camelbak water bladder, one of the best troop innovations ever. Throughout my time we had all of our ammunition pouches, canteens, medical kits, and buttpacks attached to a cartridge belt, which was hung from suspenders to ease the burden. In the Corps there are several nicknames for our load-bearing equipment, which the Army called "LBEs," a name I always detested. Being Marines, we always had a bit more color and flair than those Army doggies. Sometimes you were told to bring your "war belt," a great name, or simply "your deuce gear." To an outsider, "deuce gear" makes simply no sense for combat belts, but it's actually part of Marine Corps history.

The term *deuce gear* is actually a shortened version of "782" gear, which is Marine Corps slang for all of the individual combat equipment and field gear you were issued at each unit you were posted to. For example, when you're issued your war belt for the first time, it's given to you in pieces. There are two canteens with two canteen covers, two magazine pouches that hold three thirty-round magazine clips for your M-16, and a medical kit that comes as one unit inside of its own pouch. The main cartridge belt wraps around your hips, and the suspenders ride over your shoulders. Your field gear includes items such as your poncho and the poncho liner that is used as a blanket, a sleeping bag, half of a canvas pup tent that we absolutely never used, whereas we frequently used the three tent pole sections that were supposed to be used with the tent. This is far from all of the gear that would be issued to every U.S. Marine, and each item is of course itemized with a section for how many are issued to you and a small section for you to initial to verify that you received this gear.

Way back when before Congress forced the Pentagon to consolidate all the paperwork and stop wasting money on printing so many different types of forms, when you joined the Marine Corps and were issued all of your field gear and combat equipment say during the 1930s, guess what the number of the piece of paper was? Exactly: Form 782. Form 782 existed in the Marine Corps for so long it became part of our language. If you were having an annual inspection of all your gear, you were told to bring all of your 782 gear. If you're going to the hand grenade range for only one day of training, you would only bring your war belt and not drag on all of your 782 gear. If you're not confused enough, plenty of Marines used *war belt* and *782 gear* interchangeably.

As we all know, U.S. Marines are not normal, so it shouldn't come as a surprise that we don't talk normally either. We never go to lunch or dinner; we go to eat chow. When we have so much training to conduct that we have hardly any time to spend in the chow hall, this is known as "eating duck." What that means is we are so busy that the only thing we are going to do is duck into the chow hall, eat, and duck out. It's a little play on words that goes so far back in Marine Corps mythology that no one has the slightest idea when it started, although everyone hears it for the first time at boot camp on Parris Island or in San Diego.

As far as rank is concerned, a first sergeant is frequently called "the first shirt," and in Marine Corps slang a master sergeant is called "Top" with a capital "T" and not referred to as a top kick, which is Army slang that we always avoided. A lance corporal is frequently referred to as a "lance coolie" for reasons I never fully understood. I just assumed it was a politically incorrect bastardization of the derogatory nickname for the Chinese workers that helped—and frequently sacrificed their lives—to build the railroads of the Great American West during the 1880s. The connotation is rather obvious as lance corporal is the most common rank within the enlisted Marine Corps, as no one stays a private or private first class (PFC) for very long unless they are truly an extraordinary screw-up. Therefore since they are doing most of the dirty work, it's common to have some staff NCO tell a subordinate to "go grab some coolies" to complete a particular task.

One of the most respected and sometimes feared ranks in the Marine Corps is the gunnery sergeant or "gunny" for short. Even members of the other military branches like to use this term. Much like a sailor making the grade of chief, a gunny is almost always respected for his knowledge and simply having been around the block so much that any Marine can turn to them for help for virtually anything. Some gunnys are so slick they make con artist Bernie Madoff look like a door-to-door salesman; other gunnys are so independent that under the right circumstance they might tell the general he's wrong, out of uniform, and then beat him at a game of pickup basketball.

Virtually every radio in the U.S. military has the official designation of AN/PRC written before the set number. It's an acronym that actually stands for "Army/Navy, Portable, Radio, Communication," which is the official description that you'll usually only hear in Communication School or during a formal class on a new radio. However, since it takes too long to say all of that, virtually every radio in the Marine Corps and Army is almost always called by the name of "prick" followed by the set number. Therefore an AN/PRC 77 is always called a prick 77. An AN/

PRC 104 high-frequency radio was therefore always referred to as a prick 104, and so on and so on.

Another military designation system involves using the word *Mark* with a capital "M" to identify hundreds if not thousands of different types of military gear, weapons, bombs, vehicles, artillery pieces, and even the huge battle guns on U.S. Navy destroyers and battleships. I don't know how this got started, but it goes back so far in history, it's hard to track down. It might be something as simple as the fact that virtually everything in the military falls in the category of munitions, and it was just simply an accounting method on someone's sheet of paper back in the old days. But that's pure speculation on my part. For example, in my unit during one training seminar, the instructor could refer to Mark 82s, Mark 138s, or Mark "niner eights." What this could mean is that if we had traveled to Camp Lejeune to practice CAS missions for example, the Mark niner eights would be Motor T terminology referring to the M998 Humvee series that were transporting troops out to the bombing range, the Mark 138s would refer to the communications Humvees that we would use to contact the attacking pilots by radio, and the Mark 82s would be the 500-pound bombs the incoming fighter-bombers would be dropping during a live-fire exercise. I know this is confusing, but this is the way we spoke in virtually every sentence, and a civilian with zero military or security experience sitting in on a class wouldn't have the slightest idea of what we were talking about. As I wrote earlier, Marine ANGLICO is essentially the combination of five MOSs, and we used the terminology and slang of all five job types at the same time.

To help you understand the terminology used in this book, I've assembled a collection of Marine slang and military terms. I have also listed my favorite field gear, which anyone could, and should, include in their backpacks or daypacks whenever they take a long or short trip in the great outdoors.

Whenever someone in the U.S. Marine Corps, Army, or Air Force refers to a senior officer as a "bird colonel," they are talking about the American eagle design of an officer just below the rank of brigadier general. A bird colonel is significantly more powerful than a lieutenant colonel, and in infantry terms he would command an entire regiment with three battalions of combat infantrymen. Think of Colonel Potter in the old *M*A*S*H* television series and you'll get the idea. When things were screwing up, old Sherman would get on the phone and really chew someone's ass at headquarters down in Seoul, Korea. While we're on the topic of rear echelon types that everyone on the front lines thinks are worthless and weak, we come to the derogatory term of "pogue."

Pogue or POG refers to the thousands of support troops required to keep a fighting force in the field under combat. Some defense experts state that as many as ten troops are required to keep one infantryman in the fight and pulling the trigger. Infantrymen rightfully say that everyone in the military works for them, and basically they're right. Hell, even ANGLICO teams are there to support the infantry or tank units. However, pogue usually refers to a headquarters type who never leaves the office except for morning physical fitness and normally has a very bad attitude. Needless to say, the grunts hate these types, especially an admin type who struts around like a drill instructor. Those guys usually get beat up on Friday nights at the enlisted club, and no, there won't be any witnesses when the military police show up.

As far as the different sections of a Marine unit, the communications section is always called "Comm" and all of our Humvees and trucks are in the Motor Transport section, which is always called "Motor T." There is simply no such thing as a "motor pool" in the U.S. Marine Corps unless you're making a very bad joke at the Army's expense. If you're not feeling well or simply too hung over for physical training, you can "report to Sick Call" or "go see the Doc." Also, physical training is always called "PT" and a physical fitness test is always called a "PFT." The headquarters platoon is called the "head shed" because that's where the unit's leadership is located, and supposedly dreaming and scheming new and improved ways to save the world for democracy.

Concerning various aircraft types, AV-8B Harrier jump jets are always called "Harriers." F/A 18 Hornet jet fighters are always called "F-18s" with Air Force "birds" also being referred to by their numbers except for the mighty A-10 Thunderbolt II: the "warthog." Helicopters are different. Marines always call helicopters "helos," pronounced "HEE-lows." I haven't the slightest idea why as the word isn't spelled "helocopter," but like so many thing in the Corps, that's just the way it is. To further confuse the issue, the aviation community in the Marine Corps routinely refers to helicopters as "bubbas" for some deranged reason. But they understand each other, so there you go. A third option for helos is simply to call them by their number, which makes a CH-53E Super Stallion equipped with three jet engines the concise "53."

"How many birds are coming, Gunny?"

"Three helos. Two 46s and one 53."

"Cool. I've never jumped a 46. Can you get me on that stick?"

We understood each other just fine.

Regarding weapons, an M-16 is a rifle and not a machine gun, and machine guns are always called by the numerals such as the now retired M-60s and the powerful M-240G, which is usually called a "240 golf." The 240 golfs were so powerful that an urban legend sprang up that during the invasion of Haiti someone had to open fire on some rioter/criminal/idiot and the power of the machine-gun rounds actually held the guy up in the air until the gunner ceased fire. Of course, no one really believed this crazy story, but it shows the raw power of the 240 golf, which can easily blow a limb off an enemy soldier. The Squad Automatic Weapon fires the same 5.56mm round as the M-16 and is always referred to as a "SAW." When I was in, we never had any SAWs in the armory, but with the close-in combat of Iraq and Afghanistan, 4th ANGLICO was issued SAWs to blast bad guys during the opening stages of a fight. The NATO standard 9mm Beretta is always called a "Beretta" while the great American Colt 1911 automatic pistol is always call a ".45." And by the way, we never should have switched from the .45, for all you bean counters at the Pentagon. Also, a bean counter is someone who is more concerned with statistics and numbers while ignoring teamwork, esprit de corps, and all of the intangibles that make a military unit or sports team great. In the corporate world being called a bean counter might be a compliment, whereas in the Marine Corps it's a severe insult.

My personal list of favorite gear mainly revolves around what I carry in my backpack, buttpack, or wear on my person. I don't think anyone can overestimate the impact of Gore-Tex on the U.S. military, especially the field jackets that everyone wears even during the summer when it rains all the time. The old field jackets were first designed in the 1950s and hadn't changed much since. They were big, bulky, weren't even all that warm, they weren't waterproof, and the sleeves always extended past your wrists like you were an eight-year-old on a school playground squirming around in your big brother's coat. The Gore-Tex miracle, and it was a miracle for ground troops, changed all of that. For all of you civilian outdoorsy types, the military jacket is superior and what I would select to this day. I would be quite surprised if your average American hunter disagreed with me. Also for cold weather it is essential to have what is known as a "neck gaiter." For Mountain Warfare School or any deployment to Operation Battle Griffin in Norway, we were issued a 2-foot-long, 100 percent wool tube that you wore around your neck. Your neck loses a great deal of heat just as the top of your head does, so wearing a wool gaiter around your neck and a wool knitted watch cap on your noggin will keep you healthy and on the move for days. No hiker should go out into the cold without one; I know I never will.

Another great innovation that I've never seen used by civilians is the poncho liner, a super lightweight blanket that would attach to the inside of a poncho when it was cold and rainy. At 4th ANGLICO we always carried ponchos even after Gore-Tex hit the field, but that was because they could be strung up in an endless amount of ways for field expedient shelters. Poncho liners are routinely called a "woobie" by troops to show how much affection we have for them, especially when they get broken in all soft and comfy like the blanket your mom gave you when you were a little kid. Poncho liners are quilted patterned nylon wrapped around a polyester loft center that can easily take you down to freezing when used along with a rubber poncho and a sleep mat. I'm not joking: The poncho liner is one of the best military investments since the F-15 first took flight in the early 1970s. Ask any veteran and they'll agree.

Great military gear that I own today and always keep in my personal buttpack are the same items I carried with 4th ANGLICO. I carry a two-colored air panel with bright orange on one side and the weirdest purple/lavender "whatever the hell fuchsia means" color on the opposite. Air panels have been used since World War II, with tankers laying them flat over the engine compartments of their Sherman tanks so Allied airpower could easily spot them. If you're lost and deploy an air panel the right way and search aircraft fly over or near you, it's almost a lock you will be located and rescued. Other great items easily bought online or in stores are cyalume sticks, 550 cord (and no, I won't call it paracord!), a signal mirror, a P-38 or John Wayne can opener, and the truly awesome "British lifeboat matches."

Most people know what cyalume sticks are as they can be bought at virtually any sports store or big box home improvement store. Here's a great trick for you in case you're lost and trying to get someone's attention. Grab some 550 cord and slide out one of the skinny white threads and tie it to the open slot on the cyalume stick. Break and shake the stick to get it good and glowing and then start swinging it in a circle. I guarantee it will create a bright continuous loop that will be easily seen in the dark of night.

Plenty of the pilots we had at 4th ANGLICO told me that by far the most visible daylight method of rescue was the signal mirror. It's a small mirror with a hole cut or drilled in the center. With minimal practice you can learn to create a reflection on the ground and then "steer" the little splotch of light at the aircraft or search party looking for you. I suggest buying a 3-by-5-inch version and don't buy a glass one. I learned that lesson after a parachute landing. One jump: crack! Time to buy a new mirror.

Marines always call the little fold-up can openers a P-38 or a John Wayne. I have no idea where the nicknames came from, but the little bastard will easily open up any tin can in no time. Another tip for junior paratroops: don't try to look all cool with a P-38 strung to your dog tags. When you land and make a dynamic parachute landing fall (PLF), that cute little can opener buddy of yours will leave a quarter-inch cut right in the middle of your chest. Not that this happened to me, of course.

It seems that since the dawn of fire, humans have been arguing incessantly about the best way to start a fire. If you really want to start a so-called flame war on the Internet, go on YouTube and make some silly post about fire starting and sit back to watch the avalanche of insults and static that comes your direction. For years I carried a bottle of the afore-mentioned British lifeboat matches. Around fifty matchsticks come in a plastic bottle much like a bottle of aspirin. Each wooden matchstick has a nearly inch-long coating of flammable material just like any match. These are covered with a varnish-like coating that makes them waterproof, but they also flame like a bat out of hell. The selling point of the matches was that you can't blow them out once you strike them. Well, I put that to the test on the concrete floor of the garage one day, and it's true. Use them sparingly because they light up like little blowtorches, which is why they're so valuable.

Hopefully this little chapter will help you understand the language of this book and Marine ANGLICO.

CHAPTER FIVE

Five MOSs in One:
Spotter, FAC, Para, F/O, Frog

MARINE ANGLICO IS SORT OF AN AMERICAN COMBAT VERSION OF *Tinker, Tailor, Soldier, Spy*, the brilliant John le Carré book. We dressed differently; we talked differently. We weren't normal Marines. I fit in perfectly.

Being an ANGLICO Marine really requires five very different military occupational specialties (MOSs):

Communications

Naval Gunfire

Artillery

Close Air Support by Tactical Aircraft

Paratrooper

If you've been in ANGLICO for a long time (twelve years in my case), it's almost a guarantee that you had still another MOS. I started out in logistics and embarkation and then trained in each of the above subjects over the years. It's why one of my commanding officers had lobbied for an ANGLICO MOS just as all of the skills to become a fully qualified Recon Marine were assigned their own MOS. Of course, it's never happened and I don't expect it to, especially with the advent of the Joint Terminal Attack Controller or JTAC (Jay-Tack).

However, let's go over some terminology first and a bit of Marine slang before we get into details. ANGLICO companies have two front-line MOSs. A U.S. Marine scout/forward observer (0861) uses radios and digital communications devices to "call in" artillery shells from a Marine or Army battery or fire from U.S. Navy destroyers or battleships, or uses a radio to talk to Marine or Navy pilots to launch air strikes from jet fighters, bombers, attack helicopters, or massive gunships such as the U.S. Air Force Spectre.

The other operator MOS is called a 2531 field radio operator. They attend school at Camp Pendleton in California. Since the school is titled the "Field Radio Operators Course" or FROC, Marine radio operators (such as comedian Drew Carey) are often called "frogs." Pairing these two MOSs works well. One Marine can teach the 0861 scout/forward observers about radios, and the other can teach the frogs how to call in artillery, air, and naval gunfire.

A forward observer in a normal artillery unit in the Marines or U.S. Army will only CFF from the artillery unit he's assigned to. While this troop will refer to himself as an "FO" (eff-O), ANGLICO operators will call themselves 0861s in recognition of all the other tasks we do, such as air strikes. Which brings us to the U.S. Air Force forward air controller, or FAC (FACK).

Air Force FACs have a storied history going back to World War II. Riding like cowboys behind the turrets of Sherman tanks, they gleefully blew the crap out of Nazi troops for wild man Gen. George S. Patton's slashing attack across France. Nazi Panther tanks would show up, FACs called in P-47 Thunderbolt fighter-bombers to drop 500-pound bombs, fire rockets, and that was that. Modern U.S. Air Force FACs almost always work with the U.S. Army, and in fact, I never even saw one in twelve years of operating.

Some of the officers in 4th ANGLICO were pilots who were quali-fied to fly combat aircraft, namely F-18 Hornet jet fighters, the awesome AV-8 Harrier jump jet, A-6 Intruder bombers, or helicopter gunships such as the AH-1 Cobra or Hueys loaded with rockets or mini-guns.

Our pilots taught us how to call in air strikes, whereas Air Force FACs attend a formal school in Fallon, Nevada. For years members of the Marine Corps, or at least ANGLICO and Recon, tried to attend the school, but the Air Force wouldn't accept enlisted Marines as students. One instructor told me he would take me in and I could attend the entire course, but the Air Force wouldn't let him give me certification. It was a rule we all labeled as stupid and shortsighted, which it was.

A Marine ANGLICO unit is in fact a very odd unit. A normal infantry company has around 225 Marine riflemen operating with three platoons and a small headquarters element. Three of these companies make up one battalion, which also has an additional weapons company and a full staff for operational planning. The Marine Corps battalion is commanded by a lieutenant colonel, usually in his late thirties, with his second-in-command, called the executive officer or XO in Marine slang, with the rank of major. The senior enlisted man is a sergeant major who serves as an advisor to the battalion commander in all relations regarding enlisted personnel but also directly overseas the training and leadership development of every enlisted Marine, NCO, and staff NCO throughout the entire battalion. He is universally referred to as "the sergeant major," reflecting the respect and hopefully admiration for the longevity of his career and the knowledge that he's attained along the way.

In every military around the world, the word *battalion* is similar to the word *business* in the sense that there are an endless number of definitions, variations, and goals for what that business is supposed to do or wants to accomplish. Generally speaking a battalion is large enough to operate on its own with its own motor transport, medical, communications, supplies, a training section, plus an operations section that is constantly planning and scheming future operations. However, your typical battalion would only have assets such as food, gasoline, or other supplies to operate no more than ten to fourteen days without resupply from the higher echelon, which is always a regimental level. Marine battalions in particular are usually rather large with upwards of twelve hundred Marines forming the entire unit. In addition to the line platoons and support sections, a Marine battalion has a headquarters company that is commanded by a captain who oversees all of the support functions for the line platoons plus supply, field rations, and the training and operation sections. The headquarters company commander is usually a senior captain due to the varied tasks he has to monitor and therefore only reports directly to the battalion commander. As the Marine Corps is the smallest of the U.S. military branches, being selected as the battalion commander is one of the highest honors for a commissioned officer, and it is an essential stepping-stone for those who want to be promoted to full colonel or into the general ranks.

A Marine ANGLICO company is about the same size as a normal infantry company. During my twelve years with 4th ANGLICO, we were as small as around 170 Marines when I first joined in the late 1980s and then increased to a little under 250 during the Gulf War and after due to all of the peacetime operations we were tasked with after 1st and 2nd ANGLICO were abolished during the aftermath of the Cold War (collapse of the Soviet Union and the destruction of the Berlin Wall). A significant argument against Marine ANGLICO companies has always been the large number of assets required to field even one company, and that's excluding the airborne capability that each unit used to have. It's an argument that is easy to understand quite frankly, as we had more Marines in our headquarters platoon than in the three line platoons designed to support foreign or U.S. Army units in the field.

For example, when a regular infantry company has a broken or damaged field radio, it will need to be taken up to battalion for service or repair and a different radio set will be issued to that company. The same goes for motor transport. If you need 5- or 7-ton trucks to move an infantry platoon, battalion will send you one. We had all of that on site in West Palm Beach, Florida. It was great for training, as we were a little self-contained entity, which gave us the freedom to train all over the state of Florida or even leave the state to jump into Fort Benning, Georgia, or fly up to Camp Lejeune, North Carolina, to blow shit up.

Fourth ANGLICO consisted of:

Communications

Medical

Supply

Administration

Operations

Training

the Parachute Loft (to pack and maintain parachutes)

Motor Transport

1st Brigade Platoon

2nd Brigade Platoon

3rd Brigade Platoon

the Armory (weapons and laser designators/range finders)

The brigade platoons are designed to support a U.S. Army brigade combat team in combat. Just as battalion is a word with dozens of meanings around the world, brigade is similar. I personally consider a U.S. Army brigade to be a very large, heavy regiment frequently assigned a specific task and organized accordingly. As such, a brigade platoon in ANGLICO is led by a very experienced Marine major who interacts with the senior full-bird colonel or one-star Army general in charge of your typical brigade. A normal platoon in the infantry is led by a young lieutenant, often with less than three years in the Marine Corps. If an ANGLICO team assigned to a brigade starts to butt heads regarding a mission or usage of our assets, twenty-three-year-old Lieutenant Greenhorn won't stand a chance against Colonel Potter from *M*A*S*H* or, worse still, George Patton during the 1930s before he was promoted to general. In short, the Marine major serves with the brigade staff and runs his two SALT teams, who run two or three FCT teams serving with the line platoons locked in combat or out on their own.

All of the other sections in a Marine ANGLICO company are organized into the headquarters platoon. During my time headquarters was so large it was split into two platoons just to control everybody. Even though my first MOS was embarkation and logistics, I always worked with the communication section just to keep me occupied. Whenever we had morning formation or were dismissed at the end of the workday, the communications Marines stood in the ranks with medical, supply, administration, the parachute riggers, training, operations, and even the lone career planner whom we usually only spoke to once a year when it was time to reenlist or extend our current contract. In 4th ANGLICO we had a ton of vehicles: white Econoline vans to serve as administrative vehicles, huge 5-ton camouflaged GMC trucks for field training, and for a very long time before and after the Gulf War, we must have had almost fifty Humvees parked in our rear parking lot, which usually just sat there until they broke. As my Motor T buddy Smitty explained to me, Humvees are designed to operate at full speed basically twenty-four hours a day. If they were not run almost every day, the oil and lubricants don't cycle through the engine or the entire vehicle and they crack. So when Smitty was stationed at West Palm Beach, he spent about an hour each day firing up a small number of Humvees, laying on the gas pedal until all the black diesel smoke ran out the rear exhaust pipes, and letting them sit there and run for about ten minutes to keep the vehicles in running order. Smitty did this all the time. But as a result of all these vehicles, 4th ANGLICO had a very high number of school-trained drivers and mechanics to keep all this rolling stock on the road—which is why we split Motor T into its own platoon that stood next to the rest of head-quarters during company formations. Motor T worked extremely hard and was very tight, very proud under the leadership of Vietnam veteran and MSgt. José Vicente. There were two funny things about Motor T under Top Vicente: They were always, and I mean always, late to any formation called by the sergeant major or anybody else for that matter, but when they showed up, their close order drill—i.e., marching—was sharper than anybody I ever saw at 4th ANGLICO.

On paper a US Marine ANGLICO company only has three sections that would be deployed into the field.

THE DIVISION CELL

The aptly named Division Cell is assigned to either a U.S. Army or for-eign full-strength division, which in the U.S. military could be as many as twenty-five thousand soldiers whereas the much smaller British army operates divisions with roughly 10,000 troops that are designed to deploy very quickly. Obviously a twenty-five-year-old Marine captain who is the normal commander of the company-size unit is not going to be able to successfully interact with a two-star general from the U.S. Army, who most likely has no idea why we are there to begin with anyway. A twenty-year veteran lieutenant colonel who's had a successful career in infantry or artillery with his sergeant major tagging along behind him is going to be able to hold his own against the flag officer, in addition to his duties of planning, monitoring, and supervising his supporting arms liaison teams (SALT) and the multiple firepower control teams (FCT teams), who were the small teams of Marines actually calling in air strikes, artillery, or naval gunfire missions for the supported line companies. The Division Cell has the majority of the senior leadership of any Marine ANGLICO company, plus fifteen to twenty other Marines to help monitor the radio networks and coordinate the teams operating in the field. It's a very strange thing to see only twenty Marines in a group operating during a field exercise, and the person in charge is a Marine lieutenant colonel. Normally that would be considered a large squad of Marines and led by a buck sergeant. It's just another quirk of Marine ANGLICO.

The Supporting Arms Liaison Team

Always referred to as "the SALT" or "the SALT team," this group of Marines operates at the battalion level and is usually designed and equipped to coexist with the army's tactical operations center or "TOC." Most of the Army tactical operations centers I saw were based out of Humvees called "high backs" due to the taller canvas coverings in the rear of the Hummer or where they could use field tents to create a very small radio communications section in one place to display all of the operational maps, codebooks, and other planning gear to run their operations. The SALT teams usually were equipped with MRC 138 or MRC 110 communications Humvees to monitor every FCT team in their area of operations, plus they can pick up and move with the TOC whenever required due to a change in battlefield situation or even if they just came under attack and had to bug out. The SALT is usually not a very large section, with a senior captain who is usually a naval aviator and serves as a certified FAC for the supported battalion. In my experience, basically everybody else is there to monitor the radios twenty-four hours a day. As I've written before, the SALT is a classic example of being on radio watch forever and then playing catch-up when all hell breaks loose. After all, watching the maps and monitoring the radio traffic as FCT teams call in their various missions might not require any action on your part for quite some time. But if incoming artillery rounds or naval gunfire shells start passing battalion lines, quick action is needed to tighten or modify the mission. In another very unglamorous role, if FCTs needed more batteries or food, if the Army was either unwilling or unable to supply them to us, SALT teams then shifted roles to resupply and brought out whatever the operating teams needed.

FIREPOWER CONTROL TEAMS (FCT TEAMS)

Firepower control teams (FCT teams) are where the rubber really hits the runway in Marine ANGLICO companies. On paper these teams of operators are designed to be led by a junior captain or senior lieutenant, usually with a background in artillery. However, as an ANGLICO unit's situation tends to change constantly, most of the teams I was on were run by a staff NCO or by myself as a buck sergeant. Reflecting our "bombs on target" mentality, whoever was best qualified to lead the team was the Marine in charge. They are on the move, they are under fire, they're on lonely outposts for days on end, and they're the Marines holding the handset that brings in the full fury of American supporting arms. It could be a duo of F-18 Hornets slashing in for a lightning quick strike that lasts between the two of them less than five minutes, or the crazy Harrier pilots literally sucking dust off of the desert floor as they come in on a bombing run. Illumination rounds could light up the nighttime sky, white phosphorus could provide cover for marking a target, or naval gunfire rounds could be blasting an area the size of a football field with only one shell. All of this is the domain and purview of an FCT team, which is always called a "FICT team" by ANGLICO Marines. And yes, we were fully aware how redundant it is to use the word "team" after SALT and FCT. But we have our own language that reflects our unique operations.

Concerning the rest of the company, I served with hundreds of fine Marines in so-called support sections that were as squared away as a Parris Island drill instructor, as combative and ready to fight as any Recon Marine, or as intelligent as any computer whiz at the CIA. They never let me down.

ADMIN: ALWAYS BEHIND BUT ALWAYS BEHIND US

Every member of the U.S. military loves to make fun of rear echelon troops, especially administrative types who are seen as doing nothing more manly than using a 1930s typewriter, covered in black ink, and wearing one of those funny banker's visors you always see in cowboy movies. They weren't "front line" or "in the thick of it" or a "good operator with the teams." The nicknames reflected this attitude: REMFs for "rear echelon motherfuckers," Remington Raiders in reference to the afore-mentioned typewriters, and in the Marines they're just called Admin. Ok, we called them Admin pogues and made them out to be geeks who were "in the rear with the gear."

Reporting to the administration section was always portrayed as walking into some sort of dark cave where something bad was bound to happen. Your pay was screwed up, your vacation was screwed up, you can't go on leave to see your mom next month, you're not going to Jump School just yet, and best of all: You didn't get promoted yet. Great. All that and I get to spend tonight sleeping in the rain while the REMFs would be at Hooters drinking beer, eating chicken wings, and staring at, well, hooters. At least that's how we saw it.

This is part of the military mythology, but as always, we're ANGLICO, so it ain't gonna work out like normal. I've known some Admin chiefs, senior gunnery sergeants with twenty years of service, who wouldn't bat an eyelash about calling Camp Lejeune, the Pentagon, or Marine Corps Finance in Kansas City and screaming over the phone about some young Marine's lost paycheck.

Several times a year a young Marine would report for duty at 4th ANGLICO to check in. He or she would promptly tell the Admin chief, "I haven't been paid in nine months. Can you help me? I just had a baby." It never happened to me, but when it did it was horrible for the Marine involved. The military is just so huge, when things go bad, it's a disaster, especially when it comes to money.

Now when I say yelling at some hapless pay clerk, I mean this gunnery sergeant is *standing up at his desk bellowing* over the phone like King Kong after a bad prostate exam. The poor young Marine, who's broke, is embarrassed as hell, frozen in terror, wondering what type of lunatics are running this outfit, but also proud someone was finally listening. Gunny K. Kong was just *that man*.

"WHO CARES IF HE LEFT YOUR UNIT?
HE'S STILL IN UNIFORM ISN'T HE?
HE'S STILL YOUR FELLOW MARINE ISN'T HE?
HE JUST HAD A BABY FER CHRISSAKES AND BY THE SOUND OF IT, LITTLE JOHNNY'S GOT MORE HAIR ON HIS PEACHES THAN YOU DO CORPORAL SHITHEAD!"

It was glorious.

Funny thing is, no one in the headquarters section was alarmed, because they were loving every minute of it. The colonel or sergeant major didn't mind and used it as a "welcome aboard Marine! We care about our people" moment. Besides, if the colonel's travel pay ever gets screwed up, he'll need Gunny Kong just like the rest of us.

And then it happened. Gunny Kong lowered his voice and calmly asked the one question Corporal Shithead never wanted to hear:

"Do I have to call Kansas City?" Gunny Kong gently asked.

The two words "Kansas" and "City" usually go together just fine, conjuring all-American images of farmland, super nice people, the blues, barbecue ribs, more nice people, and Arrowhead Stadium. In the Marine Corps it's the focal point of everything financial, and you *never* want them involved unless as truly a last resort. Gunny Kong would boot everyone out of his office and call his super-secret phone line to speak with a "woman he knows in Kansas City that can solve this shit." There always seemed to be a woman in K.C. who could magically produce a paycheck for PFC Penniless. Sure enough, a five-minute phone call between a veteran gunnery sergeant and hard-working Kansas City momma, and within two days a FedEx envelope with a paper check drawn to the exact penny would arrive in West Palm Beach. It worked every time.

While every American veteran might have a story just like this one, at ANGLICO when we needed to flesh out an operational detachment, we took volunteers from the cooks, bakers, and candlestick makers and turned them into radio operators to man the midnight radio watch. For emergencies we gave them crash courses on calling in artillery if the enemy was storming the front gates. Which bring us to a young Admin clerk named Basit. Omar Basit was a young Marine who looked about twelve years old but was just the nicest kid you ever met. Everyone liked him and he always solved our crappy Admin problems with a smile on his face. So of course, we trained him for basic ANGLICO Special Ops and got him ready for the field.

After all those years of serving with 4th ANGLICO, Basit told me something I'd never considered: "We could never catch up no matter what we did." It made perfect sense as soon as he said it. Consider my own position: I lived 300 miles away. I moved every year in a college town and changed telephone numbers along the way. To get to Norway alone, I attended Mountain Warfare School in California and trained in Fort Drum, New York, for Winter Survival School. Jump School is in Georgia. Naval Gunfire School is in Coronado, California, Artillery School is in Oklahoma, while I was in Comm my security clearance needed constant upgrading, and we had teams of visiting Air Force trainers give us a crash course on how to load giant cargo planes. We had annual flight physicals to stay on jump status, monthly drug tests, plus being jabbed with syringes full of every type of shot medical could dream up. This is excluding annual trips to Camp Lejeune, North Carolina, and force-on-force battalion fights with the U.S. Army in Fort Polk, Louisiana, which, of course, is where our twelve-year-old-looking, boyish Admin pogue Basit got himself arrested on liberty call.

Of all the Marines I thought would get arrested on liberty, Basit wasn't the one. He had five or six Marines he ran with and Basit was the good one. He was the responsible one who kept his head. After a three-week fight at JRTC, Basit and company had been on the casino boats at Bossier City, Louisiana. My crew and I had gone to dinner at the awesomely named Ralph and Kacoo's, a huge Cajun place serving whole fried crabs, shrimp etouffee, crawdads, and blackened alligator tail that made my lips throb in pain. I actually took my Abita Turbo Dog bottle and held it to my lips for pain relief. It was quite a sight: a table of ten U.S. Marine paratroopers teary-eyed from the pain of Ragin' Cajun cuisine. Meanwhile, Opie Taylor was wearing a pair of silver bracelets down by the riverboat casino.

I didn't hear about the "trip downtown" until the next morning when Sgt. Jim Carty, my good Comm buddy, told me he was the one sent to County to collect our idiots from the local police. I asked about the usual suspects: Capone, Soprano, Corleone, Ace Rothstein, etc.

"No. It was Basit," Carty said with a laugh.

"Who?" I asked, stupefied.

"Basit," he repeated.

"BASIT? OUR BASIT? YOU GOTTA BE KIDDING ME?" I shouted in our hotel room.

"Of course, our Basit! How many Marines are named Omar in this fuckin' unit?" Carty countered.

Good point. But, honestly, I would've suspected Presidents Reagan or Truman or even Mickey Mouse to get caught spying for the Russians before I could have envisioned Basit in a Loosiana hoosegow for fighting, obstruction, or whatever the hell he did. While the funny story of Basit getting tossed into the can overnight is good for this book, it also highlights a constant refrain of this story. Any other Marine can get offended or upset about taking an Admin Marine into the field on an operation featuring thousands of troops. Well, tell me a solution, give me more money for training, or just get off my ass and let me do my job with my buddies—which is what we always did anyway.

MEDICAL: THE AWESOME NAVY CORPSMEN

I've always loved to tell Americans how U.S. Marines have complete faith in U.S. Navy corpsmen. They are so well trained, and are enthusiastic in their dedication and their care and concern for their fuzzy-headed flock of crazy jarheads. I was always shocked to learn of the lack of faith, and sometimes scorn and contempt, that individual soldiers in the U.S. Army had about their combat medics, at least during the 1990s. I'm sure that with more than ten years of two wars going on at the same time that the

U.S. Army's field medical programs have substantially improved. However, during the late 1980s and 1990s, the soldiers I served with regarded their field medics as nothing more than pill pushers, whereas I've always thought of U.S. Navy corpsmen as only a few steps below a field battle surgeon. I know they couldn't do surgery, but they were so much more well-rounded in their medical education, and they maintained near religious zealotry over the health of their Marines.

Marines call Navy corpsmen "Doc" no matter what their name or rank is, until they're promoted to chief and then you have to treat them with the proper military respect. I've often used a fictional account to illustrate just exactly how U.S. Marines felt about their own Navy corpsmen. I would tell people that if you're in a bar somewhere and you just can't go on living without getting into a fistfight, you look around the bar and you quickly decide you have two choices. On one side there's an entire platoon of Marine infantrymen drinking their beers, telling terrible jokes, but also minding their own business. On the other side of the bar, possibly a little tipsy from too much beer, is sitting a lone U.S. Navy corpsman. What this belligerent drunken fool doesn't realize is that tipsy corpsman is considered to be family by all of the other Marines that you decided not to start a fight with. I advise people in very strong terms: between picking a fight with one Navy corpsman or twenty-five U.S. Marines, go after the Marines. And don't think I'm exaggerating, because I'm not. And it's because of this: Every U.S. Marine around the world knows that if they get hurt during training or wounded in combat, a U.S. Navy corpsman will come charging at them like they're taking part in the annual Running of the Bulls in Pamplona, Spain.

It works like this. When we were training at Fort Drum, New York, during our one-and-a-half-year-long training cycle to deploy to Norway for Operation Battle Griffin in 1996, we were constructing survival shelters out in the field. The deal was to apply everything that we had learned from the Arctic warrior teachers of the 25th Marine Regiment, be alive the next morning, and "Hey! You get to go to Norway!" Needless to say, when you're out in the woods building your own little hut—or "hooch" in Marine Corps slang—you are going to need a lot of wood. You need wood for your hooch and you need wood for the fire you're going to keep going all night long. Our detachment was split into three- or four-man teams depending on our cold-weather experience, with the most experienced Marine deciding where and how we would build our survival shelters. This was decided regardless of rank. You could be an officer or staff NCO, but if a sergeant or even a corporal had already been inside the Arctic Circle and had a successful training evolution, then that Marine was in charge.

Marines were spread out all over our camp area collecting wood, cutting down dead trees, and getting sleeping gear ready for the night, which our instructors had warned would be remarkably cold. Later that evening one of my hooch partners was listening to his Walkman radio and heard on a Syracuse radio station that the temperature was 25 degrees below zero. Fort Drum is an hour away from Syracuse, and we were out in the field far away from the steam pipe–driven heat of any U.S. military base, so it was probably even colder than that. Even though I've slept on the snow 150 miles inside the Arctic Circle, survival night in January 1995 is my personal record and I think it will stand for the rest of my life. I was happily using my K-bar combat knife to hack away at some piece of wood that I wanted when another Marine using a hatchet or machete struck one of his fingers when he was collecting wood about 60 feet away from me. His buddy spotted what happened and did everything correctly according to the Marine Corps Way. He clapped his hand on the wounded Marines hand, forced him to sit down, and just yelled the universal call, a very loud, long drawn out "cooorrr-pppssmaaan!" If a Navy corpsman is too far away, in the Marine Corps version of playing telephone, we just pass the message on with everybody yelling "corpsman" as loud as they can and then getting the hell out of the way of the raging bull charge of the nearest corpsman. Since I was near where the Marine got hurt and his buddy was already helping him, I had one simple job: to turn myself into a traffic sign. I stopped what I was doing, looked in the direction of the corpsman running as fast as he could from my right, and used my left hand to point where the hurt Marine was located. Other Marines were doing the same thing, telling Doc little directions to his new patient.

"Over there Doc! To the right, to the right by Gonzo!" they'd say.

I can't remember how bad the wound was, and maybe it only required a few stitches, but it was still a perfect little example of how quickly Navy corpsmen are all over U.S. Marines.

The other funny point about the relationship of U.S. Marines and Navy corpsmen is the universal knowledge that U.S. Marines hate getting shots. Whether they have to administer a vaccine, painkiller, or even just vitamins, every corpsman will swear up and down that Marines are the worst patients they ever had. It's just a weird thing about Marines. We don't mind getting shot at, but we don't want to get shots. Besides we get some pretty ugly shots sometimes. During preparation for the Gulf War in 1990, every single member of 4th ANGLICO was lined up and paraded through two Navy corpsmen holding air guns that blasted a vaccine into your skin. Since there are no needles, it's supposed to be a cleaner method of administering shots. But it happens to hurt like hell regardless of what anybody says. I love to see the look on my registered nurse friends' faces when I tell them I received my shots for both the plague and typhoid in both shoulders at the same time. It just blows their mind. Needless to say, within twenty minutes the entire company felt like throwing up, and we didn't get much accomplished the rest of the day.

The Navy corpsmen in our ANGLICO unit were much more qualified than their active duty counterparts, a point I know will anger and aggravate active duty corpsmen. However, many if not most of our corpsmen were paramedics out in "the World" and were up to date on the latest in medical technology and techniques, in addition to riding rescue and fire trucks on a daily basis. One of our corpsmen, Doc Mason, worked for a doctor performing research on individual cells in the human body. Doc Mason told me how fascinated he was with cellular research as each individual cell was its own little world. I asked him about that scene from the movie *Animal House* when Boone, Katie, and the pledge nicknamed Pinto were getting stoned with their professor played by Donald Sutherland. Sutherland insisted to Pinto that all of humanity and planet Earth were merely one little cell in the finger of a giant being that made up the universe. Pinto freaks out when he realizes that Sutherland's logic would mean that Pinto has an entire tiny little universe in his own finger. I reminded Doc Mason of the scene from

Animal House and asked him in all seriousness if he agreed with that scene. He actually took a few moments to contemplate my question, and with the most serious look on his face that I'd ever seen, Mason looked me dead in the eye and said, "Yes."

And that is the type of Navy corpsman that we had at 4th ANGLICO. They are truly an overlooked national asset, and I'd put the 4th ANGLICO docs up against any in the entire Navy or Marine Corps any day of the week.

THE RIGGERS

Without the parachute riggers of 4th ANGLICO in West Palm Beach, Florida, you wouldn't be reading this book. No doubt. No debate. No dithering. I would have been buried more than fifteen years ago.

As they are fond of saying, "every time I pack a chute, I save a life," and it's the complete truth—and they do it every day.

All Army and Marine riggers attend a rigorous four-month-long school at Fort Lee in Virginia, and its students are roundly thrashed throughout the entire course. Since each branch of the U.S. military has some type of aviation assets, each pilot and aircrew member obviously needs a parachute. And each parachute needs a rigger who will repack the chute so it deploys safely and keeps the crew member alive. Riggers are also taught to pack and operate very large parachutes that are used to drop supplies or even Hummers or large light armored vehicles. Obviously the U.S. Army with the 82nd and 101st Airborne Divisions has thousands and thousands of parachutes that all need to be packed correctly, stored correctly, and given safety inspections on a tightly controlled basis. For some reason U.S. Army riggers adopted a red baseball cap as a badge of their office, much like U.S. Army Special Forces adopted their famous green beret back in the 1960s. However, I've never seen the Marine Corps riggers wearing a red baseball cap, as we're always striving to be different from the other services.

In a Marine Recon or ANGLICO unit, the riggers work inside the parachute loft in a very large space with tables that are around 40 to 50 feet long. A fully extended parachute is laid upon one of the tables for repacking after a parachute drop. It's a very specific by-the-numbers affair to repack a parachute so it will deploy in the proper order. I have to admit I wouldn't even consider going to riggers school. I've always had a bit of the lock-and-load, game-day personality type that doesn't lend well to repetitive tasks of any nature. Many people look down on autoworkers, turning their nose up at what they see as a mindless drone of the job. I've always had a certain amount of admiration for those folks, as I know I would be terrible at it. I know I could do the work up to standard, but it would bore me so much that I would hate my job and consequently would not last very long. It's one thing to work on an endless line of automobiles placing windshield after windshield, which does have to be done correctly or the windshields blow out at high speeds causing wrecks and injuries. But being a parachute rigger is just that much more demanding because if the main chute fails, a quick deployment of the reserve chute is the only thing that will keep that trooper alive. It always makes national news when an American paratrooper gets killed in an accident, but compared to the thousands of jumps performed each year, the number of jump deaths is remarkably small. During my ten years of being on jump status, I never had anything remotely malfunction on any of my parachutes. Marines who are airborne qualified don't coddle or offer special treatment to parachute riggers, but they are recognized for how special and demanding their job is.

COMMUNICATIONS

As I've written an entire chapter (chapter 9) on the importance of radio communications in Marine ANGLICO, you'll learn just how important the communication section is to our mission in the field and in combat. Always referred to as "the comm shack," it's actually two sections in one. One section consists of the communications technicians who keep the unit's radios finely tuned and within specifications, but also repair radio sets when Marines like me break them. The other half of the comm shack properly stores the unit's entire inventory of radios and antennas, and also helps to staff out the SALT and FCT teams during training and field operations.

My unit in West Palm Beach had hundreds of radios stacked to the ceiling and thousands of pieces of secondary gear ranging from 30-foot antennas that we would fight to mount on the back of the Humvee radio truck down to encryption devices that fit in your front pocket. It was an avalanche of maintenance and paperwork to keep track of it all, and if any of it ever went missing, it would mark the end of the career of the Marine involved. I can honestly say that in twelve years none of our radios ever went missing due to our oversight or lack of attention to detail. Coming back from my second trip to Norway in 1999, two embarkation boxes full of radios did somehow manage to find their way to another unit; however, once we loaded our communications Humvees onto the ship in Norway, and of course got a receipt for them, it was then the ship's crew's responsibility to deliver them to West Palm Beach on time, which they didn't do. I heard later that the Naval Investigative Service (NIS) was searching Marines' homes as a result. The radios were located out in California, returned to us, and I never heard anything further about it.

SUPPLY

Our supply section was a lot like the administration section. It was big, and it was staffed by very hardworking Marines who we gave a lot of crap to about being rear echelon Marines; however, they had a large amount of equipment to deal with and just like Admin were behind no matter what they did. With detachments ranging from five to fifty Marines deploying anywhere from the Caribbean to California, from upstate Louisiana to upstate New York and across the water to Norway, England, or Sardinia, Supply was always receiving truckloads of specialized combat gear to issue out. Ten years' worth of two wars with at least eleven separate detachments serving in Iraq and Afghanistan I'm sure only added to their existing workload.

A good example would be the multiple extreme cold weather detachments that I deployed on. Supply would get these huge boxes mounted on wooden pallets and almost 5 feet tall stuffed with Gore-Tex jackets, cross-country skis, ski poles, 4-foot-tall snowshoes, Northeast dome tents, polypro long johns, sleeping bags that were rated for subzero temperatures, and enough gloves to outfit an elementary school. The Marine Corps purchased a smaller amount of specialized gear, or STAP gear, in this case clothing that was tough enough for combat training inside the Arctic Circle, and then shipped the gear to the individual units that were deploying to that area of the world. It's a good plan as you don't need to buy a full set of extreme cold weather gear for each U.S. Marine just in case they might deploy to Scandinavia or Antarctica. In addition to all the combat gear for more than two hundred Marines, Supply had to monitor all of the special gear we needed for various adventures and then had to take it all back, take inventory, and determine if everything was in proper working order. Then they would load it all back onto a semi-truck and ship it back up to the Marines' massive supply depot in Albany, Georgia. And just like every other section of 4th ANGLICO, when we needed to fill out a detachment, we didn't hesitate to grab a Supply Marine, teach them how to use the radio, and assign them to the division team to help monitor field operations. They were good Marines and I had plenty of friends in Supply.

THE ARMORY

We didn't have a huge armory, as there weren't that many Marines in our company. The armory was mainly full of M-16s, Beretta semiautomatic pistols for the officers and staff NCOs, plus a few M203 grenade launchers. What separated a Marine ANGLICO company armory from other armories were the laser designator systems securely stored there. Far outdated with today's technology, when I was still in uniform, the laser designator we operated was known by the acronym of MULE, which stood for Modular Universal Laser Equipment. It was big, and it was bulky. Ugly, heavy, and hard to deal with, when you got it working right, it did its job just like, well, a mule. The lasers now look like something out of Star Wars, but more on that later. And no, armory Marines are not nice to you when you turn in your M-16. Not squeaky clean? Try again, Marine.

MOTOR TRANSPORT

I've already mentioned the hardworking bastards of Motor T, and I will provide much more detail in chapter 17. All things vehicle: It's their job. Suffice to say, Motor T Marines work a lot harder and get a lot less credit than they deserve. And if you really want to know what fear is, take a ride with a truck convoy in Iraq when you know you're going to get hit.

THE BRIGADE PLATOONS

As mentioned, the three line platoons are full of scout/forward observers and radio operators that make up the SALT and FCT teams that serve directly with U.S. Army or foreign troops. While there might only be thirty or so enlisted Marines in an ANGLICO platoon, I've been on plenty of field operations, mainly JRTC, that with the Division Cell, naval gunfire cell, and some Navy corpsmen thrown in, a deploying platoon could reach up to fifty at times. While Comm might be the heart and soul of ANGLICO, the brigade platoons are the Marines who serve at the tip of the spear.

OPERATIONS AND TRAINING

Operations (always referred to as "Ops") and Training basically go hand in hand. Very senior staff NCOs take guidance from the commanding officer and then figure out how to get the assignment done (Ops) and what type of activity (Training) will qualify Marines to get it done.

There are two types of Marines in Training: the lazy one and the good one. The lazy one sees it as a skate job as they usually don't go in the field that much. The only time you interact with this clown is during the annual PFT, when he climbs out of his cave holding his little clipboard and wearing a stopwatch around his neck, which most of us wanted to choke him with because he wasn't setting up better training plans for the unit. Marines always want to train hard, and then train harder. The Marine you really want in Training is the man who takes his cues from the commanding officer, walks into his own office, and thinks to himself "hmm ... if I keep the colonel happy I can basically run this outfit." This is the man you want. He's seen so many bad examples of training that all he wants to do is rock and roll and get Marines out in the field, where they should be. Also, he's too smart to be bothered with running a PFT. Jeez, give that job to a corporal for chrisakes!

Each of the now six ANGLICO companies are organized this way, except that the two Reserve units, 3rd and 4th, are the only two to retain the airborne mission.

After September 11th HQMC quickly realized the previous administration had made a mistake abolishing Marine ANGLICO. 1st and 2nd ANGLICO were promptly reactivated at Camp Lejeune in North Carolina and Camp Pendleton in California. However, for whatever reason, most likely financial, ironically the two active duty ANGLICO units were not designated as airborne-qualified units. That designation was reserved for the Reserve units, 3rd and 4th ANGLICO. With the expansion of Special Operations after September 11th, in an extremely wise and thoughtful move in my opinion, HQMC established a 5th ANGLICO unit and located it on Okinawa, Japan. I thought this made perfect sense. We would now have a unit full of universal spotters in the Western Pacific for multiple reasons. One, they could quickly deploy to Iraq or Afghanistan. Two, and this is strictly my own personal opinion, 5th ANGLICO could be rapidly deployed to assist our allies in the Pacific region, namely the Australians, who have been our staunch supporters for half a century, and the Philippines and Malaysia. Most Americans have virtually no knowledge of the Philippines and Malaysia and just how much territory they occupy in the Pacific Ocean. Malaysia covers thousands of square miles of open water, including the vital Straits of Malacca that sees virtually a quarter of the entire world's maritime traffic pass through it. Needless to say, the pirate activity is very high.

The Philippines are sovereign to seven thousand islands and have fought various rebel and communist groups for decades. During the 1970s and '80s, U.S. Marine patrols protected the fuel and ammunition dumps of the U.S. Navy that were based in Subic Bay at the time. Having the ability to quickly deploy small teams capable of calling in any type of air or naval gunfire support is invaluable. Granted this is not necessarily the thinking in Washington, D.C., but then again I don't know what they've been thinking on most things since President Reagan left the White House.

Presently the six ANGLICO units in the world are located in the following sites. 1st ANGLICO is located at Camp Pendleton, California, north of San Diego and south of Los Angeles. 2nd ANGLICO is located at Camp Lejeune in North Carolina, home to the 2nd Marine Division and 2nd Marine Air Wing. 3rd ANGLICO is located in tiny Bell, California, near the Huntington Beach area. My old unit, 4th ANGLICO, is way down south in West Palm Beach, Florida. 5th ANGLICO is stationed on Okinawa, Japan. Lastly, a brand-new ANGLICO, 6th, was formed and based in Concord, California. No one I have spoken to understands why 6th ANGLICO was created, as it seems to have only two platoons for training. The consensus seems to be, and I agree, that these resources should be added to the two West Coast units, 1st and 3rd ANGLICO. I know California is very big, but three separate ANGLICO companies in one state? Oh well, I guess this is why I'm not wearing general's stars on my shoulders.

So there you have it. The basic structure of, pound for pound, one of the most destructive units in the U.S. military, which we need to get more use out of in both wartime and peacetime.

Though I have described a "typical" ANGLICO unit, there is nothing typical about ANGLICO. Marines and soldiers who served in ground forces will easily recognize the battalion structure, but not as it relates to a unit of well under three hundred troops. ANGLICO is different, training- and cost-intensive, but as a young 4th ANGLICO staff sergeant named Teddy Pernal will detail later in the book, one FCT team staffed with four to six Marines has more firepower at its disposal than an entire platoon of American infantry.

CHAPTER SIX

The Eternal Sales Job

ANGLICO MARINES ARE ALWAYS TEACHING OTHER SERVICE MEMBERS who we are and what we do. In nearly every interview with former and active 4th ANGLICO members, subjects used the word *sales* when discussing working with other branches of the U.S. military or foreign troops. It can't be stressed enough how often we've done this since the Korean War.

While Americans in the business community, specifically sales folks obviously, might take offense or wonder why this is a problem, if you haven't been in the service, you don't understand how different the ethic is. Especially in the Marine Corps, we take pride in the fact that we don't need a bonus for every little thing we accomplish. We're here to do the dirty work civilians can't be bothered with. It is a very distinct insult to a member of the U.S. military to call them "corporate." It means you're, among other things, selfish, only out for yourself, or more concerned with picking up rank or kissing the colonel's ass all the time. In fact, staff NCOs in the Marine Corps (staff sergeant and up to sergeant major or master gunnery sergeant) are some of the most independently minded, territorial, and downright belligerent leaders I've ever seen. I've seen section chiefs butting heads with junior officers, and even a newly appointed lieutenant colonel who tried to tell a staff NCO how to do their job. To these Marines, being called "corporate" would actually be "fightin' words" and would mean they're superficial and not for real.

Marine Corps staff noncommissioned officers (staff sergeant, master sergeant, first sergeant, and sergeant major) are the Marines that actively run the day-to-day operations of the Big Green Rifle Club. There are as many different types of staff NCOs as there are turning leaves of a New England fall. Some are strict. Some are nicer than Mister Rogers and Big Bird (but don't *ever* piss these types off). Some are mean for fun, and some are funnier than Chris Rock at the Apollo Theater in Harlem. But each and every one of them has an independent streak and pride of ownership of the section they run that's a joy to be seen.

"Sir, you place me in charge of Comm, I know what I'm doing," Gunny Smith/Jones/Whatever would calmly say.

It's the polite, Marine Corps way of saying, "Hey! I've been doing this for seventeen years! Get off my ass and outta my shop, sir!"

Don't think I'm joking. But the other side of the gunny "get outta my shop" routine is that you're responsible for everything that happens: good, bad, happy, or sad. One great example of this attitude was an I&I Ops chief named Top Parks. Parks was a career 0861 man, which means he started as a scout/forward observer many moons ago. I have several enduring memories of Top Parks: He drank Añejo rum like most people drink lemonade, he wore his heart on his sleeve like Gen. Norman Schwarzkopf, and he *hated* then Florida Gator football coach Steve Spurrier. Even as a staunch Florida Gator, I chuckle to this day remembering the sight of Top Parks, all 6-foot, 5-inches of him, crouching into Spurrier's grumpy squat pose after pretending to chuck his visor on the ground. It was a perfect imitation and Parks loved to do it to me right in the middle of the company headquarters section. I'd walk into Operations to speak with Top MacMillan only to turn around to see Parks crouched and frumpy in the corner. Of course, he laughed at me in no short order.

Parks told me he had only one goal inside the Marine Corps.

"My job is to yell at colonels," he flatly told me.

With Top Parks that was a reality. What he really meant was that he was the expert with twenty-five years of experience. Officers checking into ANGLICO needed to listen and learn before they torched the unit with some stupid idea they just read in an in-flight magazine. I experienced quite a bit of this when I joined a small group of Marines traveling south to Puerto Rico for a naval gunfire shoot at the U.S. Navy's Atlantic bombing range on Vieques Island. I had yet to attend formal Naval Gunfire School in Coronado, California, and I was looking forward to a week of having a 550-foot-long Navy destroyer at our disposal. Everything was set for a great time: sitting on a Caribbean island, the week of my birthday on November 13 (yes, I was born on a Friday), and five full days of bombing the crap out of everything. It would be ANGLICO paradise. Well, since the Navy rammed their new destroyer against a coral reef on the way down, it was a bust. Again, Marines will never understand how the Navy rams ships into other objects while underway. In this case they hit a reef. In the Caribbean! Does anyone remember the pirates of the Caribbean? The reefs have been charted for the last five hundred years, for Christ's sake. You know what a reef is right? They all have names, everyone knows the *exact* location, and they tend to not move around too often. To make it worse, I heard the destroyer was named after a Marine Medal of Honor winner from Vietnam, Sgt. Alberto Gonzalez.

On our first day of the shoot, we were all ready to go and Top Parks told us that nearby Roosevelt Roads Naval Station hadn't had any radio contact with the ship. I was incredulous. First, you crash a destroyer on its shake-down cruise and now you've lost the damn thing? That's the word we received, and I never heard anyone refute it since. So of course, we went back to San Juan to party our asses off. Of course, Top Parks taught me how to play blackjack and introduced me to the power and glory of Añejo rum drinks just before we got booted out of a San Juan lounge since the drag queen show was about to start. We didn't train worth a crap, but at least we'd had some fun for my birthday.

This independent streak is even more important in ANGLICO, and as it turns out, so is sales. I honestly think the first meeting with foreign troops was easier than with the U.S. Army, as the foreign troops are so happy for the fire support. In Norway we were all amazed to learn the Norwegian Air Force's hard stance against CAS. Plenty of pilots are like this. I understand you need to be a cocky bastard to fly a supersonic jet fighter, but you can't fly down low to help your own countrymen who are under direct enemy fire? Yes, you have to chase down Russian bombers along your border, but if things really got ugly, their tanks would be on the ground and not at 20,000 feet. The Norgees fly F-16s that they buy from us, and as any Iraqi soldier from the Gulf War will tell you, it's a hell of a bomber. But that's the funny thing about our time in Norway: When the Norgees needed CAS, Americans and American aircraft are the ones who got it done.

In 1999 I sat in a Norwegian staff car with a young lieutenant as we watched several F-18 Hornets make simulated bombing runs against the Battle Griffin bad guys. We were in a perfect position to watch the fighters run in and maneuver into position to drop their ordnance. Every move the pilot did, I explained to the lieutenant, who was captivated by the entire situation. He looked like little Ralphie in *A Christmas Story* peering into the store window at his desired Red Ryder BB gun. It was yet another instance of teaching others the ANGLICO way.

Sitting in his home plastered with photographs of his two daughters while giving me digital pictures of his time in Iraq and Afghanistan, 4th ANGLICO staff sergeant Teddy Pernal instantly recognized the importance of selling the ANGLICO mission and used the word *sales* with no prompting from me. Pernal is a young father with *four* combat tours in two wars; he has been a paratrooper, jumpmaster, school-trained radio operator, and even drives 7-ton trucks at the unit. During his tours Pernal personally called in nearly a hundred air strikes as a certified Joint Terminal Attack Controller (JTAC). After trading the usual "no, we're not Italians" joke, Pernal told me he took a more formal approach when first attached to a new unit, a never-ending process with ANGLICO.

"You hit it right on the head. You've got to take a sales approach to it because no one knows who we are," Pernal said, echoing every other interview I conducted.

While I was used to being dropped off literally in the field as a unit was jumping off on an operation and blasting out a 10-minute routine on who I was, Pernal developed a thirty-minute presentation for each unit he was supporting in Iraq and Afghanistan.

"I've got four guys. I've got more skills than most commanders do in a platoon. I'm not trying to insult anybody, but can I go through this with you and brief you on our capabilities," Pernal said. "In today's war [environment] as soon as they hear I can control any aircraft from any country and blow up anything you want, then it's like 'alright cash me out.' Then they want you within arm's reach."

I've always told my friends the "arm's reach or on our own" philoso-phy was the best way to employ an ANGLICO team. Perhaps as a reflec-tion of countless mountaintops he climbed in Afghanistan, Pernal said he preferred to resist a commander's close proximity and spot his team in an "overwatch" position to cover the unit's mission with air strikes or supporting fires. In ground combat *overwatch* is a term much like *lookout*, or what fire marshals do in fire towers. Usually from an elevated position, you can see what the unit in front of you cannot. You can warn them, fire on the enemy, or, in ANGLICO's case, blow the living crap out of anything you see. In ANGLICO you're a ridiculously heavily armed big brother watching someone's back and also the surrounding areas. Whether it's a regular infantry platoon looking for a weapons cache in a lonely little ville somewhere or a Special Ops team making a prisoner snatch, do your thing skipper and I've got your back.

"You have to explain to them that you're best utilized in an offset, in an observation post somewhere. Sometimes they don't want to hear about that, because commanders these days want to have a lot of control," he said.

Hence the previous stories about various combative staff NCOs. ANGLICO Marines need to be mature enough, professional enough, know their weapons, and keep their men together and on target. Per-nal remembered one Afghan mission that actually captured too many prisoners. The bad guys needed to be brought back for interrogation loaded onto helicopters to handle the numbers. The unit Pernal's team was attached to promptly set up a guard routine and started rotating soldiers, and Pernal's Marines, through the guard routine with guidelines on when to feed them, wake them, etc. After the mission was complete, Pernal wanted to perform an after-action report (AAR) with his FCT team and the CAS they had called in. Not locating one of his Marines, Pernal learned his man was on POW detail. Pernal would have none of it.

"I literally just walk over to their staff sergeant and say, 'Hey, we don't do that shit.' We don't do point, we're not MPs. We can do it, but you didn't even talk to me first. We have our own stuff to do. When we get back we have to prep our gear for the next mission."

A photo Pernal supplied for this book shows his preference for not being tied to a commander's elbow. With Marine Adam Weinstein looking at the camera, you can see for yourself the details of any ANGLICO mission. While his weapon is *always* within reach, the big three are right next to him: radios, antennas, and a method to mark the target. To the right are two Marines looking down into a valley where a Special Ops team was searching a village for bad guys, terrorists, Nazis, or whomever. In the immediate foreground one Marine is responsible for the marking gear, in this case, two laser designators, the one he's peering through and one laying to his right. The red-headed Marine eyeballing Pernal is the Marine who will communicate with the incoming aircraft.

Obviously, a platoon commander or Special Ops team leader who understands what the "Greeks and Italians" from ANGLICO can do gets something very rare on any battlefield in return: peace of mind. With American weaponry in the hands of a properly trained troop, anyone or anything can be given a fast exit into the afterlife. Retired first sergeant Parks Nicolls, the bra-size improvement Marine from chapter 12, told me that though he'd never been thought of as an Italian trooper, plenty of times Army commanders happily butchered our unit's name. Whether on a peacetime exercise in the mid-1970s or when Nicolls deployed for six months in 1990 during the Gulf War (the crazy bastard showed me a photo of himself with his right hand under the trip wire of a land mine!), the song remained the same. The Army unit commanders had limited resources just as everyone does, and then they were told they would have to provide food, water, and an endless supply of batteries for four to six Marines. On a two- or three-day mission, it's not a large problem. On a two- to three-week exercise such as at the JRTC or deploying overseas, it's a big logistics problem. And of course, they were usually pissed at us instead of their superiors, who should have told them we were coming, much less showing up just before jumping off into the bush.

"Usually the first time that they really understood what we did was when 'it' hit the fan and all of a sudden, there's air stacked up all over the place, there's artillery coming in, and it all happens in ten minutes," he remembered. "More than one time, the company commander or battalion commander would ask 'who's doing that?' and people would just point up the hill. 'Those guys!'"

When asked who our guys were, they replied in some type of weird French or maybe even Latin: An-gelli-co. To me that sounds like a small town in Italy or Spain or maybe the new 60-foot charter boat you just bought with your state lottery ticket winnings. Come on boys! Let's set sail on my new Angellico cruiser. Bermuda here we come! Even my mom laughed when she heard that one.

"I heard An-gelli-co more than I heard ANGLICO," he remembered with a big laugh. "I guess we had an angel on our shoulders, I don't know. Cowboys, prima donnas, everything but Marine."

Fifteen years after retiring, Nicolls also said he preferred to separate himself from the unit he was supporting, just as Pernal noted. If for no other reason, prior to the newer-model digital radios, ANGLICO FCT teams had a radio for each Marine to carry, which meant at least four to six radios with antennas sticking out of our backpacks. Standing next to the command group of a company or battalion, Nicolls said, could produce as many as thirteen radio antennas in one location. An "A-1 priority target" as he termed it, and he's right. Enemy snipers and forward observers, who had the same job as us in part, were trained to spot such telltale signs of a unit acting stupid. Poor security in front or rear, bunching up, or creating a sudden antenna farm are all quick ways to be among the stupid and quickly dead.

"Down at the FCT team level, I always detached myself from them and told them I'd leave one of my junior troops and when you need us another one will come up with the appropriate radio," Nicolls said. "I didn't play that way. I was always near, 50 or 100 meters away, up a hill or wherever I had eyes [on the target]. The dumb ones who didn't know what to do with us, and that happened more than once, they'd have us down in a wadi or a ravine. What good am I down here? I can't see."

As I touched on in the first chapter of the book, when my team was attached to a scout section of the 101st Airborne Division at JRTC, we were assigned to monitor a section of the battlefield 6 kilometers behind enemy lines. After the disaster of almost freezing to death the night before, we quickly found a hide site or a "blind," in duck-hunting terms, and set up our observation/listening post. Northern Louisiana in the winter had some wispy underbrush that reminded me of wheat, and we used it to camouflage a small copse of trees right out in the open. It was perfect. What pack of idiots would place themselves right out in the open? Well, us, of course. If the bad guys think you're too stupid to go there, it's a perfect position.

In fact, our own O/C (officer/controller) left our position for some reason, and when he returned, he strode right by us, even though we'd been there for two days. It was a great hide. We lay on the ground for nearly four days acting more like a Recon team than an ANGLICO FCT team. We were so close to the enemy road supply routes that if we called in artillery or naval guns, we'd hit our own position. However, as the true heart and soul of Marine ANGLICO is our communications assets, we relayed SPOT reports to our company, battalion, and even the brigade level. A SPOT report is radioed when you "spot" an enemy unit and use a military acronym called "SALUTE" that means "size, activity, location, uniform, time of sighting, and equipment." As each level of the ANGLICO detachment monitored all of the operating teams, all of my buddies heard everything we saw: armored cars on the move, enemy patrols strolling by us like they were walking in Central Park, and even a paratroop drop that flew so close I could clearly see the jumpmaster standing in the rear door. The radio I always got screwed carrying was the nearly 30-pound, high-frequency (HF) AN/PRC 104. I was married to this pig for two weeks and I hated carrying it, but damn if it didn't have a solid 40- to 50-mile range when I needed it. I once made a lightning quick radio check using only a 10-foot whip antenna from Fort Benning, Georgia, back to West Palm Beach, Florida, nearly 800 miles. It wasn't supposed to be possible, but radio signals bounce off temperature gradients, sunspots, cloud levels, landing Martians, and all kinds of crap. But we loved it. We were on our own, watching our infantry commander's back while he was chasing bad guys and we relayed intelligence on enemy movements in real time.

Nicolls recalled one case of exactly two 4th ANGLICO Marines actually striking out on their own during a training exercise (I'm sure they got approval from their SALT commander) in front of the Forward Edge of the Battle Area or FEBA in military jargon. The term *FEBA* came out of the American experience in Vietnam, as there was no strict "front line" a la Gen. George Patton's thrust across northern Europe in 1944. Following the procedure, one of my instructors from Artillery School at Fort Sill, Oklahoma, had suggested, these two Marines located a spot on the front side of a hill where they could easily observe any enemy movement. Out in the field discussing land navigation and where to site an observation post, my instructor told us not to overthink the situation. He pointed to a lonely tree about only 10 feet tall, but offering nice shade. Out in the open, dug in under the shade with nothing but an M-16 and HF radio, who would spot him? Normally, standing out on the front of a hill is slightly suicidal, so they looked for a cave. Can't find one? Then make your own cave.

"You're out in front of the FEBA, that's a free-fire zone. They dug themselves into the side of a hill, had their radios by their lonesome, and placed their antennas on the back side of the hill so their comms came back to us. The Opposing Force [OPFOR] came through with their Mech [mechanized armor], and they hosed them. They absolutely hosed them. The OPFOR guy said 'what the hell's going on?'"

Years later on yet another trip to JRTC, Nicolls had a bad cold and hitched a ride to an on-base "seven-day store" for some cold medicine. The driver turned out to be a full colonel and a member of the OPFOR and, in a rare turn of events, knew *exactly* who ANGLICO was and what they did. Nicolls smiled his country boy grin, and never being afraid of anyone's rank, ever, asked what the OPFOR boys thought of Marine ANGLICO. The colonel smiled and said: "You're the first target we're looking for."

One of my favorite incidents from the JRTC occurred after it moved to Fort Polk in northern Louisiana from Fort Chaffee, Arkansas, where Hollywood filmed *Biloxi Blues* with Matthew Broderick. A 2nd ANGLICO FCT team was attached to an Army infantry company, set to do its normal job of "blowin' shit up." As I detailed in the JRTC chapter, the two-week fight is frequently divided into an attack phase, guerilla-hunting phase, and the big final defensive exercise when OPFOR comes in full bore with their mechanized forces and armor. This particular 2nd ANGLICO FCT team was doing the normal routine of tagging along with their host infantry company and watching their preparations. I would usually just follow along, learn their plan, and keep an eye out for intruders. OPFOR loved to send in single soldiers as suicide bombers while a company had its head down planning for a new attack. It's very common for military units in any branch to be so caught up in new technology, maintenance, reports to higher headquarters, playing with weapons, and dealing with troublemakers that they ignore the basics, including the importance of basic security. Do you have two troops posted a hundred meters down the road in front and back of the company or on listening posts out toward the suspected enemy position? Most don't and OPFOR exploited it every single time.

Well, the 2nd ANGLICO team chief was apparently a big fan of naval gunfire. It was shaping up to be a big fight, a military version of the Miami Dolphins versus the New York Jets or the Pittsburgh Steelers versus the Cleveland Browns playing in snow and mud deep in the month of November. They know you're coming and most likely from where. You know where they are and that they're already waiting. Two American infantry companies, nearly 250 soldiers each, were going to collide head on, most likely at dawn. Well, the attacking company (the visiting unit being graded) had a distinct advantage: the ANGLICO Marines. For all you future readers from the U.S. Army infantry or armor, Special Forces, SEALs, or whatever alphabet soup of Special Ops you're part of, what followed is how you need to employ an FCT team.

The team chief looked at the company commander's plan, saw a well-dug in and -fortified position, and produced a quick and easy solution: I'll drop fifty rounds of 5-inch naval artillery on this place and that should do it. It did. With one radio call, a young E-5 buck sergeant took a company-sized position and removed it from the earth. Case closed.

I can see the team chief just sitting there all ready to fire. He would have attended the final company commander's brief on the attack the previous day, so he knows the latest intelligence on the enemy position. He would know roughly how many troops, their weapons, and how well they were dug in. With one radio transmission lasting less than a minute, the ship would fire as quickly as possible. A Spruance-class destroyer at the time had two gun mounts, fore and aft, both capable of firing twenty shells per minute. Firing would last less than two minutes and flight time to the target, depending on the distance to the target, would be easily less than five minutes. Each shell has a blast pattern of 50 by 150 meters multiplied by 50. The bad guys didn't stand a chance.

The JRTC officer/controllers (the battle referees) were dumbstruck and didn't know what the hell to do. They huddled together and talked via radio to higher headquarters about what just happened. I would've loved to hear that radio conversation with regimental HQ back on the main side of Fort Polk. In less than ten minutes, a major section of the exercise was over.

"What do you mean, they got wiped out?" some incredulous staff officer would shout.

"They're gone," replied the ref, talking like a gangster from *Goodfellas*.

"Charlie Company just started their attack! What the hell happened?"

"The ANGLICO Marines called in naval gunfire and that was it," the unfortunate ref would say.

And he was right. That was it. Like an NFL referee trotting back to the center of the field to announce a penalty ruling, they made their call: a mulligan. Yes, a do-over. I know the American public gets frustrated with the costs of our military. Trust me, you have no idea how much it costs to ship units around the world for training and exercises, even without combat operations. Do you think flying home to the family back east for Thanksgiving is a pain in the arse? Try a holiday trip with eighteen hundred troops, all of their gear, weapons, Humvees, 5-ton trucks, and throw in a few 60-ton tanks and all the classified radio gear that will get you thrown in Fort Leavenworth for eighty-five years if it goes missing. It would be like flying the Mets or Yankees down to Florida for spring training just to call it off when an opposing batter cracks a grand slam. Do you quit and pack up? No. You learn what happened, create a new plan, and do it again. And again. And again.

It's precisely what the JRTC referees did. They told everyone to reset and get ready to fight the battle all over again. And they quickly told the Marines from 2nd ANGLICO to go find a nice shade tree, sit there, and don't do a damn thing. It was just another case of a good FCT team sitting around with nothing to do. It must have been one hell of a nap.

CHAPTER SEVEN

Fun in the Sun with the 4th

AFTER FIFTEEN MONTHS IN AFGHANISTAN, ANDREW KELLEY WAS excited about his next assignment in the Marine Corps. He just didn't know where it was.

In 2014, 4th ANGLICO's present inspector/instructor was sitting in the chow hall in "the 'Stan" getting ready to brief his commanding general when he got word he would take over the regular active duty staff. Lt. Col. Andrew Kelley was on the tail end of fifteen months "in country" when someone gave him the news. He was happy to join a unit he'd discovered eighteen years before, but his ANGLICO geography was off just a bit.

"I thought it was in Southern California. My boss did too," he said with a laugh.

There is a Reserve ANGLICO in sunny Southern California, 3rd ANGLICO, but 4th was on the East Coast in sunny West Palm Beach, Florida. What the heck, he was only off by 2,600 miles. Much like the rest of the Marine Corps, Kelley had gotten used to regarding the two Reserve ANGLICOs as "jump clubs" that did perform some high-speed training, but also swaggered around in board shorts, sunglasses, and flip-flops.

"They did have that kind of image," he said. "That jump part just adds to a perception that a unit is special or different or a little on their own."

The truth was that we did swagger around. But our airborne mission actually required it. Most Marines carry their K-bar combat knives on their belts or on their 782 gear, snugly fit around the waist. Nice, neat, and trim just like every other Marine in their company. Not us.

If you jump and the wind blows you into the trees, or you're just an idiot who can't jump correctly, you might have to cut your way from inside of your tangled chute or cut the 550 cord holding your stupid ass 15 feet off the ground. But any parachute rig has a 2-inch thick waistband that keeps you strapped into the entire parachute rig. The waistband always reminded me of the little metal bar you slide down on a baby swing that keeps little ones from shooting out the front of the chair when the swing halts its forward progress. Furthermore, to fit into the parachute seat, we had to fully extend our 782 gear that carried our ammo pouches, two canteens, buttpack, and medical kit. This hung out the back and during field operations always hung low on our ass. We thought it made us look cool so we kept it that way. Other Marines saw us with our gear and combat knives slung low like gunslingers, and it only added, good or bad, to our reputation as nothing more than cowboys who jumped out of planes.

That baggie-wearing, jump club image was a main factor in the abolishment of 1st and 2nd ANGLICO in 1999. There was, and still is, plenty of rumor, legend, informed opinion, flat-out BS, and ridicule as to why the two active duty ANGLICOs were disbanded. In the late 1990s Bosnia and Kosovo were in full swing, but amid further military cutbacks after winning the Cold War, many Marines began to question the value of ANGLICO units, especially as they cost so much money to maintain. For around two hundred Marines, you needed a battalion's worth of gear and administrative support to keep it going.

Equally as important is that most Marines never see us do our thing because we're supporting the Army or a foreign unit next door or down the way. Hence, even today, ANGLICO has very little political power within the Marine Corps. Two hijacked jetliners smashing into the Twin Towers on a beautiful Tuesday morning changed that in less than two hours.

However, the main factor when active duty Marines come to 4th ANGLICO is the never-ending battle royale of active versus Reserve. Active duty guys call us "weekend warriors" who can't commit and we call them morons who couldn't get a real job in the real world. None of us actually thought that, but it was a great way to piss off someone who's had one too many beers at the enlisted club. Even as Lieutenant Colonel

Kelley made his way to West Palm Beach, he said he believed that he and his peers lived, ate, slept, and wrote about the profession versus the part-timers of the Reserves.

"But in the post 9/11 Marine Corps, I was pleasantly surprised with the level of professionalism. The Reserves are different. There's no doubt about it," Kelley said. "It's not better or worse, it's just different."

A frequent complaint about Reserve Marine Corps units is that individual Marines are too narrow in their views or not as well rounded as other careerists. It's a fair criticism, but does it really matter out in the field? I served with around fifty Marines for the entire twelve years I was in 4th ANGLICO and we ran everything without even talking to each other. If Peyton Manning can just glance at a wide receiver and instantly knows which pass route to switch to, what happens when you bring in a new quarterbacks or receivers coach? Can Peyton get along with this guy? If he has new ideas, will they listen or play the grizzled veteran routine and screw everything up? A Reserve unit is the same way, and active duty Marines who come to Special Ops units learn this very quickly.

"A lot of junior Marines, all they know of the Marine Corps is West Palm Beach. They've barely set foot on major Marine Corps installations or gone on major exercises. On the other hand, unlike active duty, you have some Marines in 1st Brigade platoon that have been there for nine years and really develop an expertise and familiarity [with each other]," Kelley said.

For me, being a Marine reservist at a high-tempo, sought-after unit was extremely demanding. I've been off and on active duty plenty of times. I didn't find active duty particularly hard. Chow was free, rent was free, the PX was down the street with a ton of cheap stuff to buy, and since you're on base, focusing on training was all you did. I've also been a regular civilian schlub too and that's very easy. Put these two things together and now you have a challenge. As a bar owner, will you hire a bartender for only two days per month and have him serve your best customers Friday and Saturday night? Or on New Year's Eve? Will a garage owner have Mr. Two-a-Day work on the Rolls Royce Phantom of your richest client? Probably not, huh?

Consider everything you do in your own life. Two days from now you'll be staggering out the back door of a jet transport weighing 300 pounds with all of your gear and parachute rig, staying up all night to run simulated artillery, CAS, naval gunfire, and Evac missions, trying not to kill yourself throwing live hand grenades for the first time in a year, another parachute jump back to the Reserve Center where you'll make all of your radios, weapons, parachutes, and field gear *spotless*, and I mean *without a spot*, get dismissed at 5:00 P.M. on Sunday, drive home 300 miles, and be at work or in class on Monday at 9:00 A.M. Easy, right? Wrong.

The old stalwarts of 4th ANGLICO were a supremely dedicated group. For years I drove 300 miles one way for drill weekend. One sergeant major drove his old pickup truck in from across the Georgia line, and dozens drove from Miami, Tampa, Orlando, Jacksonville, and tiny little towns I'd never heard of. Hell, Captain Martin flew in from the Virgin Islands. He always won for longest nut-job trip. He did it for years with a smile on his face and terrible jokes for everyone. With my little government paycheck, after gas, Florida Turnpike fees, new tires each year, and little bags of Doritos for the road trip, I didn't turn a profit for half a decade. But we trained, jumped, drank beer, chased chicks, had fight scenes in bars from Palm Beach to hell and back, and loved every damn minute of it.

After only seven months at 4th ANGLICO, Lieutenant Colonel Kelley had already spotted the nature of the high-speed Reserve beast. Much to my pleasant surprise, Kelley was the first active duty officer I've ever heard wonder if he could succeed with the double life of a Marine reservist in a unit routinely tasked with "real world" and also combat missions.

"It's hard in the Reserve world. Quite frankly, I'm not sure I could do it," Kelley told me from his West Palm Beach office. "It's a challenge if you're balancing another profession. It's one thing if you're eighteen years old and not sure what to do with your life, but we have guys in law school, an architect, city planners, engineers, guys making a lot of money."

When I was in 4th ANGLICO, I always insisted that I would stack up the talent of our enlisted ranks—privates, privates first class, lance corporals, corporals, and sergeants—against nearly any unit in the world. I meant it then and still do now due to the raw talent found in the South Florida area combined with the crazies who traveled so far to be in ANGLICO. I'm sure 3rd ANGLICO is the same way, because it was nothing for us to have several lance corporals who had just graduated college, got married, had a little one on the way, and were fully operational spotters for CAS, naval gunfire, and artillery. This depth of talent and experience outside of the Marine Corps is perfect for ANGLICO as our operators needed to be well-rounded people who could operate on their own in Iraq 20 kilometers from their boss, or the nearly 7,000 miles away from their own units in West Palm Beach or Camp Lejeune, North Carolina.

That's why I chose the photo of an ANGLICO lance corporal discussing air strikes with a French aviator for this book. In the photo LCpl. Antonio J. Castillo and Pvt. Matthew J. Hurley, two radio operators with 2nd ANGLICO, are discussing American GPS gear and range-finding equipment with Lt. j.g. Jerome Laye from the French navy, a pilot based off French carrier *Charles de Gaulle*. It's a perfect "ANGLICO moment": Even the most junior Marine, in this case Private Hurley, is expected to know all aspects of ANGLICO and be able to teach it to any rank, most likely from another American service branch or foreign national. Very few, if any, U.S. Marines are tasked with this.

"We have an assistant district attorney that's like a lance corporal generator operator (MOS). The expertise and life maturity is something that you don't see in guys with the equivalent rank on the active duty side," Kelley said.

I have to admit, I often bristled when someone said, "what's the big deal? It's only two days a month and two weeks in the summer, right?" Well, no you're wrong. Since no one knows about ANGLICO, and it takes too damn long to explain it to someone who's had a couple of beers already, I rarely told anyone what I did. From twelve years of personal experience, the "Reserve thing" for 4th ANGLICO was just the opposite of what the American public, and also active duty military, believes. I only took three trips of Annual Training Duty, during a dozen years. That's because I would help out at the unit when money was available for pay so I could help with the Mount Everest of paperwork every section owned.

Or I was at Airborne School at Fort Benning, Georgia. Or I was at a three-week simulated battle at Fort Polk in Louisiana. Or I was at Coronado, California, first for Long-Range Maritime Navigation School, then Naval Gunfire School years later. Plus there was Artillery School in Fort Sill, Oklahoma, a one-week U.S. Air Force crash course on how to load jet transports with trucks and tanks without the planes falling out of the sky, innumerable flights to Camp Lejeune for regular drills, and two separate trips to Norway. Keep in mind, this was all before September 11th.

GySgt. Arturo Guzman is the I&I operations chief, ops chief in Marine slang, and is a prime example of how the active and Reserve staff of a modern Reserve unit interact. A veteran of two tours in Iraq and one in Afghanistan and a qualified JTAC, Guzman had already served with 1st ANGLICO and had been briefed on what to expect from reservists by a former 4th ANGLICO ops chief.

Guzman had his own "you ANGLICO guys" moment when he deployed with the 11th Marine Expeditionary Unit and was actually chastised as soon as he walked in the door. Even on the active duty side of the house, Guzman saw the cowboy misconception surrounding all things ANGLICO.

"Their 'welcome aboard' package was: You're not special. You're Marines just like everyone else. We didn't even say anything. We just got here!" he remembered with a laugh. "You don't even know who we are and you're getting at us for not being special."

Or, as I like to tell my friends: ANGLICO is so specialized it's not even Special Ops, which is true. A large part of ANGLICO's independent streak stems from the fact that when a Marine new to the ANGLICO community fully realizes the nature of the job, training is going to get a lot more detailed and varied than he expected. For example, every U.S. Marine is fully trained in combat first aid, wound treatment, and evacuation. Well what if you're 20 kilometers from the nearest friendly troops because the Army didn't know what to do with you and, as Gunny Unay Cruz told me, parked your ass under the Iraqi sun and left you there to spot any enemy movement?

One of your Marines is suffering heat stroke and a Navy corpsman gave you a saline IV drip "just in case." I can assure you neither the

Marine Corps nor the U.S. Navy medical establishment wants just anyone inserting needles into a sick Marine's veins. I carried one in my pack for years for just such a situation. During a two-week stint at Camp Lejeune in the late 1990s, we practiced just that. I won't name anyone or even what year it was, but one of our corpsmen was a paramedic in the real world and, like us, felt if we had a piece of gear, we should know how to use it. It was completely unauthorized, which is why we didn't tell anyone. But again, I ask you? What do I do when we're out on our own or with a unit that doesn't speak English? As Gunny Guzman's "welcome aboard" party attests to, you want to take me down a few notches, but also parcel me out to whoever needs our support, and, of course, without any more money or gear to accomplish the mission. If you ANGLICO guys are so special, how come you can't just handle it? Gee, thanks guys.

"We're not Special Forces, we don't fall under any of that, but we have a very specialized mission that needs to be understood by the Marine Corps, because they're the one that are going to task us out to these other units," Guzman said. "They're non–Marine Corps units. We have to play by their rules and at the same time still play by Marine rules."

Just like Lieutenant Colonel Kelley, Guzman was pleased to see the high number of Reserve Marines that took their profession seriously, even while doing two days a month or two weeks in the summer. That's excluding the eleven deployments 4th ANGLICO has made during the seemingly never-ending war on terror.

When I first pitched this book idea to my publisher, as discussed in chapter 1, I wrote how I developed a "sales pitch" to quickly teach the U.S. Army just what the hell we did for a living. Meeting Gunny Guzman for the first time, he started using the same "sales" or "sell it" type of language, and this is fifteen years after I did it on my own. For Guzman this meant working with the Reserve staff, learning the commanding officer's intent and focus, and then convincing, or "selling," the regular staff on why training should happen a certain way. Remember, ANGLICO units are almost always on their own in some way and each Marine needs much deeper training in all areas. In fact, *Always on Our Own* was one of the original titles I suggested for this book.

"We have to spend our money wisely and the little time we have has to be spent the right way," Guzman said. "It helps out on both sides. I take it as a check and balance."

A "normal" Marine unit, whether an infantry company or combat engineers, when they hit the field they're accustomed to everyone being together at once. Lieutenant Colonel Kelley said it's easier for younger Marines to rely on that "salty" platoon sergeant or stalwart captain for guidance, leadership, or simply the correct way to do their job.

"In ANGLICO I don't have that. Everybody has to have the ability to operate independently as a small team. I send that five-man FCT team and they attach to some nation's infantry company 20 kilometers to my east and that other FCT team is attached to another company 15 kilometers to the north. I don't necessarily even *see* those guys," Kelley emphasized. "Go attach to these guys, figure what they need, and make it happen. The nature of the job requires more highly trained guys than other jobs in the Marine Corps. That's just the nature of it."

Take communications for example. Kelley said, and I know from past experience, it's not enough to know basic radio operations to perform a task "because Staff Sergeant told me to": What about when things go wrong? A radio is a machine and machines break. Just like your home computer, your car, or whatever cable/satellite/Internet service you use to watch television, when it ain't working, you need to call someone to fix it. With an operating FCT team, very junior Marines are in a combat situation troubleshooting, fixing, restarting, reassuring your very pissed off host unit that you'll quickly be back on line with good comm, and this dude might not even speak English. And they don't care about your problems. They care about the Navy destroyer that *you* said could cover their coastal operation or about that F-18 Hornet that will scream in and drop a 500-pound bomb *exactly* where they want and also not kill their troops. Remember that private and lance corporal speaking with the French navy's Lieutenant Laye I just wrote about?

"So one, you need more experience, confident guys to function in that role. And you don't know what that role is. You could be working with the U.S. Army, First World or Third World countries. It really requires embracing the leadership principles the Marine Corps preaches.

ANGLICO really epitomizes that. Mission tactics, decentralized command, trust tactics, you need junior Marines to be trusted to be placed into a situation that I really don't know what to tell them," Kelley said.

I know this sounds crazy. A U.S. Marine lieutenant colonel with eighteen years of active duty, a master's degree from Wisconsin, almost five rows of ribbons, and three tours of duty in combat zones, and he's a little hazy on what's facing his troops. As I will write time and again in this book: What are we supposed to do? You fling us into these nut-bag situations and then just walk off. Then, when we pull off some screwball solution, you're mad because we're not acting like "real Marines." Well, walk 20 miles in my jungle boots, carrying a 60-pound backpack, eating one MRE per day, purifying creek water with iodine tablets to stay hydrated (and hence alive), and it's two weeks until you get a shower or clean cammies. And, yes, that was a peacetime operation.

A prime example for me was the third time I went to ANGLICO's favorite playground, the force-on-force battle exercises run by the Army at the JRTC. I warned the fifty or so Marines to repack their gear and get ready to step off the bus wearing combat gear, drop your seabag (duffle bag) for the SALT or division team to collect, hold out one hand for ammunition, the other hand for MREs, and follow your newly assigned unit right into the bush. They thought I was joking. I wasn't.

I was given my own team to run. Since Congress was always too cheap to send 4th ANGLICO to JRTC for the entire evolution, we would arrive about three days before the fight started and had to haul ass to get everything done. Radio frequencies for four radio sets, food, ammo, weapons testing, getting MILES gear assigned and tested, radio call signs, new maps that we always had to laminate ourselves, weather forecasts, and, of course, the ten times in three days when the unit we would be supporting was changed. MILES gear stands for "multiple integrated laser engagement" that is attached to all troops and vehicles during war games. I always called it laser tag on steroids, but it eliminates any doubt of who's been "shot" or not and adds quite a bit of realism to field exercises. Plus, we spent quite a bit of time in the Army field kitchens, stealing as much food as we could. They had a ton of it, and the Marine

Corps gave us exactly three MREs per day. As usual, the Army wasn't telling us much of anything, and when they did, that got changed too.

One of my Marines walked back into our tent and told me he spotted a huge sand table in a nearby GP tent, a "general purpose" tent the military uses for damn near everything from makeshift tear gas chambers to private quarters for the general. As team leader, and being quite fed up with the lack of "word," (the official plan from battalion or regiment), I instantly decided I was taking my FCT team to the briefing. We asked around and some Army guys told us it was going to be the brief for the entire regiment, how it would fight, what the goals were, and where everyone was supposed to be on D-Day and at the end of the fight. As Lieutenant Colonel Kelley noted, I was so used to being in ANGLICO, it didn't even enter my cranium to ask permission, con my way in, or even mention it for that matter. I just did it.

The main reason I attended the regimental brief was that I started to catch wind that I was going to support an infantry company, who later turned out to be the Nasty Dogs from Orlando. Frankly, they got a crappy assignment guarding the Main Supply Route (MSR). I wanted to see where the MSR was and which weapons I could use to protect it. At the appointed time I grabbed my team and told them we were going to the regimental brief.

"Just walk in like someone has already invited us and it'll be fine. What are they going to do? Kick us out?" I told them.

I've never seen so many dirty looks in my life. The entire regimental staff, three battalion commanders with their full staff and their sergeants major, every company commander and their first sergeants, probably the medical staff and chaplain were there too. And also four U.S. Marines who no one had invited. It was also the largest sand table I had ever seen. It showed the entire plan for around four thousand troops in the field at once. Every unit was marked, and every route of attack was highlighted with large red arrows and "phase lines" snaked across the ground showing where each unit was supposed to be at a certain time.

A sand table is a great tool. They've been used for centuries by every military that has ever existed. In its most basic form, a sand table is this:

As a child, have you ever stuck your finger in the dirt and created a sports play for your friends to follow? That's it.

"Jerry, go get yourself double covered, and free up Peter. Jeff, make a beeline for the Johnson's station wagon and wait for the ball, 'cause it's comin' at ya'. Jackie, since you can't catch or run, at least get yourself run over before Big Harold kills me. Ready? BREAK!"

It's not much different except that combat operations are far more serious than backyard football games, and now they're being made with high-tech lasers and moving terrain models. For being outside of a classroom, this sand table was huge, probably 25 by 25 feet, and showed the entire operation. It was like looking at a landing map for Omaha Beach on June 6, 1944. I always felt the Army went a bit bonkers with field sand tables. Picking up leaves, twigs, rocks, and larger sticks works just fine for a sand table if everyone is paying attention. It's usually what we did. What I saw didn't make me very happy. The MSR snaked right across the battlefield. This meant that the Nasty Dogs, and us, would be constantly on the move, getting hit, and most likely I would never get a battalion Fire Direction Center to clear me to fire naval gunfire across battalion lines. What that means is, if I'm in 3rd Battalion's area of operations and want to blast some bad guys with naval gunfire, I have to launch twenty rounds sailing over the heads of two other battalions. Needless to say, it didn't happen too much on that gig and we were stuck riding shotgun and playing Recon as needed. If I had sat back and waited for the Army to tell me this information, well, I'd still be waiting. Just as Kelley remarked on "figuring it out," we did just that. And that's Marine ANGLICO, even without the board shorts and flip-flops. I'll pick my own sunglasses, thank you.

Chapter Eight

Reach Out and Touch Someone

IT'S FOUR O'CLOCK IN THE MORNING, PITCH BLACK, AND GUNNY HENRY is creeping south down a skinny Norwegian dirt road as we sidestep German tanks and Dutch Marines looking for us. After a very close encounter that almost saw us get captured the first hour of the exercise, we were on full alert.

Hours earlier, Gunny Henry was driving our radio truck Humvee north toward a tiny Norwegian town called Moen, which is pronounced just like the popular plumbing and faucet company. I was working three radios at once and two Marines in the rear were talking on portable radios. Our platoon commander had told us to drive as far north as we could on Highway E6 to determine how far our communications network would extend. As usual, 4th ANGLICO had set aside our well-prepared plans when faced with the realities on the ground. At this point we were an hour and a half north of Narvik, roughly 150 miles north of the Arctic Circle. Not bad for a unit based in West Palm Beach. Every minute I would send out a radio check on a different radio.

"Lightning rear this is Lightning forward, radio check," I droned.

"Roger. Lima Charlie," which is slang for "loud and clear."

If they can barely hear you, the response is "weak but readable," and if a mountain blocks your signal entirely, all you hear is static, until you drive around the other side and it sounds like they're inside the Humvee with you. With everyone preoccupied we drove straight out in front of our own lines. There's nothing like the sound of a Dutch Marine with a fully automatic weapon to help you focus.

Pop, pop, pop, braaaappp!

We were lucky. Since the "war" had just started, both sides were a little slack and both parties were surprised to see each other. Military history books are full of stories about enemy troops just walking into each other, especially in jungle warfare. We had even driven by German tanks, which just kept driving past us, south toward Narvik just like the terrible Nazi takeover of Norway in 1940. It was an amazing sight: German tank commanders standing in the turrets wearing black leather jackets. It looked like a photograph straight from a history book. Yet, we stayed with the mission, right on the outskirts of friendly lines.

Every three years Norway activates its national defense plan for one-third of the entire 1,200-mile long Arctic nation. Titled Battle Griffin, in 1996 the war mobilization would be staged in the northern parts of Norway centered on the ancient town of Narvik and its deep-water harbor. In the early 1980s someone in the Pentagon realized a fault with NATO plans for central Europe. With hundreds of NATO and Soviet divisions facing each other on the central front, Scandinavia was the weak spot. The Warsaw Pact troops could hang a right through Scandinavia and NATO would be in trouble. Therefore, the Northern Front was born. Who would the Pentagon select to freeze in the Norwegian fjords and snowbound mountains? The Marine Corps, of course.

Like many European nations during the Cold War, Norway (whom we always called "the Norgees") has a draft. Even Switzerland had a draft for the entire Cold War. I like the Norgees draft system. When you turn eighteen years old, you're off to boot camp. No exceptions. Oh, you're a pacifist? Now you're a medic. NEXT! What? You're a blonde chick that doesn't like guns? Fine. Now you're a truck driver. NEXT! Norwegian citizens go to boot camp, then get a specialty (truck driver, infantryman, radar man) and get sent home with all of their combat gear including an assault rifle made at home in Norway. They aren't even required to cut their hair while in uniform. Norgees might not be called up for years. But, when the call rings out, they can put thousands of troops on the street in a matter of hours. (And yes, that means you, Washington, D.C., after Hurricane Katrina.)

I was hoping I would be a team chief on one of the FCT teams assigned to the Norwegians. Resting up after being in charge of transporting all our gear from West Palm Beach to the Arctic Circle, I was excited to hit the field and go kill some fake Commies. Fat chance, buddy.

Since my initial MOS had been logistics/embarkation, every deployment I signed up for, I was instantly assigned Embark NCO to shepherd all of our gear to the final destination. That's fifty Marines worth of backpacks, M-16s, Beretta pistols, live ammunition, sea bags, and with ANGLICO we have hundreds of pounds of radio gear. Plus, extra bags and crap some officer always brought because he thought he was above the rules.

Since no one wants to travel to the other side of the Earth and not be ready, we brought three of every set we needed. Each FCT team needed at least three radios plus crypto gear to scramble radio traffic, and the SALT and Division had twice as many to monitor all the activity and approve CAS and fire missions, plus the even larger radios on our radio truck Humvees.

We could use our most powerful radio Humvee to talk to aircraft, destroyers and battleships, and artillery battalions, and with 400 watts it truly had a worldwide range on the proper frequency. But, in the wrong hands, the electric power could kill a man with the click of a radio handset. Long before the horn-rimmed advertising scourge of "Can You Hear Me Now?," my high-speed, airborne-all-the-way combat assignment was simple. Drive around for two weeks in the Arctic Circle as a mobile retransmission site. Yippee.

Major Fernandez was our platoon commander. A Gulf War veteran and firefighter in the civilian world who'd been to Norway, Fernandez knew communications were key. With his FCT teams on the move, radio contact could be established, lost, and regained in mere minutes if not less. His solution was to bring 4th ANGLICO's most powerful radio trucks to serve as a sort of mobile cellular phone tower.

As I wrote in the introduction, most Americans think a cell phone alone can send a voice message across the nation. It can't; telecommunications firms use fixed towers to retransmit the messages. In a combat situation that's impossible. American intelligence locates these towers long before hostilities start, and they are destroyed early in any conflict. This is why the military uses man-packed radios that are completely self-sufficient in the field.

In '96 I stood on a road surface marveling at the perfect V shape of twin 900-foot peaks on either side. The mountains, fjords, ice flows, and rivers all played tricks on radio communications, while the aurora borealis dumped millions of ionized particles throughout the atmosphere. In short, Norway is a communicator's nightmare. If ANGLICO can't talk on a radio, then there is no ANGLICO.

No air strikes. No naval gunfire. No artillery or swiftly relaying enemy intelligence to Regiment in the blink of a digital eye. You're just standing there with a Norwegian battalion commander staring at you like you're an idiot. And since you can't talk, well, you are an idiot. Years before, a Marine buddy had warned me: "Never become a communications officer. If there's a mountain in the way, it's your fault," he admonished.

Amen, brother, but it doesn't help me now.

But, I got my boring, necessary assignment and I would do my best. It's an ethic largely missing from American society today: doing the dirty work without complaint or looking for reward. Ronald Reagan did it in World War II. He left his movie career to join the Army and fight the Nazis. Reagan's reward? Go make movies. Do you mean combat footage of our boys in action? No. Go make training films with the First Motion Picture Unit where everyone in the audience knows you can't actually fly a fighter plane. Conservative icon Senator Barry Goldwater graduated flight school and for his efforts received the glamorous job of ferrying new aircraft to combat theaters and flying supply planes "over the Hump" in Burma and China. And while everyone thought Senator George McGovern was a peacenik due to his anti–Vietnam War stance, he was actually a decorated pilot on B-24 Liberators during World War II who flew a full slate of thirty-five combat missions. Goldwater and Reagan might have asked for a transfer to a combat assignment, but they did their assigned tasks and so did we.

But it's also how we drove head on into a column of 50-ton Panther tanks. It was the first time German troops had trained outside their nation since World War II, and a lot of Norwegian locals were none too happy about it.

At the moment, we were known to have a better present situation since it was four o'clock in the morning, we had Danish Marines and German tankers driving all around us, and we had no idea if they were looking for us or just moving to their own positions. Gunny Henry decided that we needed to start moving back to where we came from, so we took a quick break to grab some quick chow, drink a couple of hot wets, and also to burn all of our codes in case we got captured. Cpl. Troy Sutton was given the task of burning all the codes without getting spotted by the enemy. While Troy did a very good job of digging a hole in the snow and burning our codes and disguising it from any prying eyes, he also took the opportunity to slip and fall into a creek 150 miles inside the Arctic Circle. Not good. Not only was Gunny Henry now extremely pissed off, he made a quick decision for both of our Humvees to load up and get back to the safety of our own front lines. Gunny Henry took over driving and put on a pair of night vision goggles and started creeping down a tiny Norwegian dirt road at God knows what time in the morning while Lance Corporal Torres and I tried to make contact with the rear through a digital communications terminal, or DCT for short.

DCTs were a great piece of gear. It was a digital terminal that was hooked up to our PRC 104 high-frequency radios. To send encrypted messages for an air strike, enemy sighting, or even just food resupply, all you had to do was type in the message regardless of how long it was, press "send," and the message was sent off in a compacted burst of data that was almost impossible to catch by the enemy. Hence the term "burst transmission." While Torres and I were playing with the DCT, Gunny Henry was creeping down the dirt road keeping an eye out for any sign of bad guys. He quickly got what he was looking for. Two Dutch Marines running in single file ran right in front of our Humvee, and that was all Gunny Henry needed to turn into General Patton after creeping for a couple miles at only 5 miles an hour. Henry exploded into action.

"They're here! Grab your 16s!" Gunny Henry shouted.

Torres and I were in the backseat of the Humvee and quickly grabbed our M-16s to start firing out the rear window. We were all keyed up from almost being run over by German tanks and getting shot at by Dutch Marines, and Troy trying to drown himself inside the Arctic Circle didn't help the situation either. I grabbed my M-16 and leaned over Torres's shoulder to get ready to open up on anybody I can spot. Instead I saw the biggest damn moose I've ever seen in my entire life. A moose! It was *huge*. Its antlers were huge, its body was huge, and I thought I was going crazy. Just as I started to question my own sanity, Torres turned around and looked at me and said, "did you just see a moose?" Indeed I did.

What caused Gunny Henry such alarm was that he spotted the white vapor barrier boots of what he thought were Dutch Marines.

Vapor barrier boots are made out of rubber and have a cushion of air in between the inside boot and the outside boot, hence the term *vapor barrier*. Just like a wetsuit for divers, your body heat warms that air barrier and keeps your feet warm. You look like a dork, but your feet are never cold and all you have to wear is white athletic socks. Since they're so oversized and it looks like your feet are swelling, anyone wearing vapor barrier boots looks like Walt Disney's Mickey Mouse. So therefore vapor barrier boots are universally known in the U.S. military as Mickey Mouse boots. Even my mom knows they are called Mickey Mouse boots because I showed her all my gear before we went to Norway. What Gunny Henry thought was two Dutch Marines running in single file, was actually the four white hooves of a giant moose. Since this runaway Norwegian moose was dark brown with white feet and it was four o'clock in the morning deep in the countryside, Bullwinkle actually did look like two troops getting ready to attack us.

Now this caused me a bit of amusement, especially since I wasn't going crazy. I then realized it was up to me to tell Gunny "damn the torpedoes, full-speed ahead, set phasers on kill" Henry that it wasn't the Mongol hordes coming to get us. It was Bullwinkle. And his buddy Rocky wasn't tagging along with him.

I could never understand Motor T Marines who told me they had a hard time reading Gunny Henry's mood. I thought it was the easiest thing in the world since he only had two moods: One, he's laughing so hard he can barely talk. Two, he's so stinking mad that he can barely talk.

"Why can't you just do what I asked you to do?" he'd shout at some hapless Marine, who invariably didn't do what he was supposed to. "If I have to tell you one-more-god-damn-time . . ." Henry would spit out, emphasizing each word as he went.

Needless to say, almost running over a moose wasn't going to bring out the happy in Gunny Henry. Since this is the Marine Corps, Torres was a corporal and I was a sergeant, we both knew who got to tell Gunny lead foot about Bullwinkle's sudden appearance.

"Hey Gunny?" I asked.

"WHAT!" he shouted as we flew through the Arctic night.

"I don't think that was the enemy," I offered.

"What! Then who the hell was it?" he demanded.

Here we go.

"I think it was a moose!" I yelled over the racing engine.

"WHAT! THAT WASN'T NO GOD-DAMN-MOOSE!" he spat out as he looked at me like I was the one with antlers sticking out of my helmet.

Torres came to my rescue.

"No, Gunny, it was a moose. I saw it too," he insisted.

Gunny Henry slowed down to a reasonable speed and stopped for the other Humvee to catch up.

"Hey, did you guys see that giant moose?" someone shouted.

I thought Gunny Henry was going to kill all of us, but soon he started to laugh.

"Damn, Mes, I thought it was two Dutch guys in Mickey Mouse boots. Those NVGs aren't working too good in this dark," he told me.

He was right. It was so damn dark and the pine trees were so thick, the night vision goggles were struggling with the ambient light. However, this didn't prevent us from giving Gunny Henry a rash of shit about being a bigoted moose killer. Now it was back to the laughing version of Gunny Henry and he took it all like a champ. Even better, Norway actually has roadside traffic signs warning of moose crossings just like deer crossing signs in the United States, so he had a laugh whenever we passed them. Needless to say, we busted Gunny Henry's chops the 4,500 miles back to South Florida.

So there you have it: the enduring story of the Norwegian moose in the Mickey Mouse boots.

While this is a funny story that I love to tell my friends, it's completely typical of ANGLICO. It shows how we took everything we learned and practiced and almost always ended up "winging it" once we made it into the field. The moose in Mickey Mouse boots had all the ANGLICO elements: foreign troops, working out in front all on our own, shooting from the hip (or Humvee as it were), and the never-ending task of establishing "good comms" with our bosses for FCT teams in the field. But it all centered around one thing: communications, the topic of our next chapter.

CHAPTER NINE

MOS 1: Heart and Soul

THERE ARE PLENTY OF THINGS TO WRITE AND TALK ABOUT WITH Marine Corps ANGLICO. It's fun and glamorous to jump out of planes. Some ANGLICO Marines even get to go to high-altitude parachute school depending on their assignments, usually when they are attached to one of the units of the U.S. Army. Since it has battalion assets, the units draw a lot of money and much more equipment than a normal-sized company of 225 Marines. But while it's easy to focus on the glamour of the gold jump wings, the independent duty, and almost always working with foreign troops from another service, the one true common denominator for every ANGLICO Marine is the man-packed radio in his backpack. Communications, or comm, the Marine Corps slang, is truly the heart and soul of every Marine ANGLICO company.

During my time in West Palm Beach with the Marines of 4th ANGLICO, I spent six full years in the communications section even though my original MOS was as an embarkation and logistics man. When I first reported to West Palm Beach in late 1987, the embarkation section consisted of myself, a brand-new PFC, and Staff Sergeant Barry, a Broward County sheriff's deputy who rode Harleys for the department and was also wounded as an infantryman in the Vietnam War. Barry was a great guy and easy to get along with; the problem was since the unit was not being deployed anywhere anytime soon, he didn't have anything for me to do. Since no one in the Marine Corps in any capacity sits around with nothing to do, Barry loaned me out to the communications section run by a Florida state investigator, M/Sgt. Ronnie Lee, who would go on to become the sheriff of Hendry County on the southwest coast of Florida. Needless to say, since I did not go to Communication School to become a field radio operator, I didn't have a clue as to what I was doing or what I was supposed to do. Both Staff Sergeant Barry and Top Lee looked after me just fine, and I started to learn about all of the radios that were literally stacked to the ceiling of our section.

One thing about the comm shack back then was that we undoubtedly worked at least as hard as any other Marines in the unit, and we definitely worked longer hours. For years, on a Friday or Saturday night of the monthly drill weekend as the rest of the company was being dismissed for the evening, Top Lee would invariably quickly turn around and shout out "comm don't go anywhere!" After the three line platoons, the headquarters section, the parachute riggers, and medical and supply were dismissed, all of the Marines in comm would trudge back into the comm shack to finish all of our work with the radios. We didn't have to clean them, because whichever Marine checked them out for training was responsible for that. But we always performed monthly maintenance on the radios that didn't go to the field, we had a snowstorm of paperwork to keep up with as each radio set has its own service jacket just like we did, and we were constantly doing inventory to ensure each piece of gear down to 3-foot-long coaxial cables was properly stored in the proper place. Plus a plastic bag stuck to the end of each embarkation box held the packing slip for each one, and Top Lee insisted that every box had the proper packing slip. Top Lee was a very calm, friendly, and relaxed Florida country boy who rarely raised his voice with us much less got angry. However, when it came to doing the job right, he was as ruthless in his attention to detail as a surgeon or an operator at a nuclear power plant. I remember one commanding general's inspection where we were allowed a 10 percent margin of error. In other words, on this test you have to score a 90 to get a passing grade. In the civilian world scoring 80 percent is a B, whereas in the Marine Corps that was simply passing. When the inspectors got done examining every box, radio, and cable that we had and ran their numbers, our margin of error was only 1 percent. My buddies and I did all the work, but Lee was the one who really got it done. I was really very sad the day he decided to retire and leave 4th ANGLICO.

Even after twelve straight years in the same unit and working with so many ground military units around the world, I still don't consider myself to be an expert in patrolling or even infantry tactics. I'm very well versed in both aspects of these types of combat operations, but I'm just not the one that should be the lead instructor when it comes to teaching these subjects. Experienced Marine infantry are much better at these tasks than I am, and Recon Marines are always going to be better in patrolling than me, and I would go so far as to say plenty of the ANGLICO Marines I served with. While this might sound like an insult, if you deploy to Iraq and the assignment that you draw is to work with U.S. Navy River Marine forces along the Euphrates River and you haven't done any infantry patrolling for the last nine months, this young Marine lance corporal is not the one you want to teach patrolling to a group of privates or PFCs who just joined your unit.

By the same token, when my buddy Joe Macantee "deployed for active duty" during the Gulf War in 1991, he spent more than a half year with the Norwegians. Somebody in the Pentagon correctly deduced that while half a million American forces were deployed to the Gulf States, we didn't want to see the Russians start fooling around with our good friends the Norwegians. While Joe and his fellow Marines did a great job providing backup for Norwegian ground forces, his so-called combat service in the Gulf War consisted of snowcapped mountains in the dark waters of Norwegian fjords. It was just the luck of the draw for him. He later got hit by a roadside bomb in Iraq, and I spotted my old friend getting pinned with a Purple Heart in the local newspaper. Joe returned to the States after the war and for a while actually traveled to West Palm Beach from Syracuse because he wanted to be a member of ANGLICO so badly. If Mac had been an ANGLICO Marine during his Norwegian interlude, he wouldn't have performed a parachute mission in almost a year. Not jumping for a year makes you pretty rusty very quickly. While we rehearse for every parachute drop just like a theater company does, Mac and other Marines, namely the ones that had just returned from combat duty, would need a little bit more extra attention before the next job for safety measures.

But as I said, whether a Marine is serving with the Norwegian army, serving with the riverine forces, or spending only three days learning how to drive and fire the main gun on a Bradley Fighting Vehicle in the Gulf War such as my buddy Chip Hanke, the thread that runs through every team out in the field is their communications assets.

Put simply: Comm is the heart and soul of ANGLICO. I remember how one SALT team Marine captain responded to my young PFC question about being in a field operation (JRTC 1990, and, yes, it was colder than hell) without carrying an M-16. Since we were in a "normal" ANGLICO SALT configuration with the Army's 101st Airborne Division, we were attached to one of their battalion's tactical operations centers, or TOC, which is always pronounced as "TOCK." The only weapon this aviator captain was carrying was a Beretta 9mm pistol, a weapon I never cared for. Give me the Colt .45 automatic any day of any combat assignment. In fact, he wasn't even rated to carry one, which means he didn't withdraw an M-16 from the armory, even for this trip. He taught me an important ANGLICO lesson: You're not there to pull the trigger; you're there to blow the shit out of the entire valley if required. With a wave of his hand, he gestured to the surrounding terrain and mentioned an enemy attack. The TOC was surrounded by a ring of troops including two 60-ton M1 Abrams main battle tanks.

"Besides, if they get this close to the battalion TOC, there will be plenty of wounded troops for me to pick up their rifle and fire it. If they're hit bad, they won't need it anyway," he said. "We're here to call in assets from air, land, and sea."

I've mentioned how glad I was to see how much smaller the laser designators had become during the fifteen years since I left 4th ANGLICO. In the digital world fifteen years is more than a few lifetimes; toss in two hot wars and technology really takes off. The same thing has happened to the radios used by U.S. forces. Old First Sergeant Nicolls spoke of his refusal to be within 100 meters of a company command group during field exercises, I'm sure because every radio was bigger and each had its own 10-foot antenna. Nicolls was right: Ten to twelve antennas in a group is a priority target.

During my time in the late 1980s and all of the '90s, I saw some digitizing of our HF radio, the AN/PRC 104, the advent of the SINGARS AN/PRC 119, and the first satellite field radios (SATCOM), the PSC-5 series that could easily be carried by one Marine. (Please be advised that anything I write in this book about communications, weapons, or field gear is readily found in the public domain or on the Internet.)

If I ran or was assigned to an FCT team, it meant that each Marine was fully loaded with comm gear. That meant radios, multiple antennas for each set, handsets to talk into, slash wire to make field-expedient antennas, large and heavy batteries for three days of operation, code books with unit call signs and radio frequencies, and cleaning gear for field maintenance.

The AN/PRC 113 was the smallest and lightest, an ultra-high frequency (UHF) radio that only worked on "line of sight" and was designed for FACs, recon, and for ANGLICO to talk to pilots in the aircraft for CAS or incoming medevac missions. We used it exclusively for air support. In my experience, since it was the lightest radio, the team chief always got to carry it. It was built by Magnavox, the old television manufacturer, weighed 13 pounds, operated with two batteries weighing 5 pounds total, could operate in UHF and VHF, could communicate on eighty-four hundred separate channels, and was fully functional in an astounding temperature range from minus 20 degrees to 154 degrees Fahrenheit. It almost always was operated with a 16-inch-long omni-directional antenna, universally referred to as a "donkey dick." If you didn't call it that, no one knew what the hell you were talking about.

My favorite feature of the 113 was frequency hopping. We could load in eight frequencies, or "freqs" (pronounced "freaks" you freaks!), press a button, and the internal classified guts of the radio would skip between freqs to keep the enemy from hearing our transmissions. Plus, you could set up an entire radio network (net) with this. It was hard and took practice, but I loved hearing that rapid "tick, tick, tick" sound the hopping emitted into my handset.

I always got stuck with the heavy AN/PRC 104, a 25-pound HF pig of a radio that, I have to admit, was our most reliable long-range radio. It was nothing to throw up a 10-foot whip antenna and send message traffic to my SALT team nearly 50 miles away. The 104 was made by the Harris Corporation and was a very tough radio that could handle 280,000 frequencies to transmit voice message traffic and data, and even came with its own old-fashioned Morse code key that could be attached to your knee with a horseshoe-shaped clamp. It came in a fiberglass transit case that truly was a self-contained unit. The receiver, amplifier, and coupler were all held together with metal clamps and came with three battery boxes that were attached to the bottom of the radios and contained the 5-pound BA-5590 lithium batteries. It came with electrical cables that would allow the radio to be powered by an outside source or a Jeep or Humvee, and a 10-inch round base for a 15-foot-tall radio antenna called an AS 2259 that could extend the range of the radio up to 300 miles by bouncing radio signals off of the ionosphere to a distant station. The ubiquitous 10-foot whip antenna was attached to the radio with the hard rubber base that allowed the antenna to sway with the movement of the Marine carrying it so it didn't snap off. The 104's transit case interior was a foam rubber molding that had a space for every component of the radio, which kept everything safe and sound and meant maintenance and storage were a snap because the parts only fitted into the right spot. The cases even came with their own ALICE backpack (All-Purpose Light-weight Individual Carrying Equipment) to carry the radio. Just like the PRC-113, it had an insane temperature operating range from minus 50 up to 160. Our unit had these cases stacked to the ceiling of our communications section, or comm shack.

The AS 2259 radio antenna was rolled up in an olive drab canvas bag with seven pole sections that were attached to the round base that came inside the 104's transit case, which never made any sense to me. Since the 2259 was most likely going to be used with a PRC 104 anyway, why wouldn't the antenna base be included with the antenna kit instead of the carrying case it's shipped in? The transit cases were always left at the unit inside the comm shack in the antenna kits all rolled up and strapped together, and were usually tossed in the back of the Humvee for transport to the field. With four guy wires necessary to hold the 15-foot antenna, the base was a necessity and it just made sense that it would be included with the kit. It struck me like having to change the tire in your car by the side of the road and discovering when you take the spare tire and jack out of your trunk that the car dealer had placed the crowbar somewhere else.

The other field antenna that we used, but not as much, was the AS 292, which was always referred to as the two-niner-two. Thirty feet tall, heavier, more robust but also with a longer range, the 292 needed at least two Marines, maybe three, to set it up. It also needed more area to operate, which is why it was usually erected in a rear echelon area such as a regimental command post, as they moved around less than the maneuver units such as infantry companies, platoons, and of course Marine ANGLICO FCT or SALT teams. If we could avoid bringing it out into the field just for the weekend, we certainly did. However for a two- to three-week operation overseas or training with the U.S. Army, we always brought at least two or three along just in case we needed them. It was all part of the avalanche of communications gear that any Marine ANGLICO detachment deployed with.

Another Marine carried the Vietnam War–era AN/PRC 77 frequency-modulated (FM) radio. It was big, bulky with barely a 5-mile range, but it was incredibly reliable and is still used by militaries friendly to the United States to this day.

The PRC-77 was first deployed with the U.S. military in 1968 during the height of the Vietnam War. At the time it was seen as a miracle of a small unit radio and excelled at close-range and tactical communications during combat operations. The PRC-77 has had an amazingly long life for any piece of military equipment, right up there with such long-term American military products as the B-52 Stratofortress, which first flew in the early 1950s, or the C-130 Hercules cargo aircraft that first flew in 1958 when Elvis Presley was hot on the music charts. Even today, nations with a worldwide reputation for technical prowess such as the Austrians, the Norwegians, and even the Swiss are still using the PRC-77 in one capacity or another. While most of the radio sets have been updated and improved over the decades, most of the 77s are used to teach new radio operators basic communication techniques, using rear areas for administration; however, the Filipino military still actively uses 77s in military operations. An FM radio that operated over 920 frequencies, it weighed at least 13 pounds and came with its own frame attached to shoulder straps for a radioman to carry next to his company commander, plus the standard 10-foot whip antenna and also a 3-foot-long metal tape antenna that can be turned upside down using a metal gooseneck attachment so the radio operator wouldn't be so obvious to snipers or enemy forward observers.

I know some Americans might think it's odd that a military radio would have such short range. I know we spend a lot of money in the military, but one thing that civilians don't take into consideration is the huge number of people who are in the field at the same time. In the civilian world, if you have two thousand employees, you are considered to be a very large company. Well, in the military I call that morning chow at every large training base in the country. What this means is a radio communications officer is allotted a certain section of the radio spectrum. Most people don't realize that the radio spectrum is a finite space, which is why it is so tightly regulated by the Federal Communications Commission, and even why the dial on your car radio only has a set number of frequencies. Now if every military radio had a range of a thousand miles, everybody would be talking over everyone else's radio transmissions and nothing would get accomplished. A communications officer for an entire division, which in the U.S. military could be from twenty-five to thirty-five thousand troops, could use the same frequencies multiple times by employing short-range radios. When the entire 1st Marine Division was deployed to Iraq during the early part of the Gulf War, platoons on patrol could be as much as 20 miles apart. Handheld walkie-talkies or small radios with a shorter range means that a communications officer can get more mileage out of all of the allotted frequencies. This is just one of the aspects of being a communications officer. When units can't talk to each other, it's your fault and someone with a lot higher rank than you is always going to be extremely angry.

I'll write one sentence about "crypto" (slang for cryptology or encryption), the super-secret data codes and machines used to encrypt our radios so the enemy can't listen in, actually I won't, so that's that.

I've often been asked by my civilian friends why the military's radios have always been so big and bulky as opposed to a home telephone, or the small walkie-talkies that American police officers attach to their shoulder with no difficulty, much less the small and getting smaller by the day cellular phones that virtually everyone in the world owns. As a young

Marine I held a lot of those same beliefs, especially when I got stuck carrying the heavy 104 and a three-day supply of 5-pound batteries plus all my combat gear and M-16. One year when I was living in Gainesville and taking classes, a friend of mine got me a job working the midnight shift at a convenience store. Cops always came by to grab a cup of coffee or a snack, and after getting to know one police officer a little bit, I told him what I did with the Marine Corps, and we began talking about various weapons, gear, and tactics, and eventually got around to radios. I told him how powerful our radios were but also how big and heavy as well. I asked him how police use such small walkie-talkies every day of the week and could seemingly speak to the police dispatcher, the county jail, or City Hall with such ease. He cleared the situation up for me very quickly. Nearly everyone has seen a police officer leaning his or her head over toward their walkie-talkie, typically attached to their uniform just next to their shirtsleeve, usually on the opposite side of their badge. But the officer told me what most people don't realize: His police cruiser had a radio unit and repeater in its trunk.

As soon as he told me this, I understood why military radios were bigger and heavier. A radio repeater or retransmission unit does just what it sounds like: It repeats or resends a message with an added power boost to a distant receiving antenna. Therefore Officer Friendly out on patrol is not using a tiny handset to communicate directly with the police dispatcher. Instead of one tiny walkie-talkie sending radio transmissions all the way across town or the county, the signal is retransmitted by a heavy base unit in a police cruiser and received by an even larger antenna at the police station or county jail that is attached to a 150-foot cell tower and powered by the local electric company. A military radio needs to do all of this in one unit and also fit in a backpack carried by one soldier, hence the term *man-packed radio*. For example, take a heavy HF PRC 104 that has a receiver, coupler, and amplifier powered by two 5-pound batteries with a radio handset and antenna attached to it. Taking this into consideration (and how you can't fit a cell tower in a vehicle radio base unit in your backpack), it starts to make sense why military batteries such as the lithium BA-5590 retail for almost $100 a pop. As I'll explain in chapter 18, the capabilities of modern military radios and how extensively trained me and my Marine buddies were became an extreme source of frustration for me viewing all of the mayhem and chaos in the city of New Orleans just after Hurricane Katrina. As you learn later, the military could have easily blanketed the Crescent City with a radio network that could have kept the White House informed of the situation in almost real time. Why not just use cellular phones, you ask? They aren't encrypted, which means the bad guys hear everything you say, and in combat or during a natural disaster, you can assume the power stations are going to be knocked off line. So as soon as your cellular phone battery runs out of juice, so do you. I saw this in Pascagoula when I reported on Hurricane Katrina. I can still see the disgust on the face of a conservative, blue-blood southerner holding up his cell phone and calling it "worthless" after the storm. He told me he had almost begged the local telephone company to buy electrical generators for the cellular towers located throughout the area. They bought the generators all right. But they placed them at the base of the tower in low ground so they were promptly swamped with the floodwaters of the tidal surge pushed in front of any hurricane. Good job, men!

Now we'll turn our attention to the 50-year, constant scourge of Marine ANGLICO. It's not the U.S. Army, although sometimes it feels like they are when we work with them. It's not the U.S. Air Force refusing to drop our jumpers a whopping 1,000 feet higher than normal to give our "junior jumpers" more "canopy time."

"You asked for 1,500 feet, you get 1,500 feet," a 12-year-old looking Air Force lieutenant arrogantly dismissed Master Sergeant MacMillan one day. I saw it happen.

It's not even the fact that the American public has never heard of us. Ever.

It's batteries. Yes, confused reader, you read that correctly. Batteries. Thousands of them that seemingly reproduce like furry Tribbles falling on the head of Captain Kirk in the original *Star Trek* television series (shut up nerds, it's still the best version of the show and you know it). They're big. They're bulky. They're heavy and rumor had it they tended to explode when they got wet. I've seen them start to smoke, emit little showers of sparks, and crust over with powder like some weird fungus from a 1950s science fiction movie at the drive-in. On any type of mission, peacetime or combat, you're loaded down with two in each radio and four more to last for up to six days. As I wrote in chapter 1, each battery is about the size of a large watch case you get as a graduation, retirement, or promotion gift. You quickly take out your shiny new watch and chuck the packaging. For us that's exactly one battery. The U.S. military has millions of them.

We used mainly three types of batteries: the BA-5590, BA-5598 (a bit smaller and lighter), and a BA-3186 for the older PRC-77s. Since the 3186 is 9 by 3.5 by 2 inches, it was universally referred to as "a brick" due to its being nearly identical in size to a red housing brick. Bricks weigh 4 pounds, put out 15 volts, and since so many militaries around the world are still using PRC-77s, companies from as far and wide as Buckingham, England, and little Sanford, Florida, just north of Orlando, are still manufacturing them. I'm not even sure if they had the same numeric designation when I was in, because we always called them bricks.

To give you an idea of just what a burden all of these batteries are, the 14-volt 5598 and 5590s are sold on the commercial market for nearly one hundred dollars *for each one*. One website I found online claimed that the U.S. Army alone bought 350,000 batteries in one year, or $35 million. That's excluding the other services and all of the other battery types. Small wonder that the Marine Corps has switched over entirely to rechargeable nickel-cadmium batteries, which, of course, are heavier. While it might seem obvious to change to rechargeable batteries, well now your comm techs have the fun task of constantly recharging batteries in a combat zone, plus carrying the battery-charging gear itself. If you've ever bought a battery recharger yourself, you learn very quickly you need three times the amount of batteries you thought you would to cycle through new and charging units. Like I said: Batteries are just a damn scourge.

Everyone just loves their SATCOM. It's small. It's light. The antenna looks like something out of *Star Wars* and snaps right open like a little kid's pop-up book. Plus, the no-static sound quality is so good, it's like talking to your mom on a landline telephone. However, there are a few little quirks. The PSC-5 system I first learned how to operate had this small canvas bag (olive drab in color, of course) so you could carry the entire radio and antenna draped over one shoulder like a purse. No one called it a purse or said you looked like a Frenchman, but we all overlooked that because "hey, it's SATCOM and it's cool!" The PSC-5 was so good that you could actually not take it off your body, pop open the antenna, attach the coaxial cable, and just start talking. There was one slight drawback as one instructor told me: The radio was so powerful if you did that too much, it might fry your nads like a microwave.

"You'd be better off placing the radio set 3 to 5 feet away and stretching out the handset cord," he deadpanned.

Thanks for the important safety tip there, staff sergeant.

Now don't get me wrong, SATCOM is terrific, but what nearly no one outside the military knows is that any SATCOM device needs an *exact* frequency to operate on, and if you have a man-packed set like the military, you need coordination from the proper authorities as to when and where you'll operate the system. Since everyone wants to use it, it's strictly controlled. And if you don't follow the rules, the "men in black" will make a very nasty phone call to your command to get your sorry ass in line. Also, out in the field, the higher command will assign you a certain angle to orient your cool-looking antenna so your signal hits the right antenna. On one mission it might be low on the horizon, on another it might be shooting nearly straight up at a satellite just above you. Hence the need for such tight supervision from spooks upstairs.

For you civilian operators who read this and say "gee, I own a satellite phone and don't need to do this," there's a very simple reason Mr. Snotty. Your signal is actually being transmitted to a ground station that retransmits your signal to the person you're calling. Hurricane Katrina, the big killer that exposed all of the flaws in American civil defense, showed this. I spent almost a week in the Pascagoula, Mississippi, area immediately after Katrina. I was a staff writer for a trade journal, *The Credit Union Journal*, expertly run by publisher Frank Diekmann and editor Lisa Freeman, who went to New Orleans after Katrina. Speaking with locals who tried to use their newfangled SATCOM phones after the storm, it wasn't the miracle worker they thought it would be. One credit union official complained that she had to go outside to use it, and since the radio frequency spectrum was so jammed with traffic, she had a hard time getting through to her bosses to update her status. Transmitting data? You can forget about that after a hurricane.

After Lisa Freeman and I both returned from the Gulf states and began a year-long series of stories about how Katrina affected credit unions and the financial system, I mentioned the total destruction of the communication system. I pitched the idea of using radios and SATCOM for each credit union and we subsequently published a large story on it. During my research into the civilian use of SATCOM, I was astonished to learn of the ground link that commercial satellite companies were employing. Even more shocking was the site of the ground station: *South Florida!*

Just in case you've lived under a very large rock for the last six hundred years, South Florida tends to be hit with very nasty storms called hurricanes on a rather steady basis. Look up the path of Hurricane Katrina in 2005. People forget it struck Florida first and promptly stressed out the entire SATCOM system even before its eventual Category 5 landfall along the Gulf shoreline. So before you shell out a ton of money for civilian SATCOM, I would highly suggest asking your vendor if it has a ground relay system and where it's located. If your bad-ass SATCOM phone has a ground relay, why bother?

Present 4th ANGLICO I&I communications chief S/Sgt. Carlos Torres has had quite a career. The youthful-looking, fourteen-year veteran of the Marine Corps served combat tours in Iraq and Afghanistan before arriving in West Palm Beach. Starting his career in 2000, he had the extraordinary experience of graduating boot camp on Parris Island, South Carolina, not only on his birthday, but on November 10, which is the birthday of the Marine Corps, a date Marines have been celebrating since our founding in 1775. To really kickstart his career, Torres graduated from Field Radio Operator School and was promptly assigned to Hawaii for his first assignment. The ensuing years brought duty on Okinawa with 5th ANGLICO and then deployment to Afghanistan with the 3rd Recon Battalion. Along the way he also served a term as a recruiter, one of the more high-pressure jobs in the Marine Corps that plenty of Marines get relieved from for not fulfilling quotas sent down by HQMC. I never wanted to be a recruiter because the job is such a pain in the ass, and plenty of Marines think you're nothing more than a professional liar, whereas serving as a drill instructor is met with near universal praise and admiration.

Sitting in the office of my old comm shack with Torres fifteen years after I got out of uniform was a bit surreal and yet familiar at the same time. I had asked to meet with him to discuss which aspects of present-day communications and radios I can write about in this book without having any kind of security breach, which I have been dead set against from the beginning of this project. The thing about military radios is they are basically metal boxes containing the classified guts that really matter. Manufacturers of military radios such as Motorola, Magnavox in the old days, the Harris Corporation based near Cape Canaveral in Florida, they all have datasheets on their radio systems that are published on the World Wide Web and are even handed out at military shows around the world.

Torres brought out four radios to show me they were two-thirds smaller than some of the radios I used during my time with 4th ANGLICO. Not only were they physically smaller and that much lighter, most of the radios were running computer software that allowed almost any type of data transmission and even web applications. Plus instead of having one radio for high-frequency transmissions, one radio for FM, one radio for UHF to talk to incoming aircraft, and possibly a separate radio set specifically for SATCOM, this new generation of radios could function on two different radio spectrums as well as having a SATCOM function included. These new radios felt like something out of *Star Trek* to me. However, just like so many things in Marine ANGLICO that never seem to change, whether it's the eternal sales job of what we do, the jealousy and anger of other Marines over our independent cowboy nature, or how we struggle for political power even with HQMC, I just had to ask about "the scourge." And after reading this chapter you know what I'm talking about: that's right folks, batteries.

Not only have the batteries not gotten smaller, they are now heavier, because of the Marine Corps' move to "go green" to reduce its environmental footprint and to not require as much energy in forward combat areas. The batteries I used were never rechargeable and had to be sent back and treated one for one when they ran out of power. Rechargeable batteries existed, but I guess the Marine Corps just didn't have the money to buy them. After explaining the amazing new capabilities of the new-to-me radios, Torres had a sad look on his face when I asked about whether batteries were still the thorn in the side of Marine ANGLICO.

"They are still the same size [the radio batteries]," Torres told me. "I wish they would make them smaller [versus the radios] to be honest with you."

Torres told me that on a typical mission in Iraq or Afghanistan, if you are part of a team going out of the perimeter defenses on a five-day mission, each Marine would have a different radio set and he would take around thirty batteries and spread the load among each team member. Military radios have such a need for power that Torres said thirty batteries putting out upwards of 15 volts each would barely last for the five-day mission. And trust me, in the Marine Corps you just don't chuck things away, you bring them back and turn them in to the comm shack.

"Of all the equipment we had for five days, the batteries were the heaviest," Torres said. "It adds like 40 pounds to your pack right there."

Another entire field unknown to the public involves what's known as "field expedient antennas." Even training for combat is a rough game, far tougher than most civilians will ever know. Worldwide, U.S. troops are hurt or killed during training accidents virtually every day. Recon and ANGLICO Marines are airborne qualified and need to learn how to properly pack their backpacks to ensure their radios will work after landing. During paratroop operations backpacks are released from the jumper's body on a 30-foot-long lanyard that hits the earth before they do. If you hit the ground with all of your combat gear, the 70 pounds of a parachute rig, and a 65-pound backpack, you're not walking off of the drop zone on your own two feet. In other words radios and their antennas can get broken at any time and in combat they can be shot away by incoming fire.

A field expedient antenna can be as simple as using green duct tape to keep a 10-foot whip held together or using communications wire (which we always called "slash wire") to build a completely new antenna. When I was on an FCT team out in the field, I never used a fully extended 10-foot whip as it looked like a flag shouting out "Hey! Enemy sniper! Please put a bullet through my forehead!" As I was usually stuck carrying the heavy AN/PRC 104, I would take the rubber hard base the whip antenna was supposed to screw into and attach it to the radio. Just before the brass fitting fully seated in the radio, I would take a 10- to 15-foot section of slash wire, strip the end of it, and use the bare metal as a connector to the radio. The wire length worked great as an antenna and would simply trail behind me on the ground. Since it was covered with a slick plastic coating, it didn't even catch on anything. As we usually tagged along with another unit, there wasn't even anyone behind me to step on it. If I couldn't get comm with the artillery battery, a U.S. Navy destroyer sailing off shore, or my SALT, I would just take out a canteen, tie it to the trailing end, and toss it up into a tree facing the distant station I was trying to contact. It worked fine and I did this for years.

Other units in combat facing a problem with a busted antenna need to quickly improvise with pieces of wood, bamboo, or rubber to create insulators for their new antennas. ANGLICO Marines very commonly create their own kits full of slash wire, wire strippers they bought on their own, wire splitters from Radio Shack, coax cable and coax cutters also bought from Radio Shack, and one of the easiest, most available insulators throughout the U.S. military: the little plastic spoons in every MRE.

Our Marines would grab a plastic spoon and use a knife to cut little holes on each end to hold slash wire or carve notches to use as a spacer. While other units used these in emergencies, ANGLICO Marines used them as a first choice to avoid being spotted by the enemy. Official Marine training manuals have plenty of diagrams on how to build your own insulators. The diagrams showed what worked the best (plastic spoons, buttons, the busted-off neck of a glass bottle, or even a section of plastic bag), what was OK (a piece of wood with holes drilled on each end), or only very average (cloth, or a small loop of nylon rope).

I won't even begin to try to describe all the separate types of field expedient antennas. Entire books have been written by communications types on the subject of antennas, how they operate, and the best way to emplace them without electrocuting yourself or your buddies. Plus I'm heeding the warning of my mom, who told me to not get too technical "because otherwise I'm just going to skip over it."

Some of the more common methods used when I served were the above described slash wire trail method to reproduce a 10-foot whip, placing antennas on the rear slope of a hill or mountain to reach the rear stations and keep the signal away from the bad guys in front of you, or using larger antennas such as the 2259 and 292 described before to bounce radio signals off of the ionosphere. Once you started playing with sky wave radio shots, then you had to pay attention to sunspot activity and when they were occurring. Sky wave is a tactic of literally bouncing radio signals off of the ionosphere a section of earth's upper atmosphere full of ionized particles from the sun's radiation. As early as the 1920s, amateur radio operators were having two-way conversations with radio stations across expanses as large at the Pacific Ocean. But as I wrote, you'd better pay attention to sunspot activity to achieve good radio communications.

One common field expedient antenna was called the sloping vee antenna. Radio antennas are usually omnidirectional or directional. A directional antenna means just that: I want my radio signal to go in one direction only, the distant station you're calling. An omnidirectional antenna, such as a 10-foot whip or the fat rubber-coated antennas usually used to talk to aircraft, emits its energy in a 360-degree pattern. Omni-directional antennas work great to broadcast to everyone (a music radio station, for example), but the enemy can also pick it up, which is where encryption and frequency hopping come into play. The sloping vee would be built and emplaced with the open section of the V facing the station you were trying to call. A simple sloping wire would generally work as a directional antenna and could be taken down immediately. A sloping vee is more static and takes time to construct and displace.

I won't go into every antenna type, as it would bore you to death and I'm not an expert in the field anyway. There are dozens of types with names that sound like plays that Vince Lombardi or Don Shula drew up for the Super Bowl. There's the Flying Vee. The Inverted Vee. The Vertical Whip and the Half Wave Dipole. How about the Inverted L, the Long Wire, or the always popular Vertical Half-Rhombic? If the End-Fed Half Wave doesn't work then we'll try the Center Fed Dou-blet. Of course! Who wouldn't? What the heck: If the Vee or Sloping

Vee doesn't work, then we'll just have to try a Yagi. I told you that you wouldn't want the details. But, in addition to CAS, artillery, and naval gunfire missions, each ANGLICO Marine needs to know the details of field communications.

For any member of a foreign military unit or the U.S. Army, the following can't be overstated: An ANGLICO Marine is there to help any way he can, but it's with his radio and not his M-16. Of course we can shoot, move, and communicate like any U.S. Marine, and in fact, ANGLICO Marines are some of the most extensively trained troops in the Corps. But don't put us on point, don't look at us as a little team to do the shit work you should be doing on your own anyway. We're here to blow shit up for you, we're great at it, and we use the radio.

The standard method in any possible sighting was to use the radio to send a SALUTE report up the chain of command as soon as possible. SALUTE stands for size, activity, location, unit, time, and equipment being carried by the enemy troops. For example, when Gonzo and I were 6 kilometers in front of friendly lines at JRTC in Fort Polk and a C-130 Hercules loaded with OPFOR paratroopers flew directly over our observation post, it was a perfect time for a SALUTE report. However, as the aircraft was on its final approach to the drop zone (I could clearly see the jumpmaster standing in the cargo door ready to launch his jumpers), I stammered out a quick and dirty message to my SALT and to Regiment without any regard for standard operating procedures. This later drew a slight rebuke and reminder for all FCT teams to use the SALUTE format, but I was surprised by the sudden appearance of the C-130 full of paratroopers. Since we always arrived at JRTC with only around three days to prepare, we hadn't gone to the formal Intell brief run by the Army and I simply wasn't aware the "bad guys" had any airborne capability on that operation.

As I wrote before, very large and complex books have been written on radios and antennas, and by experts much more qualified than I. However, radios are at the center of everything and members of other military branches should always remember: An ANGLICO Marine not talking on a radio is not doing his job.

CHAPTER TEN

MOS 2: Marking the Target

CHIP HANKE IS THE ONLY ANGLICO MARINE WHO EVER USED HIS own body as a method to mark a target.

Marking the target means employing some type of identification for the pilot of a jet fighter or helicopter gunship to fixate on the correct target and release their ordnance. You can mark a target with smoke rounds from the artillery by either having a round impact as close as possible to the target or placing the incoming round in a spot that easily can be seen by the pilot and then give directions from that point. Though everyone is enamored with laser-guided bombs these days—and they are extremely accurate, there's no doubt about that—they are simply the latest and greatest method of marking the target, a process that goes back hundreds of years in the world's militaries.

Chip and I were on the same 1996 deployment to Norway for Operation Battle Griffin, the tri-annual mobilization of Norway's military with the primary focus of being a deterrent to the Russians. As I'll detail in chapter 20, Chip's FCT team was so effective in being such a colossal pain in the ass to the opposing force that on the final day of the exercise the Dutch Marines fighting on the other side simulating the enemy broadcast on an open, unsecured radio net that they were climbing up the mountain where Chip and his team were operating. The Dutch Marines' sole purpose was to wipe them out. While Chip was calling in one CAS mission, a Cobra gunship was sent in to fire simulated missiles at whatever target Chip was trying to hit. As a result of too many civilian casualties in the Vietnam War, throughout all of the military operations in the 1980s and 1990s, the Pentagon required "eyes on" whatever target a FAC or ANGLICO Marine was trying to destroy. In fact, it became so prevalent that during the NATO bombings in Bosnia in 1999 jet fighters would actually make at least one pass over the target just to make sure it was the right one and attack it on the final pass, which greatly exposed the pilots to potential enemy fire.

On this particular mission the gunship pilot couldn't see Chip and his team members and wouldn't fire as he didn't want to create a friendly fire incident. During the '80s and '90s, there was a wildly popular brand of sunglasses made by Revo. They were cool-looking glasses that had different-colored lenses with a mirrored sheen to them and were popular with the American surfer set and all over South Florida. Chip was wearing his Revo sunglasses during this mission while the helicopter pilot was settled into a hover repeatedly asking where Chip was standing. While Chip had sent in a proper nine-line brief used for all CAS missions, since the pilot did not know where his team was located, he refused to fire. Both Chip and the gunship pilot were getting very frustrated, as pilots don't like to just burn off gas waiting for a mission to go down, and in an act of desperation, Chip finally picked up his PRC-113 UHF radio handset and yelled:

"LOOK TO YOUR LEFT! I'M THE ONE WEARING THE FAGGY PURPLE SUNGLASSES!"

The gunship pilot looked to his left and quickly spotted Chip waving his hands and arms like a madman and, of course, sporting his "faggy" purple sunglasses.

"Oh! There you are!" said the pilot, then promptly located Chip's target and destroyed it. Mission accomplished.

I've always loved this story about Chip, plus it's a perfect example of ANGLICO Marines making things up as we went along, because we had to. However, it does create friction with the rest of the mainline Marine Corps, who use these as examples when they accuse us of being just a bunch of cowboys.

Chip Hanke (HAN-kee) was just a great guy and one hell of a Marine. He was probably a little under 6 feet tall and calling him barrel chested is an understatement, as at one point he could bench press 415 pounds on a regular basis. He was a big goombah guy who virtually everybody loved, but also respected as a leader, a great operator, and just all-around good guy. Hanke served in the first Gulf War and Kosovo and had made so many peacetime deployments that even before September 11th Chip had four full rows of ribbons from all of his military operations. He had even been awarded an Army commendation medal for his great work during one of 4th ANGLICO's regular deployments to the JRTC in Fort Polk, Louisiana. Though we always make fun of the Army for giving out medals to everyone simply for doing their job, we never gave Chip a hard time as we all knew he probably deserved it.

For being such a two-fisted beer-drinking U.S. Marine paratrooper (who also serves in the civilian world as a police officer), Chip was never a hard case with junior Marines and just wanted everyone to do their jobs to the best of their abilities. I can still see the look on his face after he returned from the Gulf War and how much seeing dead bodies for the first time in his life had affected him, especially because so many Iraqi soldiers were wiped out toward the end. I'll also never forget a Sunday afternoon after we were dismissed and having our monthly little beer bash (situated off government property of course) as I kept quiet and listened to Chip and 1st Sgt. Parks Nicolls discussing how to deal with the bad memories they were still carrying with them even a few years after the end of the war. I still take it as a great compliment that both of them trusted me enough to speak so openly about their feelings and how much it affected their lives. Plus I was smart enough to keep my mouth shut when combat veterans started to reveal their true feelings, which I do to this day. Today Chip is married and living in the Orlando area serving as a police officer and having a grand old time raising his two little boys. Nobody deserves a happy home life more than Chip does.

Probably the most common methods of marking a target are calling in either an artillery shell or naval gunfire using white phosphorus, which creates a bright white cloud upon impact. White phosphorus, or "Willy Pete" as it's almost always called, has been used by numerous world militaries as far back as 1916, can be used in hand grenades, artillery shells, mortar shells, naval gunfire, and fired from aircraft that are equipped with missiles that carry the substance. Though they are most commonly used to create smokescreens for ground troops to assault a position or cross a danger area, being an ANGLICO Marine I usually thought of Willy Pete rounds as a terrific way to mark a target, as they are blindingly white and rise almost straight up in the air after bursting on the ground.

Willy Pete is not without controversy, as militaries including our own can fire over the heads of an enemy position and correct the fuse to allow the shell to burst in midair over the target, which sends the burning white phosphorus onto the enemy position below. U.S. forces in Iraq were using Willy Pete rounds to force enemy fighters out into the open to be attacked, while many human rights groups condemned the Israeli Defense Force for using white phosphorus to target terrorist groups such as Hamas in southern Lebanon during the first part of the twenty-first century. One of the better ideas I heard for using white phosphorus came from 1st Sgt. Parks Nicolls, who told me as a young corporal that the Germans fighting on the Russian front during World War II would lay down a straight line of white smoke or Willy Pete that an attacking Russian tank force had to drive through. In the movies everything is a close-up to show the good-looking actors' faces as they fight the forces of evil, but in real life tanks and aircraft are usually rather far away, and of course look a heck of a lot smaller than when they're just across the street. The Germans would lay down this line of white smoke with their own tanks and antitank artillery pieces ready to fire as each tank popped out of the smoke, creating a black or dark green color against the curtain of white smoke. I have to admit it's a great technique as the German gunners simply picked off the Russian tanks one by one.

Back during the 1930s CAS techniques were being developed by various militaries around the world, but especially the U.S. Marine Corps as it spent years fighting in the so-called Banana Wars in Haiti and Nicaragua. While crude by today's standards, it was a new development to place radios in aircraft that would be bombing the enemy. It was also a new development at the time for an aircrew to speak with troops serving on the ground in contact with the enemy. Often flags, semaphores, or what is now known as an air panel would be spread out on the ground to mark the location of friendly troops. Just as you can mark the target, you can and should mark your own location by various methods, whether it is using a radio to send a grid location on the map or with today's GPS systems or even using small signal mirrors that are given to aircrews for their survival kits. I always carried a single mirror, and to this day in my own hiking gear, after a 4th ANGLICO helicopter pilot told me in no uncertain terms that if it was daytime the most effective means of signaling by far was with a single mirror and not the strobes that were coming into fashion at the time. However, strobes are obviously terrific at night.

Later in 1944 during the Allies' mad dash across Western Europe after the Normandy landings on June 6, 1944, many U.S. Army FACs would ride along with Sherman tanks talking with their fellow pilots by radio to call in dive bombers on Nazi troops. A frequent technique would be to tie an air panel on the flat section of a Sherman just behind the turret, which would show attacking pilots where the FAC was. As I said before, it's always good for an attacking aircraft to know where you are in relation to the target. It's the same reason that Chip Hanke was jumping around like a madman waving his purple Revos at the attacking Cobra pilot during Battle Griffin '96. An air panel is a great tool that is really nothing more than a piece of canvas around 4 by 6 feet with two very bright almost neon colors on either side of the panel. One side is usually a bright rescue orange and the other side is a very odd purplish, lavender mix of color that I think was created by the U.S. military just for the purpose of being easily seen from the air. I'm sure a painter or graphic designer could quickly identify which fancy shade of purple/lavender/ whatever on the color wheels that they use, but personally I have never seen the exact color in any wildflowers or plants, from the Florida Everglades to Louisiana or North Carolina and up into Indiana and Kentucky where my extended family lives. Just like a small signal mirror, it's another piece of gear I carry in my hiking buttpack to this day. Obviously I don't have any intention of being lost in the woods sitting there with no food or water while search helicopters fly over me without seeing me.

Illumination rounds, sometimes called "star shells," are rounds fired by artillery or naval gunfire that do just that; they illuminate a certain area most likely occupied by enemy troops. A forward observer might use illumination rounds to make it easier for an infantry company during a nighttime attack, or they can be used simply to harass an enemy force.

For example, if I'm sitting with my FCT team on top of a mountain and a distant area of open ground is a little too far away for me to effectively observe, I would have one of my Marines randomly send illumination rounds over the area to discourage any enemy movement on the ground or to possibly catch them in the open. If you catch them in the open, then it's time to send in high explosive rounds to get rid of them. As far as marking a target with illumination rounds, believe it or not, pilots flying nighttime missions will actually penetrate under the cone of light provided by illumination rounds to strike a target. In addition to allowing the pilot to actually see what they're about to hit with bombs, rockets, or missiles, the elimination round, since it bursts directly over the target, also serves as a marker for the incoming aircraft.

Another very effective piece of gear that we had in 4th ANGLICO was a self-contained transponder called an AN/PPN-19 that we referred to simply as a "beacon." We didn't have too many and it was probably the heaviest, fattest bastard of a piece of gear that we had in the comm shack. I hoped and prayed that I would never be in the field with this monster stuck in my backpack, and as it turns out I never was as we always carried it in our Humvees, usually when we went to Camp Lejeune to blow stuff up at OP (Observation Post) 5 or OP 6. The PPN-19 was like a giant green box with a short, round, rubber-coated omnidirectional antenna sticking out of the top. The antenna was removable in case you were going to use the beacon for naval gunfire instead of calling in air strikes. Keeping the round rubber antenna on top allowed aircraft to pick up your location and adjust their attack route off of the electronic signal using the compass heading you radioed to the pilot. Before the near universal use of laser designation systems, almost every mission employed some type of method to ensure that attacking aircraft, a naval ship on station ready to fire, or the supporting artillery unit knew exactly what your position was. The reports that you would send back as part of your fire mission order relayed information about the target, what it was, the compass heading from your position to the target, and the distance measured in meters. For further assurance during the day, you can land a Willy Pete round just next to the target, or at night you could use illumination for the same purpose, as we've just learned in this chapter.

The PPN-19 was also very effective for naval gunfire. For example, suppose I was on the reverse slope of a hill or mountain, which means that the crest of the mountain would be blocking the enemy located in front of me. Friendly forces, other Marines, and the ship that was about to fire in support of my mission would all be located behind me. The stubby little rubber omnidirectional antenna that sits on top of the PPN-19 was removable as I wrote before. Removing the antenna then redirected the electronic signal out a very small window located on one side of the PPN-19. The reason for this was that instead of omnidirectional, which means a 360-degree radiation pattern, now the transponder's signal can be directed precisely to the unit or ship that's about to provide fire for your mission. Yet another idea for a PPN-19 was to have an ANGLICO or Recon team inserted into a very dangerous location, most likely behind enemy lines, and use the beacon as a nonhuman marker that artillery, naval gunfire, or strike aircraft can use as a reference point to attack the enemy. This type of mission wasn't talked about too often, as it would usually include the destruction of the emplaced PPN-19 that during the mid-1980s I was told cost sixty thousand dollars per unit. The high cost of this chunky little piece of gear that resembled R2D2's mutant little cousin from *Star Wars* wasn't lost on any of us. After all, in the mid- to late 1980s, a small condominium, even in the pricey Sunshine State, cost about that much. The PPN-19 was such a great piece of self-contained gear that we could fit that sixty thousand dollars into our mountain rucksacks.

The first time I used the PPN-19 was as a very young lance corporal on a trip to Camp Lejeune as we ran nighttime CAS missions at OP 6, one of our favorite places to blow shit up. It was one of the few times that I took part in calling in CAS with the Grumman A-6 Intruder attack aircraft. The Intruder was a bulbous-nosed bomber that could carry virtually every type of bomb, missile, rocket, cluster bomb, anti-radiation missile, fuel tank, and even nuclear weapons in the U.S. inventory and hit the enemy in any type of weather. Plus, it had large fuel tanks, so it could hang around and drop bombs for quite some time, while faster fighters such as the F-18 Hornet blasted in, dropped two loads, and hit the bricks. The Intruder was so effective as a strike aircraft that it served in the U.S.

Navy and Marine Corps from 1963 until its retirement in 1997. Author Stephen Coonts even wrote a book titled *Flight of the Intruder* that was made into a movie.

As every weapon system of any type has its quirks that need to be learned, trained with, and adjusted to, both the A-6 Intruder and PPN-19 that we were using that night showed they both could be a bit temperamental, yet ultimately worked like a charm together. As I sat there watching the team work the mission, time and time again the aircraft crew would pick up the PPN-19 only to lose it before they could start their final bombing run. Fortunately, since we were using Intruders, their large fuel capacity meant they could hang around and try plenty of times until they got a good lock on our location at OP 6. Granted as Marine pilots, they dropped bombs at OP 6 hundreds of times, but that's not the way to train for combat. You train the way you're going to fight with no exceptions, which meant we were to get all the gear online and get it working together. The flight crew finally got a solid lock on the PPN-19, came in screaming at around 500 feet, and placed their practice bomb exactly on the target we were trying to hit, which was an old abandoned amphibious tractor. Americans are used to seeing direct hits with lasers on television newscasts and online video services, but this was before the Gulf War and we weren't using lasers then. Still, we were calling in CAS missions with jet aircraft in the dark and got a perfect hit on the first drop. As I said, the PPN-19, though I never wanted the fat little bastard in my backpack, worked and it worked well. I gave it the nickname of "the portable airport" as he could be taken anywhere in the world and was so powerful that jet pilots could almost always fix its location.

As you'll discover when you read chapter 18 about how Marine ANGLICO could have helped out after Hurricane Katrina in New Orleans or after Hurricane Andrew in South Florida, the PPN-19 beacon/transponder would have been invaluable helping to fix the location of the observation teams that we inserted, plus we could have deployed other sets to every airport in the region that had suffered damage. After the runways had been cleared of debris, aircraft of all shapes and sizes bringing in supplies and personnel would have had no problem locating those airports.

Today, lasers are everywhere. Presenters in business meetings use lasers to point out various aspects of pie charts and bar graphs, combat troops and police officers mount them on their weapons for accuracy, and unfortunately since there's always at least one jerk in every crowd, some have chosen to use small lasers to point in the cockpits of landing jetliners, which is an offense that will get you thrown in prison very quickly. During my time with 4th ANGLICO, the most reliable and capable laser we used was the MULE. Training manuals always said that the bulky laser could be fired similar to a rifle, which was a claim that we all took as completely ridiculous. The weight and bulk of the older style MULEs prevented them from being held steady for any length of time, which was necessary for the aircraft to pick up the "sparkle" of the laser reflecting off of the target you were trying to destroy. As a result, it had to be mounted one way or another, whether it was on the hood of the Humvee, a stable pile of sandbags, or on the large tripod that it came equipped with. MULEs were always kept in the 4th ANGLICO armory as lasers are both delicate and dangerous, plus I was told they cost $250,000 for each complete set.

During one of my visits back with 4th ANGLICO, Gunny Cruz was taking me around speaking with different Marines and I was going back and forth with a young lance corporal speaking through the locked, reinforced steel cage door of the armory discussing all the old equipment versus the new. Gunny Cruz and I were trying to tell this young Marine just how large and heavier the older laser designators were, which he'd never seen. Cruz quickly pulled out his cell phone and did an image search for a MULE, which astounded the young Marine.

"Wow! Look at the size of that tripod!" he exclaimed.

"Exactly. That's why we almost always carry them around in the Humvees because they were so big," I said.

With a range supposedly out to 5 kilometers, we usually planned on illuminating a target from 3 kilometers away. And I don't know who came up with the trite expression of "painting the target," but I never heard anyone say that during my twelve-year stretch at 4th ANGLICO. We always said "mark the target," no matter what method we were using, and if it was a laser, we always said that we were going to "illuminate" it as a laser is a beam of light in the first place.

Now's the time when I'm gonna get a little jarhead all over your ass. And that is to warn others not to rely only on lasers for marking the target. I'm also perfectly aware that every member of the U.S. military that went to Iraq and Afghanistan just declared me an idiot who doesn't know what he's talking about. Really? Equipment never breaks down? You'll never face a situation where you are calling in so many air strikes with your laser equipment that it drains every one of your batteries? Since you were raised in the post-Reagan era of "it's all about self-confidence" and the always arrogant and irritating "trust me I know what I'm doing" attitude of stupid white boys everywhere, you didn't bring any backup batteries with you. What about the enemy? They don't have a say in any of this? Are you sure? In Afghanistan the enemy broke through the line at a Marine airfield, destroyed six Harriers, and killed the squadron commander. If that can happen, anything can happen. In other words don't ignore the older methods of marking the target due to the current rage of using lasers for everything. While artillery units were withdrawn from the combat zones several years ago, plenty of 81mm mortar platoons are operating in country and can expertly fire Willy Pete rounds, smoke, or illumination whenever tasked with a fire mission. Mortar crews work extremely hard and never get credit from anyone in the media or Hollywood.

It reminds me of the early 1990s when GPS was cheap enough that troops were using it for everything and ignoring the tried-and-true methods of basic land navigation. My Marine buddies at 4th ANGLICO saw this plenty of times when we deployed to JRTC and U.S. Army soldiers were in the field in a supposed force-on-force exercise navigating through the bush with their heads down focusing on the GPS gear in their hands. How can you be on the lookout for an enemy waiting in ambush if your eyes are pointed down looking at your new fancy piece of digital technology? Again, don't get me wrong: GPS is a terrific tool that I wouldn't leave the rear area without. However, the Marine Corps has never abandoned teaching Marines basic land navigation skills and making them practice as much as possible.

CHAPTER ELEVEN

MOS 3: Airborne Country

JUST TO BE CLEAR: I HATED JUMP SCHOOL.

I loved the idea of getting my jump wings and setting myself apart from other U.S. Marines; I just couldn't stomach how the U.S. Army got the job done. It was everything Marines believed the Army was. Ponderous. Overblown. Much ado about *everything*, the PT wasn't hard enough, the food sucked, the staff hated our guts along with the SEALs, Navy Explosive Ordnance Disposal, deep-sea divers, and Recon, and for some reason, every day we were getting awakened at *four o'clock in the damn morning*! Is it June 6, 1944, and Ike's outside with a pep talk to go kill some Nazis? Are we replanting Old Glory on top of Suribachi? Are Neil and Buzz suited up for landing the lunar module on Tranquility Base? No, we'll be spending the day jumping into sawdust pits until each of us, including Army privates and captains, are ready to machete the teaching staff.

I've met very few Marines who wouldn't go to Jump School given the chance. Even if it was a three-week gut check or a manly-man test getting ready for combat, Marines want to go to Fort Benning, Georgia. But Jump School is owned and operated by the U.S. Army and that's that. I fully acknowledge and respect that the Army created the first American airborne units and developed the tactics we still use today.

In 1940 with the war clouds of World War II gathering over Europe and around the Pacific Rim, the Army started a test platoon of volunteers led by Lt. William Ryder. Ryder's platoon took over an old aircraft hangar at Lawson Field, just across the border from Alabama, and started to train with parachutes. After only eighteen days the test platoon was sent to New Jersey to train with 250-foot steel towers that dropped visitors during the New York World's Fair in 1939. Jump School evolved into three phases: ground week, tower week, and jump week. Ground week was spent in huge sawdust pits while you perfected a parachute landing fall. Tower week was spent waiting for low winds to be dropped from the 250-foot tower, and the third week was for jumping out of a perfectly good military aircraft five times to earn your basic paratrooper wings. Jump School is staffed by veteran paratroopers from the 82nd and 101st Airborne Divisions, plus the Rangers and Green Berets, who all wear black baseball caps, hence their nickname, the Black Hats. My primary Black Hat was Sergeant First Class King, who lost one eye in an M-16 bad ammo accident. He was ruthless with our instruction, but it made us good, and safe, jumpers out in the field.

The 250-foot tower was my favorite part of Jump School and the most productive. Jumpers donned a chute harness with the parachute attached to aluminum connectors on top on the shoulders. Just like the 1939 World's Fair, the parachute was attached to a ring that carried the jumper aloft. Two steel cables were attached and you were hauled 250 feet in the air. On signal from Sergeant King below, you were released and hopefully you remembered what he taught you in ground week, because you were coming down in your first parachute fall. All the Marines, SEALs, and Navy Explosive Ordnance troops in my platoon got our wings after our fifth jump and went our separate ways in the military. I knew it was a rare opportunity within the Corps, but I wanted my gold wings even more.

But to have such a monopoly on airborne training that every member of the U.S. military goes there? My second week of training had thirty Recon Marines from Okinawa, Japan, fly in for Jump School. How much did that cost in jet fuel alone? Hell, I pay taxes too. Why not partner with the Australians, Japanese, Filipinos, Malaysia, and Taiwan to create another Jump School in the Western Pacific? It would cost a hell of a lot less and would be great for team building with our Allies. Needless to say, the Army is very tight-fisted about school slots, and the Marine Corps doesn't get many. It droves us nuts that the Army used Jump School as a recruiting and retention tool and allowed almost any soldier to go just for the asking, when an ANGLICO Marine might wait two years for a chance. I joined 4th ANGLICO in December 1987 and didn't get to Benning until spring of 1990.

In the Marine Corps only Recon, Force Recon, ANGLICO, Air Delivery Platoon (ADP), and parachute riggers are designated paratroopers. Other Marines might catch a slot as a reward for great service, but they might not ever jump again. Oliver North is a great example of this. During his public introduction in the Iran Contra fiasco, North's uniform showed the silver-tinted U.S. Army wings, or "lead sleds" as we derisively called them. I have no idea how many jumps North did, but a fact is a fact and every Marine who went to Jump School wanted gold wings. Some Marines have taken as long as seventeen years to get the proper combination of night jumps, combat gear, and even altitude. In the Marines you can't just hang out with the SEALs or Green Berets and stack up jumps. It's the right order or you don't pin on the Gold.

Reconnaissance companies (Recon) perform area surveillance for a Marine battalion and also go to dive school. Force Reconnaissance (Force Recon) run deep or long-range missions and provide hostage rescue missions for a Marine Expeditionary Force staffed with upwards of fifty thousand Marines locked in major ground operations. ADP are the lunatics who shove tons of supplies, vehicles, or water out of the rear of cargo planes. They need to be airborne so they won't fall out of the back of the plane over Afghanistan. Riggers are all jumpers as they are the experts who repack all of the parachutes in the Corps. I'm alive because of them, no doubt. ANGLICO is the only other jump unit. Out of 250,000 active and reserve Marines, that ain't a lot.

We hated the silver wings because they were "Army," "lead sleds" or "training wheels." After I got back from Jump School in 1990, my Goldwinger buddy Karl Duce showed me the ropes and successfully guided me through my "cherry jump," the all-important sixth jump. It doesn't sound like much. Number six? Big deal! You made it through Jump School, right? In the Marines you might not jump again for months or even a year and you get rusty fast. In short, this means cherry jumpers are dangerous as hell. They're rigging their own pack for the first time, a Black Hat isn't monitoring every movement they make, and they're nervous as hell or flat-out scared. After all, jumping out of a perfectly good airplane isn't the most natural thing to do. Jump school is a very tightly controlled environment with instructors literally about every 30 feet for the entire three-week course, and nothing is left to chance. When you're back with your unit, you are expected to ramp it up and get your gear ready on your own and on time, and keep your eyes open for a clean safe exit from the aircraft. If your unit is jumping all the time, this might not be such a bad thing as there's no long break from jumping between the time you graduate Jump School and make your sixth jump. However, sometimes there were long dry spells for jumps, such as during the late 1990s when the missions in Bosnia sucked up so much transport aircraft that after Jump School many people had to wait as long as a year to start jumping again. These poor souls are basket cases of nerves and some of them are just freaking out and get lazy with their procedures. Obviously these types can be very dangerous to themselves and others and are usually paired up with an experienced Goldwinger to literally keep them alive.

Plus, military static line jumps are at very low altitude. Training jumps are at 1,250 feet at Fort Benning, nothing like the videos you see of skydivers jumping from 10,000 feet. But my cherry jump was at around 900 feet over a local wildlife refuge called J. W. Corbett Wildlife Management Area run by the Florida Wildlife Commission. How we ever got permission to jump into a protected area I'll never know.

My sixth jump had me standing about fifth in line in my "stick," or the group of Marines I would be exiting the aircraft with, and I could clearly see out the door and was a bit shocked to see just how low we were. In a real mission you might have hundreds if not thousands of troops falling from the sky, plus a highly armed enemy might be shooting at you the entire time. In other words you need to get on the ground and fast. I could clearly see every detail over Corbett including various pine trees and Sable palms that I might land on top of or smash into. I always had pregame jitters like an athlete before the game, except that we couldn't get up and pace back and forth in the locker room or take turns pounding on each other's shoulder pads to get each other fired up. On any jump you have to stay calm and in control of yourself despite your fears and apprehensions. It was one of the main reasons I wanted to go to Jump School in the first place. If I can't successfully jump out of an airplane, how could I possibly withstand the rigors of a combat assignment? Once my stick stood up and moved toward the open door under the explicit control of the jumpmasters, I could see out the door and see the ground passing below us.

I could see the passing farmland and there was something about the patterns of the agricultural community that calmed me down instantly. In a split second I lost my pregame jitters and literally wanted to run out the door. It might sound strange, but everybody reacts to jumping out of airplanes differently, with some actually jumping out of the aircraft with their eyes closed, which we mockingly referred to as making a "night jump" during the daytime. As weird, wild, and wonderful as jumping out of planes can be, I thought the only thing crazier was doing it with my eyes closed and never did it once. Out the door I went, my chute popped, and I looked down into deep saw grass and Sable palm trees that I didn't want to land on. Grabbing my right toggle, I corkscrewed down to the spot where I wanted to land and nailed it. This was why I always wanted to be a paratrooper: weighted down at 300 pounds, willingly charging out the back of a jet transport, and staying calm enough to land just where I wanted. It was a great feeling and I truly felt like an ANGLICO Marine after almost two years of training on radios, land navigation, CAS, artillery, and whatever else my leaders could dream up.

While the way the Army conducted Jump School might have driven me crazy, being airborne in the U.S. military is ultimately a great thing to be. Once you have checked off your specific jumps and gotten your gold wings, other members of the military do look at you differently even if they think you're crazy for jumping out of "a perfectly good airplane": We always responded that there was no such thing as a perfect airplane, and if the bird went down, we had a way to get out while you rode the bird down to your own death and destruction. Neither side ever won the argument, nor did either side ever give in. I had one strange reaction to being on jump status for ten years. It completely ruined me for being on civilian jet airliners, because if there is an accident and a plane began a rapid descent, I was trapped until the plane burst into flames as it hit the ground. As a paratrooper, I had two parachutes, a helmet on my head, a three-day supply of food, water, a survival kit, my poncho liner, a shiny new space blanket I bought for a whopping two dollars at Target, plus all of the rescue signaling devices I carried in my buttpack. Whenever I flew with my mom and big brother Jeffrey to Kentucky for the family reunion in late June or the Kentucky State Fair in August, it always freaked me out when the pilot made some quick turn or climbed at a very steep angle on takeoff. It took me years to get over these feelings. I'm sure the world's airlines are very pleased to know I no longer feel like a trapped rat on their sinking airborne ships coursing through the skies.

Every month for twelve years, I received a letter that served as my drill notice. It was a simple one-page plan for the weekend folded in threes and stapled together with my name and address on the front. The drill notices were one of the main reasons that we constantly updated our addresses before leaving each month, as so many people in the United States move around so much, especially young people in their twenties either attending school or just getting started in life. I've seen some drill notices that were eleven pages long, which is way too much, and ours, in my opinion, were too short on detail at only one page for each month. If an airborne operation was scheduled, I would already have my combat gear packed up and ready to go before I left my home as I would be too busy getting ready for the jump to play around with individual gear.

If it was strictly a training jump, only the Marines who were paratroopers would be involved, plus three or four Humvees fitted with radios would drive to the drop zone in advance carrying communications Marines, at least one Navy corpsman, and usually two jumpmasters who would communicate with the aircraft and check whether the winds were too high to drop the incoming paratroopers. If the entire company was flying to Fort Benning, for example, which we did almost every year, Marines that hadn't earned their jump wings were placed on one aircraft while two other planes would be packed to the rafters with paratroopers who were so close to each other that when the jumpmasters checked us before we jumped they actually walked across the top of our packs that were resting on our thighs. It sounds demeaning but the only way the jumpmasters could move around was to literally walk on top of us.

If the entire company was going to Benning, then everyone knew there would be a mad dash for the comm shack to get radios and have them properly packed inside their backpacks for the job. The old ALICE backpacks had a pouch in the main section of the pack that rested along a soldier's or Marine's back, and this is where we placed our radios. By using a harness that was strapped to the pack and then connected to a 30-foot lanyard that we would drop prior to landing, if a paratrooper packed correctly, it would fall to the ground at a 90-degree angle and your individual sleeping gear, spare sweater or nightshirt, or your Gore-Tex jacket would serve as a cushion to protect the radio. Always remember as you read anything about Marine ANGLICO: Without a radio you're not doing your job. Period.

After pulling as many as two hundred individual radios, antennas, and the rest of the mountain of communications gear an ANGLICO Marine uses in the field, we each made it to the paraloft to sign out what was known as "air items." Air items included the harness that I just discussed, the 30-foot lanyard that ensured you didn't strike the ground while wearing a 65-pound backpack subsequently breaking your ankles or something worse, a large bag called an aviator's kitbag that would be used later to fold up your chute and carry it out of the drop zone, and one odd-looking loop of tubular nylon known as a knife extender.

Each paratrooper unbuckled their belt and passed it through the loops of the knife extender after attaching it to the K-bar combat knives that each jumper was required to wear. As anyone who has gone skydiving will tell you, parachute rigs are incredibly strong, built of very thick synthetic material that I think might not be penetrated by a round from a .22-caliber pistol. They are strapped on over your individual combat gear, so if you normally wore a knife attached to your belt, you wouldn't be able to reach it anyway if you came down in a forest. Therefore a knife extender was created that literally "extends" a knife's sheath down the side of the paratrooper's leg much like hostage rescue teams and modern-day SWAT teams carry their pistols down on their leg like gunfighters during the Wild West years of the late nineteenth century.

Frequently, individual Marines would use the military's version of duct tape to secure either a flashing strobe light or a small flare to their knives for use during a survival situation. In one of the Marine Corps' wiser moves, after too many injuries with knives, a special hard plastic sheath made by a company called Kydex was mandated for each jumper carrying a K-bar as it kept it from cutting through the traditional leather sheath of a Marine K-bar and stabbing the Marine in the leg with his own knife. Of course, we all had to buy them ourselves, but it was a smart move and solved the problem almost overnight.

Safety issues aside, I have to admit I always loved wearing my knife extender because it made us look like gunfighters. In addition to that we had to fully extend the old load-bearing equipment as all of our magazine pouches, first aid kits, canteens, and buttpacks were placed through the loop that made up the seat of the parachute harness. It also made it easier when we were carrying our large mountain ALICE packs that we always had with us because we were always carrying radios and needed the larger-sized packs. It hardly fit the spit-and-polish image of the Marine Corps when a group of ANGLICO Marines walked across base with their equipment bouncing off their butts and their K-bars slung low like Wyatt Earp. But we thought it looked cool, and it was definitely part of the ANGLICO swagger that we strutted around on display much to the chagrin and sometimes flat-out anger of other U.S. Marines.

Two items that entered into pop culture with the Iraqi and Afghan wars going on for so long were para cord bracelets and heavy nylon belts for outdoorsmen that everyone now calls riggers' belts. During the entire time I was with 4th ANGLICO, I never even heard the term "para cord," which I suspect is what the U.S. Army calls it. My Marine buddies and I universally called them parachute shroud lines, which is what they are, made of what we called 550 cord. When you're descending in a fully open parachute, your backpack is on a 30-foot lanyard hanging below you, your combat gear and your M-16 rifle are strapped together with the heavy harness of whichever parachute you are using, and you are attached to the main parachute by dozens of very thin synthetic shroud lines.

They are actually tubes with seven tiny white strands on the inside of each one, which gives the shroud lines their strength. The Marine

Corps rumor mill had it that each individual strand could withstand 550 pounds of pressure, hence the name 550 cord. The paraloft had miles of this stuff, and we used it for everything from stringing up our ponchos in between two trees to create a small tent to tying them around cyalume sticks to swing them around the circle to signal in a landing helicopter; we even extracted the black shoelaces from our jungle boots and replaced them with 550 cord. I'm sure the first Marines to come up with the idea of using the 550 cord in jungle boots intended for them to be used in an extreme emergency, but eventually it became part of our particular look, just like our knife extenders and how we wore our 782 gear slung low.

For anyone in the civilian world who wants to buy 550 cord on the market, you need to be careful about what you're buying. After it got popular with the public and became known as para cord, plenty of knockoff brands started being sold. The easiest way to spot them is by looking at one of the ends of the cord to see if the seven telltale white strands are inside the tube of the shroud line, and not some crappy nylon mesh as I've seen plenty of times. If you really need to have some real 550 cord, I highly recommend a store located outside of Fort Benning that is a mecca for the airborne community called Ranger Joe's. They have an extensive website for ordering and you can purchase as much as 500 feet of 550 cord for any hiking, boating, or outdoor use you might need. Unless you need rope for rappelling, which is its own specialized product, 550 cord will serve your needs better than anything else on the market as far as I'm concerned. And don't buy it at the flea market; buy it from Ranger Joe's.

It seems now everybody on police and fire rescue teams are all wearing riggers' belts of some sort. I guess it's not all that bad, as they are remarkably strong and last forever. The original riggers' belts were the invention of the U.S. Army, most likely created by the parachute riggers at Fort Benning. With so many jumps happening every single day for decades, sooner or later some hapless little student is going to land in the trees, and the parachute gets shredded like toilet paper as the poor bastard crashes through pine tree branches on his way down to the ground and most likely breaks his leg. That's one parachute that died for his country. Plus everything in the military has a service life, and once it is reached the item can no longer be used and is usually sold as surplus.

The main rig of a military parachute envelops the entire body of the jumper and is incredibly strong and well made. Once you have been in one, you will never have any fear of accidentally falling out of the chute, unless you're either making a water jump and getting out of the harness on purpose or you are suicidal. Each parachute rig also has a belt that wraps around your waist just like the belt that holds up your pants. Like all of the metal connectors on the U.S. military parachute, the buckle is made out of aircraft aluminum. It is a simple rectangle with the belt slipped in one side over the center section and cinched down on the other side like many fashion belts that women wear. Sometime over the years one rigger looked at a trashed or otherwise unserviceable parachute rig, pulled out his knife, cut the belt off, and made himself a nice new belt that eventually became part of the look of school-trained parachute riggers throughout the U.S. military. Much like the Green Berets sport their famous headgear, parachute riggers at Fort Benning can be seen standing outside of their main paraloft taking a ten-minute break wearing red baseball caps and belts made from destroyed parachute rigs. It's part of their look and part of their culture, and they're the ones that invented it.

Almost everybody I knew in the airborne community would have paid cash money to have a real riggers' belt. I know I would have. Somewhere along the line someone took some nylon strapping and decided to make a belt out of it as a sort of imitation riggers' belt. Hell, he was probably a rigger himself as they all know how to sew with very large industrial sewing machines as they have to repair parachutes that have been torn during airborne operations. It might seem funny to some people that big tough American paratroopers know how to sew, but they also run quite the little side business designing and building various modified buttpacks, pouches, and field kits especially for Special Operations teams. 4th ANGLICO had four full-size sewing machines when I was in, and they were part of our TO just as our M-16s and Humvees were.

To help keep straps that were wrapped around your backpack from unraveling, we used what we call riggers' tape, which looks like an olive drab roll of duct tape that might be found in any American home. But riggers' tape, if made by the right government contractor, was the stickiest, most obnoxious piece of fastening gear I've ever encountered. Marines almost always use what we call the "buddy system," just like scuba divers when under the sea. When two Marines were getting their gear ready for a parachute jump, one Marine would be working on their pack and deuce gear as his buddy was tearing off long strips of riggers' tape to hand to him as he secured his gear before getting on the jet transport. The great thing about riggers' tape was also the bad thing about riggers' tape. If it was a windy day, particularly in South Florida where a tropical gust of wind can come out of anywhere at any time, riggers' tape will fold over on itself and that was the end of it. Trust me when I say this: No matter how hard or how long you tried to separate the fold in doubled-over riggers' tape, you were not going to succeed. I know it sounds strange, but when you're peeling off long strips of riggers' tape for your buddy, you really had to pay attention, because otherwise you have to take that long strip of tape and throw it away. But when it worked, it kept your gear secure even as you were blasted out of the back of a jet transport.

I've never seen any type of adhesive tape on the civilian market that was in the same league as real riggers' tape. But not all riggers' tape was the same. When some idiot congressmen's little brother or crooked cousin was awarded a government contract to make riggers' tape, they produced an inferior version that was worse than anything we could buy at a local hardware or home improvement store. We went from a great product that would practically stick to a rolling wave at the beach to something that wouldn't stick to our nylon packs at all, so therefore we never used it.

Everyone knows that parachuting has inherent dangers. After all, that's why we got hazardous duty pay for being on jump status. Everyone has seen a movie, television show, or advertising parody of a parachutist yanking on their rip cord only to have the chute not deploy from its bag at all. Paratroopers jumping at lower altitudes always use what is called static line, an incredibly tough and durable lanyard with an aircraft aluminum lock attached to a quarter-inch steel cable running the length of a transport aircraft. When you go out the door, you pass the static line to the jumpmaster, who grabs it and pulls away from you, and after you exit the door, the static line poles the parachute out of the deployment bag, or D bag in paraloft lingo. Therefore, having a parachute simply not come out of the bag at all is virtually impossible. However, there are plenty of other things that can go wrong, usually due to a paratrooper not performing the proper procedures taught at airborne school. As I've written before, I couldn't stand the way the Army ran Airborne School but the Black Hats taught us the right way to be paratroopers, and they wouldn't let us advance until we got it right.

If a paratrooper is walking out the door, hands off his static line to the jumpmaster, but doesn't exit the door at a proper 45-degree angle, he or she could hit their shoulder on the side of the aircraft door causing them to spin. If they spin too much as the parachute is extracted from the D bag by the static line, it will roll up like a handkerchief causing the jumper to plummet to the earth unless they regain their senses and deploy the reserve chute. This is usually referred to as a Roman candle, or by some people who smoke as a cigarette roll. Not too many people survive a Roman candle. I prided myself on keeping my wits about me during parachute jumps, so I wasn't too concerned with a Roman candle and was more focused on worrying about a catastrophic failure of the parachute.

Another nightmare scenario for paratroopers is what's known as a "tow jumper." A tow jumper is pretty much just what it sounds like, which is a paratrooper who has a chute that won't detach from its static line and is literally being towed by the aircraft like a speedboat pulling a water skier. This can lead to a very bad accident as military aircraft slow down to around 125 knots to get the jumpers out the back door. As the deployment bags of the previous paratroopers are dangling on the side of the aircraft, usually well out of the way of the succession of jumpers, sometimes the wind will simply blow one of them down, tangling your chute in the massive ball of flapping D-bags causing you to be towed behind the aircraft. It's a great reason to wear a helmet on any type of parachute jump, as the turbulent air behind a large military aircraft will be flinging you all over the place and most likely smacking your head up against the side of the bird. It's an incredibly violent accident that no one ever wants to go through, but it does happen a few times per year, although I can't remember any towed jumpers during my twelve years with 4th ANGLICO.

After each stick of jumpers exits the door, the jumpmaster will instantly look out the door to count the number of open chutes and to see if he has any towed jumpers. Believe it or not paratroopers are trained to stay in a nice tight position with legs, feet, and knees together in the event of a tow jumper incident, with your arms tight at your sides and your hands around your reserve chute just like any good exit. Now how anybody could remember all this while being towed behind a jet transport I don't know, and I doubt very seriously if I would have the presence of mind to stay in this position while I was being whipped around like a raggedy Ann doll being dangled outside the car window on a family vacation. One option is for the jumpmasters and aircrew to use a pulley to drag you back inside of the aircraft, which of course would result in you being beaten half to death on the side of the aircraft as they haul you in like a swordfish dangling on a line. The reason they want you to stay tucked into a tight jumping position is that to them that indicates you are conscious and keeping your wits about you, however far-fetched that seems. If they make the determination that you're conscious, they will pull out a sharp instrument and cut you loose into the slipstream. Hopefully your main chute will deploy, but if it doesn't, you'll have to deploy the reserve chute strapped to your stomach in order to save your own life.

The fear of being a tow jumper is why I took our jump rehearsals so seriously. Every single jump I took part in in the U.S. military, whether it was with the Marine Corps or the Army, we always trained in mock-ups of various aircraft and practiced our actions inside the aircraft and exiting the aircraft while counting to four before looking up to see if our chute was fully inflated. The funny thing about the military chutes we used when I was in the military was that they were the classic olive drab green of damn near everything in the military, but if you jumped on a sunny day, the sun shining through the green somehow turned into the most beautiful gold that I think I've ever seen. If you think that you have seen a halo effect in your life, try to get blasted out of the back of a military transport, heading toward the ground weighing upwards of 300 pounds, and looking up to see that golden canopy above your head. Trust me, that's always a great feeling.

Some of the other potential disasters any American paratrooper faces include landing in high-powered electrical wires or their towers, or being dragged along the ground due to high winds in the drop zone. While on a military base, out in the desert, or during a peacetime exercise, military planners always try to stay as far away from electrical lines as possible, but in a combat situation sometimes you cannot completely avoid them. As military chutes are almost all round-top chutes that drop straight down, if the wind pushes you into the electrical wires the jumper doesn't have much choice. While it sounds crazy (and it is), the U.S. military teaches you to do the following: If you are dropping through the live wires with their humming tone of electrocution buzzing in your ears, before your chute gets snagged or entangled on the lines, they want you to rock forward and backward in your parachute harness to keep the momentum going so you might possibly slip through the lines and get free. While I always felt the odds of this technique succeeding were rather small, I certainly would be rocking back and forth like grandpa back on the porch in Kentucky to slide my ass through the lines as quickly as possible if I found myself in that situation. In addition to that, if it works you will quickly need to deploy your reserve chute, and that will only be helpful if the power line towers are so high that your reserve chute will have the time to open. If you come down in a residential area with standard 30- to 50-foot-tall telephone poles, all you can do is jettison your backpack and get ready for what airborne instructors referred to as a "dynamic parachute landing fall." In other words, get ready to bust your ass on the ground.

If you truly get hung up on the wires or on a telephone pole, if you are somewhere near Mother Earth, the last thing you want to do is climb down like you're on a ladder. Because if you do, you will be the connection between that power line and the ground and the only thing they'll find of you is a pair of smoking combat boots because you grounded yourself. One method is to calmly deploy your reserve parachute and use it as a rope to climb down from whatever height you are hanging from. If you're still 10 feet off the ground and you get to do yet another "dynamic parachute landing fall," or if you are so close to the ground you think you can just stand right up, to avoid being grounded and being

4th ANGLICO SSgt. Teddy Pernal having a bad day at work as he walks away from an attack site not wearing his helmet. His own title for this picture is "Real men don't look at explosions."
TEDDY PERNAL

Unidentified 4th ANGLICO Marine crossing a no-name street in Iraq under fire and a green smoke screen. DEPARTMENT OF DEFENSE PHOTO BY PH2 SAMUEL C. PETERSON, U.S. NAVY

2nd ANGLICO Marines in the middle of combat in yet another nameless Iraqi town. If you look close enough, you can see the round fired by the grenade-launching Marine on the right side of the photo. DEPARTMENT OF DEFENSE PHOTO BY PH2 SAMUEL C. PETERSON, U.S. NAVY

A Marine throws a smoke grenade to provide concealment for troops crossing a danger zone. DEPARTMENT OF DEFENSE PHOTO BY PH2 SAMUEL C. PETERSON, U.S. NAVY

4th ANGLICO Marines blow open a door in Iraq while searching for weapons and other contraband during Operation Iraqi Freedom. DEPARTMENT OF DEFENSE PHOTO BY SGT. ARTHUR HAMILTON

4th ANGLICO Marines from West Palm Beach, Florida, occupy an "overlook" position covering the helicopter insert of Australian Special Forces searching for "high value targets" in the tiny village below. ANGLICO units have run countless missions like this, but this photograph shows the varied gear placed near each Marine to quickly employ. TEDDY PERNAL

View from the overlook position. TEDDY PERNAL

A Marine carries an unassembled drone up the mountain. Drones are now so small a single Marine can throw it in the air to send back aerial photos of the target. TEDDY PERNAL

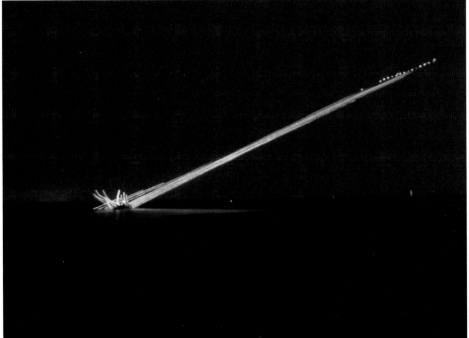

U.S. Marine Cobra attack helicopters strike targets in the western U.S. during day and night training. More rockets can be seen streaking in from the left side of the top photograph.

This U.S. Air Force A-10 "Warthog"—seen in clear detail—shows how near attack aircraft can be and how dedicated pilots are to ground troops. DEPARTMENT OF DEFENSE PHOTO BY 1ST LT. ALICIA LACY

Some ANGLICO companies are jump qualified, which requires constant practice and provides a regional commander with the capability to insert Firepower Control Teams as far as their aircraft can carry them. These three photos are great examples of the wild experience of military paratrooping.

Ramp jump out of the rear of a CH-53 Sea Stallion helicopter. DEPARTMENT OF DEFENSE

A "stick" of eight jumpers with fully deployed parachutes. What every jumpmaster wants to see. DEPARTMENT OF DEFENSE

A ramp jump from the new Osprey aircraft. This photo shows the chutes as they deploy after being pulled out of their deployment bags. DEPARTMENT OF DEFENSE

A Marine provides terminal control for a U.S. Navy F-14 Tomcat. Before they were phased out in the 1990s, Tomcats were equipped with sensors that enabled them to drop various ordnance. These photographs show exactly what it's like searching for an incoming attack aircraft. Visual recognition is critical to ensure the "bird" isn't pointing directly at you. It usually takes several Marines to spot the small image of an aircraft possibly arriving at 450 knots. DEPARTMENT OF DEFENSE

ANGLICO Marines struggle to maintain proficiency in close air support, artillery, naval gunfire, and communications. Each ANGLICO company has at least one Naval Gunfire Liaison officer to teach and advise on firing guns from navy ships as Lt. Salvia is doing with this young Marine. DEPARTMENT OF DEFENSE

5th ANGLICO Marines practice supporting fires with a combination of field radios and a field laptop. DEPARTMENT OF DEFENSE PHOTO BY LCPL. MARGRETTE DORN

To be a Marine is to be a teacher. Here, 1st ANGLICO GySgt. Jonathon Chesnutt monitors LCpl. Trey Ellingson during a call for fire exercise at Camp Pendleton, California—mostly likely with live ordnance. DEPARTMENT OF DEFENSE PHOTO BY CPL. MONTY BURTON

One of the main missions of U.S. Marine ANGLICO is to work with foreign troops. It's actually part of the mission statement. Even as very junior Marines, ANGLICOs work with much higher ranks teaching and advising what ANGLICOs could do for their services. Here, 2nd ANGLICO Pvt. Matthew Hurley (left) and LCpl. Antonio Castillo are showing French aviator Lt. Jerome Laye how one version of GPS operates. DEPARTMENT OF DEFENSE PHOTO BY CPL. STEPHEN M. DEBOARD

Marines practicing live artillery shoots in the United Kingdom. The smoke in the distance is most likely burning peat or moss and not smoke rounds. DEPARTMENT OF DEFENSE

SSgt. Teddy Pernal prepares to give a mission brief to the unit his team is assigned to for the day. The various maps he is using cover the entire area of operations for the mission. An orange panel marker in the upper right of the photograph identifies them as "friendlies" to overhead aircraft. A radio antenna sticks out of his nearby backpack, and the team's automatic weapons are within arm's reach. TEDDY PERNAL

With the renewed focus on the Pacific Rim, America's commitment to Japanese defense will only increase. Here, 1st ANGLICO Cpl. Robert T. Ruiz and a Japanese soldier use a laser designator to mark a target on San Clemente Island, California. DEPARTMENT OF DEFENSE PHOTO BY LCPL. TIMOTHY CHILDERS

A 1st ANGLICO Marine on patrol in Helmand province, Afghanistan, with the British Army's 9th/12th Royal Lancers. DEPARTMENT OF DEFENSE PHOTO BY LCPL. DANIEL WULZ

Two Marines operate laser designators and call in a mission. DEPARTMENT OF DEFENSE

The operating end of a laser range finder and designator. The user peers through the center aperture to locate the target and focus the laser on it, which ordnance will then strike. DEPART-MENT OF DEFENSE

The end result of everything ANGLICO does: bombs on target. DEPARTMENT OF DEFENSE

This is where the rubber hits the runway, with small teams of ANGLICO Marines either calling in fire or observing the enemy. Additionally, as discussed in the chapter on civil disasters in America, this photo shows how ANGLICO teams could occupy rooftops to observe a damaged city or relay information to higher headquarters. During this mission in Haditha, Iraq, this 2nd ANGLICO FCT team worked with helicopter and attack aircraft including an AC-130 Spectre gunship. DEPARTMENT OF DEFENSE PHOTO BY CPL. JAN BENDER converted into a piece of burnt toast, then you had better let go with your hands and make a complete disconnection from the entire parachute rig that's hanging from the electrical wires and free fall to the ground, which means you live. Needless to say, I never wanted to try these methods. My 4th ANGLICO jumpmasters were always very good about selecting and identifying safe drop zones for us. But also as a jumper, you simply have to keep your wits about you and observe your situation on an x, y, and z axis to avoid other jumpers and any obstacles on the ground such as trees, canals, small black ponds that are always deeper than you think, and of course the dreaded power lines. After ten years on jump status, I never came near a power line and I don't have any regrets whatsoever.

When you're on jump status for a matter of several years, sooner or later you'll get dragged after you land on the drop zone. I had a couple small instances where I hit so hard that I just bounced along like a giant G.I. Joe doll. The one time I really got dragged was when we arrived back from a three-day drill at Fort Benning and landed at the giant sod farm that a Marine Corps–friendly farmer allowed us to use out in the center of the state near Belle Glade, Florida, where so many NFL players are born and raised. Par for the course for being a paratrooper is that the drop zone safety officer (DZSO) on the ground is holding some type of instrument to measure wind velocity to ensure high winds don't scatter paratroopers all over creation. However, every once in a while when they really want the jump to go down, as soon as that piece of gear known as an anemometer lists the airspeed as safe for a jump, the DZSO radios the aircraft and the jumpmasters start sending paratroopers out the back door. However, since it's a gusty day, while you're floating down weighing 300 pounds due to all your gear and weapons, the wind obviously picks up and you're coming down faster than you ever have before and you know that you're going to bust your ass. That's what happened the first time I was dragged more than just a couple of feet. I came down in the black muck of the fertile central Florida farmlands with a good parachute landing fall about 100 meters in front of the line of 5-ton trucks that would transport us back to 4th ANGLICO in West Palm Beach, about an hour's drive away. My landing was good because I kept my head about myself; however, my chute was fully inflated at a perfect 90-degree angle along the ground and it wasn't going to deflate for anything. On a parachute rig there are two connectors made out of aircraft aluminum that are situated on the front part of both shoulders almost in the exact same place where American police officers have their little walkie-talkies that they use to talk to dispatch. These are two main disconnects for the parachute risers to the entire parachute rig. If you pop these two connectors in midair, you would simply fall out of your chute entirely. Every jumper is taught in Jump School that if you're getting dragged across the ground, to let the air out of an inflated chute, you have to perform what is called "popping a riser." A fully inflated chute on the ground is doing exactly what a parachute is supposed to do, mainly, hold onto air. This is precisely what my chute was doing as it dragged me 50 to 60 feet through the black mud with a dozen of my Marine buddies screaming at me to pop a riser. My own personal pride would not let me do this. At that point I had been on jump status for almost a decade, and I had never had an accident or situation of any type up until that day. The parachutes that the Marine Corps had purchased had 110 feet cut out of the back that gave us a slight forward momentum and the ability to place the chute in a corkscrew pattern that made us dive straight down and land where we wanted to. They were nowhere near as maneuverable as the small square chutes used by civilian skydivers or the larger rectangular chutes used by military freefall jumpers that dive out the back door at heights up to 30,000 feet.

I found myself smack dab in the middle of nearly 70 feet of parachute military equipment, stuck in the mud and not going anywhere with all my buddies yelling at me. Too bad. I was not going to pop a riser. I never had, and I was not about to start now. To get our type of chutes to collapse, you have to grab the opposite side riser and pull on it as hard as you can to force the air out of the open 110-square-foot section. Just like any other time we try to take on Mother Nature, it was one of the most strenuous things I have ever done in my entire life. I pulled and pulled and pulled and even almost gave up but with one more pull the chute collapsed. I let my helmeted head hit the ground in exhaustion and looked back in my pack. My backpack was stuck in the mud serving as an anchor, and I was being pulled in the center like a medieval torture method and the chute was fully inflated on the other side of me. It looked like a 100-foot-long exclamation point that I had created for other jumpers to see on their way down to the drop zone. However, I kept my promise to myself: Ten years of jumping and I never lost control of one of my parachutes.

The one accident that I was truly terrified of during my decade-long jump career was the Popeye. Named after the world-famous, spinach-eating cartoon sailor with the massive forearms, despite its funny-sounding namec the Popeye was a dreaded situation that could be avoided by simply following your training and staying completely focused. The static line that will extract the chute after you exit the aircraft is well above almost every paratrooper's head, so a line of paratroopers walking toward the door look as if they're all raising the same hand for attention. The 30-foot lanyard that is attached to the aircraft and the back of your parachute needs to snake across the shoulder opposite of the door you are exiting. For example, if I'm making a right turn exit, the static line and the lanyard pulling out my parachute needs to be over and behind my left shoulder. If you remember from your childhood playing with plastic toy paratroopers, the toy soldier was always in a nice tight, tucked-in position with his head down and hands over his stomach, which is actually covering his reserve parachute so it won't open by accident.

This is where the total concentration of being a paratrooper comes in. That yellow 30-foot lanyard is designed to simply never break in any normal circumstance. It's also connected via an aircraft aluminum lock that closes with a spring-loaded pin to a jet transport that is flying in the opposite direction that you're dropping out of the bird. When you approach the door, your jumpmaster is standing right there grabbing your yellow lanyard to keep it under control and keep it away from you, partially so it doesn't wrap around your neck (that would be the end of your life instantly) but also to give you a little bit of separation to bring your arms underneath it to place your hands on top of the reserve chute. If a paratrooper hasn't paid attention in Jump School, hasn't jumped in a couple of years, or possibly even as long as ten years as I've seen several times with individual Marines, or he is just too scared and rattled to follow proper procedure, then they will screw up this very simple step in the door exit. A Popeye happens when the paratrooper hands off his lanyard to the jumpmaster and instead of moving his hand underneath the cord much like an uppercut punch in boxing, he performs a windmill-like action going over the top of the lanyard, which as soon as he exits the door will cinch around his arm like a cowboy's lasso around a fleeing steer.

With paratrooper and transport plane moving in opposite directions, the lanyard will crush the upper part of the arm, most likely breaking it, and then proceed to rip apart every muscle, tendon, vein, and artery, and strip it down to the end of your arm where most likely the loop will slip off of your hand possibly taking a couple of fingers with it, and hopefully your parachute will open. Since all of your well-toned and studly military muscle, tissue, and tendons has now been violently relocated down to around your hand, you now have a huge forearms just like our cartoon friend Popeye, albeit only on one side of your body. No one in 4th ANGLICO ever had this horrible and almost unbelievable accident happen to them, and I don't think I've ever known someone who participated in a jump where a Popeye happened. I've seen plenty of reserve chutes deployed out of caution; I've seen plenty of jumpers collide in midair. I met one first sergeant who was a tow jumper as he limped around the French Creek area of Camp Lejeune the week after his accident. But fortunately I never came anywhere near a dreaded Popeye. As disgusting as this description sounds, in real life it would be even more horrific than anything I can imagine. If you are lucky enough to have the chute deploy, I would hope that you would have passed out from the excruciating pain as you drift down out of the sky. Plus, since you would most likely be unconscious, you couldn't perform a proper parachute landing fall, which means you might end up with two broken ankles on top of having a crippled arm most likely for the rest of your life. This is but one of the accidents that could befall any American paratrooper every day around the world.

Other more common accidents that paratroopers face are midair collisions or landing directly on top of the jumper below you. It's much more common than you would think, especially for the Army since they chuck out so many paratroopers in one jump. When the Army has an airborne mission involving hundreds if not thousands of paratroopers, they use old-school round parachutes that don't have any sections cut out like the

MC1-1b that I jumped for years. Again, this is an easy target for critics of the military, whether it be extremist liberals who hate everything we do unless it had something to do with World War II, the one conflict they approve of, or extremist conservatives trying to skewer the Pentagon on wasteful spending while they're campaigning for Congress. Why would the military still be using parachutes that were designed possibly in the 1950s and have hardly changed at all since World War II?

It's very simple: Round parachutes tend to fall straight down unless there is too much wind. It's always fun to watch civilian skydivers in their very small square chutes who can actually fly around in circles and almost make a loop. However, civilian skydivers aren't carrying any combat gear or weapons and they don't have anybody shooting at them. Paratroopers need to get on the ground fast, which is why we jump so low to the ground, and with chutes dropping straight down or drifting with the wind to the proper point in the drop zone, the old round-top design keeps them from colliding with each other. If two chutes become entangled, the parachute that stays inflated performs an action called "stealing air" from the other chute, which will subsequently collapse causing the second jumper to fall to the earth unless they are able to deploy their reserve chute.

Toward the end of my time at 4th ANGLICO, I was already on the ground after my jump and two paratroopers got entangled in their combat gear and could not pull themselves apart. Everybody on the ground was yelling for one of them to deploy the reserve chute, which the lower jumper eventually did and both Marines safely landed on the ground with one main chute and two reserve chutes deployed. It reminded me of watching the Apollo landings when I was a kid as the astronauts would be coming down under three very large chutes. They kept their heads, followed procedure, and everything worked out just fine. And that's one of the main reasons to go to Jump School in the first place, to see if you are that kind of man. Kipling would have been proud.

CHAPTER TWELVE

The Kids Are All Right

DURING ONE OF MY MANY VISITS BACK TO MY OLD UNIT, 4TH ANGLICO, in West Palm Beach, I was waiting for the company gunnery sergeant, Gunny Cruz, to meet me at the front gate. Around two dozen Marines were milling about out front while others arrived in their trucks and sports cars after running a PFT that morning, smoking and joking before returning to the tasks of the day. Without notice two Marines walked out the front door of the reserve center, one of them carrying the American flag folded into a neat triangle and one of them shouted out one word:

"Colors!"

Every Marine, whether in uniform or not, immediately faced the flagpole and stood at attention as the entire area promptly fell silent. Then the two-man color detail gave a short to-work command of "present ARMS!" that prompted everyone to snap a sharp hand salute and hold it as the national ensign climbed into the blue Florida sky and reached the top of the flagpole, whereupon everybody dropped their salute after the command of "carry on." It wasn't lost on me that I was the middle-aged veteran looking on from across the street undergoing a mixture of feelings—how sometimes I wish I was still in uniform, the pride that I still carry each day that I was once as good as they are today—but mostly I was proud of how sharp they looked snapping to attention, each Marine displaying a perfect salute with their right hands and arms held at a perfect 45-degree angle. And yes, they were all perfect salutes. You know how you learn to render a perfect salute for your flag? It's easy: You stand in front of a mirror and practice until it feels like your arm is going to fall off and land beside your body. Precise, quality repetition is one of the great secrets of the Marine Corps. That's actually not a secret; most people just don't put the work in.

Gunny Cruz showed up with his left arm in a sling after freakishly popping it while he was doing pullups during the PFT that morning. Since he obviously wasn't going to perform any training that day due to his injury, he took me on a grand tour of my old stomping grounds. As Cruz introduced me to various younger Marines in the paraloft, my old comm shack, the armory, and even supply, it struck me yet again that every ANGLICO Marine has virtually the same stories to tell over and over again: the "sales pitch" that is necessary for every single unit we are ever attached to, the critical importance of communications and how "an ANGLICO Marine who is pulling the trigger of a weapon and not talking on a radio is not doing his job," the completely independent nature of the job, and of course the never-ending complaints about our huge and very heavy batteries that power all of our radio gear. I've heard the same stories from Marines who served in the West Palm Beach unit forty years previously in the 1970s all the way forward to the most recent combat deployments to Iraq and Afghanistan. I told each Marine how this book was evolving almost every day and that most likely they wouldn't learn much from the book, as I was writing it for the American public, who doesn't know we exist. I promised to put in as many strange and funny stories as I could to illustrate the odd situations we are placed into and asked for as many of their photographs as they could provide for publication.

They were in great physical shape. I wasn't. They had sharp, clean haircuts. I needed one badly as I was starting to resemble Ron Burgundy in *Anchorman*. I just stood in the shade and tried to not look like some creepy guy eyeballing a bunch of U.S. Marines who were in tip-top condition and ready to defend America, while I was the one who never had the guts to join like they did. It sounds odd, and a bit funny, but that is how I felt. It reminded me of an interview with world-renowned chef Anthony Bourdain in which he observed that after being out of the restaurant game for several years of doing television that there was just no way he could go back into "the life" and pull it off with the same standards he used to practice and enforce.

I have to admit it was weird being back at my old unit. I don't even know why. Everyone was friendly or at least professional, asking who I was as soon as I walked through the security gate.

The trucks were bigger, the radios were smaller, and the Hummers were laden down with 1-inch-thick steel doors and even had air-conditioning. Armored-up vehicles were always buttoned up in Iraq, which I can't imagine during the summer months, although the armor did protect against the incoming rounds and roadside bombs.

The current company of 4th ANGLICO Marines looked and acted just like me and my buddies in the old days. They were squared away, lean with tight haircuts and happily busting each others' chops as they went about their daily duties. The uniforms look different, but luckily for me, and most importantly the country, each Marine is still the same. I commented on this to the current inspector-instructor, Lt. Col. Andrew Kelley, who quickly agreed it's always the Marine and not the gear.

"The only thing that changes is this," he said as he tugged on his digital cammie top.

Throughout this book I have told the stories of some retired Marines, some who served only four years, some who served with me for my entire twelve-year ANGLICO stint, and some who are still in uniform. Initially I struggled with how to tell the ANGLICO story that reaches back sixty years to the Korean War. It was the first time in twenty years of writing that I honestly had a hard case of writer's block. I was simply overwhelmed with more than a half century of combat, training, and a long, long list of wild and crazy Marines who I could never track down. I decided to write the book as if I was talking to one of my friends as we drank a few beers at our favorite pub. They were always interested, sometimes amazed, and frequently laughed at our antics and accidents. You'll hear about my Motor T buddy Smitty torturing new Humvee drivers in the black mud bogs of South Florida, a truly great story of my team almost running over a 600-pound moose in Norway, me being dragged by my parachute after a jump over a sod farm in Belle Glade, Florida, and of one Marine I re-named "Marco" to protect his identity. He was so wild I gave him his own small chapter. Some Marine standouts that I call "the twelve-year club" served with me my entire time at 4th ANGLICO in West Palm Beach, Florida. Two of the more memorable Marines are as follows.

MORENO

One of 4th ANGLICO's more popular and "productive" Marines was Edrick Moreno, whom I served with for twelve years. Moreno was what is known in the U.S. military as a "scrounge." My laptop's dictionary lists the word as to "beg, borrow, or cadge" for items. The civilian world calls it "stealing other people's stuff." Moreno was the best. Part cat burglar, part confidence man and big goombah guy, Moreno could have made off with the front door of the White House and had the Secret Service help him load it into the trunk of his car. I marveled about his ability to flat out steal military supplies from the Army and not get caught. The Marine Corps has the smallest budget of all the services. The Army has a lot more than us and, to us, are very sloppy with their gear accountability. The Air Force is filthy rich compared to us. If some Army doggie left gear around, we took it and put it to use, because we were always short of something. But there were rules: Don't take any weapons, classified gear, or anything that was "signed for." For a guy like Moreno, it was like being unleashed into a candy store after closing time. I'd ask him how he did it and he'd just give me his crooked smile and say: "Messmore, if you need a good scrounge, you need a Puerto Rican from Brooklyn!"

Who was I to argue? He was a great Marine, fun to be around, and seemed like everyone's crazy first cousin from Brooklyn. With my extended family hailing from Indiana and Kentucky, how I had a Puerto Rican cousin, I don't know. But no worries mate, Moreno would just forge his own birth certificate and all would be well in the land of the jarheads.

Ask for a doughnut of slash wire, he'd produce two new rolls, a bag of real doughnuts with coffee, and maybe the phone number of the base commander's daughter. He was our greatest "liberator" of Army gear ever. The first time I was at JRTC, one of our master sergeants who was a Huey door gunner in Vietnam turned to Moreno and said: "Moreno I need some ——. Go find some!" Without a word Moreno turned around, ran out of the canvas tent, and returned in exactly one hour with whatever the hell the door gunner had requested. Place your order and Chef Moreno will fill it. Just like that. And I will now officially nominate Edrick Moreno as *The* BEST SCROUNGE IN THE HISTORY OF THE MARINE CORPS! DO YOU HEAR ME, MARINES? *THE* BEST! There can only be one; and it was Moreno.

Years later after being promoted to warrant officer and training in California, Moreno pulled over on Interstate 5 north of San Diego to help out after a nasty car accident. As was his nature, he just wanted to help, whether it was his country, fellow Marine, friend, or stranger. Deeply involved with the accident victims, Moreno didn't see the speeding car coming from behind. It was on the shoulder of the road, probably doing about 70 miles per hour. On-scene police investigators later said the speeder hit the wrecked car and almost split it in half. Edrick was right in the middle. He didn't feel a thing. Other than being killed in combat, this is the only honorable way for a Marine to go out prematurely. I don't cry too often, but I did after that. I have an old boonie hat I traded with Moreno for a two-quart canteen. One of my prized possessions, it leaves my home only on Veterans Day and Memorial Day.

FIRST SERGEANT NICOLLS

When I first joined 4th ANGLICO, Parks Nicolls was a hellion, country boy staff sergeant who served as the platoon sergeant of 3rd Platoon, or the "Third Herd" in Marine Corps slang. He was a classic: squared away, cussing like a mule skinner in front of the chaplain, badgering his Marines with a million questions on weapons and tactics, becoming unfailingly polite when introducing himself to your mother, and always making his Marines do pushups before he'd hand over their paychecks. We got along fine.

I never get along with posers, fake tough guys, yuppie bikers, troublemakers, bad boys, etc. The more hardcore they were, the more I sought them out. Why? Because hardcore types are all about quality and doing it the right way. For all you blue-suit Wall Street types screaming and yelling "Failure is not an option!," real tough guys yell when it doesn't get done the right way. Not controlling the muzzle of your M-16? You might get a fist rammed in your chest. Can't load the proper frequency in your radio because you didn't pay attention in class? That's fifty pushups to start, on the black pavement underneath the beating South Florida sun. Talk back? Now you get to do a handstand, with your boots against the wall, and you'll stay there as long as I like. To make this clear, you're upside down, at a 70-degree angle, and all that weight falls on your shoulders. And that's called real pain. Nicolls had no problem with any of this stuff. We got along fine. Why? Because I pestered every Marine I knew for more information. Nicolls was excellent with naval guns and artillery and gave me my first class on artillery CFF. But the next time he sees you, Nicolls is going to hit you with a three-question quiz. If you pass:

"Good job, shithead!"

If you fail?

Well, we all know the magic number of pushups we'll be shoving out. Plus, if it's your lucky day, or he just likes you, Nicolls would stand on your back for added effect. If your back wasn't straight as a two-by-four or you didn't come within 3 inches of the ground, then you started over. True hardcore guys love to teach no matter what they do, but they also want it done correctly. Lombardi was a great teacher, Tony Dungy never raised his voice or swore in practice, and Dick Vermeil cried in the locker room. All three won the Super Bowl.

For virtually all of 1993, I was training with the Third Herd as we got ready to deploy to Mountain Warfare School, high in the Sierra Nevada of California. Top MacMillan had given each Marine on the deployment a list of exercises geared toward mountain operations, including skiing. For example, troops don't use downhill skis; they use cross-country skis for backcountry work, but also carry all the weight of combat gear plus stoves, tents, etc. To reflect this, calf raises and thigh lunges were part of the exercise regimen. Each month of 1993 the mountain warfare detachment would gather for physical training away from the rest of the company for our specialized exercises. With around fifty of us in a large circle, one Marine would stand in the center and lead different exercises. Nicolls, by now a Gunny, had selected one newly promoted sergeant to lead the session. I can't remember who it was, but this new sergeant wasn't taking his duties too seriously, and worse still, his two best buddies were snickering at him like little schoolboys.

Most Marine exercises have a four-beat pattern, with pushups and pull ups as exceptions, counted one per repetition. If you count to four while doing a jumping jack, you actually perform only one repetition. Everyone performs at the same time, at the same pace, and the same rhythm. It has its uses. As a sergeant, if your Marines are all young privates and PFCs with poor self-control, you can use this method to slow them down, grind out their sweat when they're acting up, and it shows who's in control. Well, this particular new sergeant wasn't in control, and I could see Gunny Nicolls already in a slow burn.

One mountain warfare exercise didn't make any sense to me. To work the chest muscles, we ran through twenty-five or so reps of standing chest flys like middle-school girls did in 1950s gyms across the country. How perky boobs would make me a better Arctic warrior I don't know to this day, but we ran through it. Unfortunately, newbie Sergeant Smartass got us out of synch and Gunny Nicolls struck like a Cobra.

"YOU! Get back in line!" he ordered, almost shoving the Marine back next to his snickering partners.

"KEEP GOING!" he shouted. "EVERYONE ON ME!"

We all instantly got in rhythm as Nicolls stood in the center of the ring like a bullfighter and, pointing at the three offending Marines, commanded possibly the three most dreaded words in the Marine Corps: "See me later!" Yes, they saw him later, and yes, they would pay.

"ONE, TWO, THREE!" he thundered.

"ONE!" we all shouted back in perfect synch.

Good trainers can offer encouragement, alter tone, exact revenge, all while controlling the tempo of the physical workout. Nicolls was a master.

"ONE, TWO, THREE!"

"TWO!"

"SLOW-IT-DOWN."

"THREE!"

"KEEP IT TO-GETHER."

"FOUR!"

He was like a singer changing the tone and pronunciation of lyrics to fit the beat of the song or the mood of a particular audience. And it is an art form that not everyone is great at. What happened next I never could have foreseen, and it remains my favorite memory of Parks Nicolls. How a tobacco-chewing country boy knew this I'll never know. Assembled in a giant circle flapping away like little birdies hoping to increase our bra size, Nicolls started singing the oldies.

"ONE, TWO, THREE!"

"FIVE!"

"WE MUST, WE MUST, WE MUST IN-CREASE OUR BUST!" he screamed.

"SIX!"

How we didn't all burst out laughing escapes me, but I thought it was hilarious as I'd never heard it before. Today, a quick Internet search reveals that every American woman apparently did this exercise all the way back in sixth grade. It was a classic little piece of the Marine Corps: carry out the training, take over if you need to, correct the idiots, finish the job, and be a smartass to boot. Only Nicolls.

While prepping interviews for this book, I met a crew of older Marines at the Key Lime House in Lantana, Florida, for lunch, memories, and a few cold ones. Sitting around the table were around a dozen Marines with roughly two hundred years of combined military service. They had taught me a lot, and I admire them to this day. I told Nicolls how I was going to include the story about the mountain warfare physical training and related how I made a woman laugh out loud regarding the "WE MUST IN-CREASE OUR BUST!" chant. Nicolls cut me short.

"Improve."

"Excuse me?" I asked.

"It's 'improve your bust' not 'increase.' My old girlfriend used to do it in front of the bathroom mirror," Nicolls corrected.

Now keep this in mind: We had never discussed this incident, and the conversation occurred more than twenty years after it happened. Like a proper first sergeant, he instantly corrected a wayward underling. Only Nicolls.

After nearly ten years of 4th ANGLICO continually sending detachments to two separate combat zones, it was a reassuring feeling to see my old unit in great shape and made me proud to be one of them. Even if now I was the middle-aged older Marine walking around reliving past glories, they're in fighting trim and ready to go thirteen years after September 11th. But I was the one who would tell America about them.

It was yet another example of the true strength of the U.S. Marine Corps. Civilians like to get on the backs of Marine veterans charging that we "are all the same" and that "we never change." Well why would we? We've been doing this since 1775, so we can understand why you don't understand. One of the great lessons the Marine Corps taught me is how every good to great organization should actually run itself. Don't get me wrong, Marines are rowdy and tough individuals who can trade shots and "jaw-jack" with the best of them. However, once boot camp and your initial MOS training is complete, every Marine is considered a self-contained unit who is supposed to carry out his or her duty twenty-four hours a day no matter where they find themselves around the world.

The uniforms were different. But they looked great, behaved politely and professionally whenever I dealt with them ("Oh! You're the guy who's writing the book!"), and virtually all of them had seen a hell of a lot more combat time than I ever had. In other words, just like Roger Daltrey sang on The Who's first album in 1965: The kids were all right. And every American citizen should take great pride in the U.S. Marine Corps and how efficiently it uses taxpayer money. It's no joke: The Marine Corps squeaks more out of every taxpayer dollar it gets than all the other services combined. Call me a jarhead all you want, but just like the 1980s Bruce Hornsby song, that's just the way it is.

And now I'll have that damn song by The Who stuck in my head for the rest of the day.

CHAPTER THIRTEEN

Two More MOSs

"DANGER CLOSE" IS A DRAMATIC EXPRESSION. IT WOULD BE A GREAT title for a James Bond movie. *Danger Close: James Bond Gets the Bad Guy and Your Sister!* It also would be a great name for a band, preferably an original punk rock group from the birth of that movement. "Yeah man, when I was in Danger Close, we opened for The Ramones at CBGBs in '74!" said the aging rocker still wearing the same clothes from the Nixon era.

Danger close is a term sent over a radio during a CFF mission of any type when any incoming ordnance is targeted to impact close to American troops or friendly units such as the British, Australians, or our Canadian neighbors from the Great White North. During my twelve years in the Big Green Rifle Club, danger close generally meant from 500 meters to 750 meters away from the closest ANGLICO team. Like most things in the military, danger close can change depending on the mission, an emergency situation (Viet Cong climbing over the wire trying to kill you, for example), or even the terrain.

The closest danger close figure I've ever heard was from our pony-tailed retired MGySt. Glenn Mize. Mize served with an artillery battery during the Vietnam War before spending another twenty years with 4th ANGLICO. Maybe it was during the massive and bloody Tet Offensive or because the enemy was firing into thick, sticky mud that reduced the effect of the incoming artillery rounds, but Mize brought up the closest danger close I've ever heard: 50 meters. During the Vietnam War the Viet Cong and North Vietnamese Army had an expression that if you wanted to beat the Americans, you had to hold on to their belts. What that meant was if you get close enough, then our overwhelming superiority in airpower and supporting arms (e.g., artillery and naval gunfire) wouldn't do us any good, because we wouldn't be able to use it too close to our own soldiers or Marines. Well Mize's unit was so good, they fired their shells and rolled them back to the American positions and saved the day time after time. No one complained about how close the shells were or a few shrapnel wounds if you lived through the night. The old-school nickname for the infantry is the "Queen of Battle," whereas artillery, traditionally the largest killer of enemy troops, is called the "King of Battle." Countless times in Vietnam the American Kings and Queens got together to beat off murderous communist attacks.

"And the grunts loved it," Mize remembered nearly fifty years later. "They wanted to buy us beer all the time because we saved their asses. We had a saying: The King puts it where the Queen wants it!"

Expert that he is, when I asked Mize about how I should write about a subject that would seem so boring to the general public, he quickly rattled off improvements starting nearly a century ago in World War I. After all, the general public sees artillery and naval gunfire as "big cannons" like the one at the circus that shoots that crazy white dude in the ugly helmet (who somehow doesn't get killed) all the way across the tent. There's a little bit more to it than that.

After turning to Master Gunny Mize for advice on how to teach the general public on the "super-sexy" topic of big guns that make a big bang, he quickly started running down developments over the last one hundred years. Mize said the majority of improvements in artillery have actually come in the development of the shell itself, beginning with the invention of shells that detonate on contact, and in a large leap of technology, the variable-timed fuse. Just like you see in the pirate movies or in paintings of British admiral Horatio Nelson beating up on the French navy during the 1700s, original cannons simply fired solid ball shots that tore apart your ship and its masts or flung timed bombs that blew up inside the vessel. Needless to say, the range and accuracy of these naval cannons were simply terrible, which is why all of the old classical paintings showed two massive sailing ships blasting away at such close range. Otherwise, no one was hitting the broad side of a barn or even the farm it was located on. An artillery shell with a variable-timed fuse has dozens of applications, which is why a school-trained forward observer is so critical. In the old days, if all you had in your ammo dump was old-school contact fuses, your artillery shells would explode on contact. If you find a group of very dumb enemy soldiers caught in the open in farmland or the desert, a contact fuse will explode on the surface and cut the troops down like daisies in the meadow. However, if they are dug into the side of a rocky mountain inside a fortified cave, such as the Japanese Imperial Army during World War II fighting in the battles of Iwo Jima and Okinawa, it won't have any effect at all.

Your artillery unit would be firing at a small cave entrance from a few thousand meters away, and without a direct hit you're not gaining any ground at all. However, if you adjust your rounds to detonate after impact even only a half of a second, the round will bury itself in the mountainside above the cave, creating a small landslide and sealing the entrance to the cave. I know this sounds harsh, but it is the reality of war, especially in the terrible fights of the Pacific War between the United States and Japan. The U.S. Army Air Corps (or the present-day U.S. Air Force) used this delayed detonation technique when attacking German industry during the great bomber campaign over Europe in World War II.

"The Mighty Eighth" Air Force leaders such as Generals Jimmy Doolittle, Ira Eaker, and Carl Spaatz could clearly see American B-17 Flying Fortress and B-24 Liberator crews were placing their bombs on target. However, subsequent photo reconnaissance flights revealed that the Germans were bringing their factories back into production in near record time. Much of this was due to the almost supernatural organizational abilities of Albert Speer, Hitler's favorite architect and the Third Reich's wartime minister of armaments and war production. What 8th Air Force leaders quickly learned was that the bomber boys were definitely dropping their "bombs on target," but the bombs were exploding on contact, and while severely damaging the factory structure, most importantly, the machinery operating *inside* the factory was only minimally disrupted. Setting aside the murderous and demented group of supposed humans he worked for, a man like Albert Speer would make quick work of such a situation. There was an easy solution: place a fuse on each American bomb that delayed the explosion maybe less than half of a second. A 500-pound bomb falling from 25,000 feet with a forward speed of hundreds of miles per hour will punch through any factory roof, blow up inside, and therefore destroy aircraft under construction, machine shops, raw materials, and even skilled technicians. Now we were cookin' and the Mighty Eighth's daytime raids started to sow havoc and destruction across the occupied Nazi territories.

I'm not sure what type of fuses Mize and his artillery buddies used when placing 105mm rounds only 50 meters from U.S. troops, but each mission calls for its own settings. High explosive, quick-detonating rounds are known as "HE Quick," and are the near universal default rounds for a generic mission. This type of round will most likely create a crater like most people see in the movies and is a good round against troops dug into earthen fortifications. If I were targeting an airfield with military aircraft parked all over the tarmac, I would call in an artillery mission using "HE Point Detonating" rounds. With fifty or one hundred of these rounds, I could hit the concrete runways and instantly explode and either destroy or set on fire the enemy's attack aircraft. However, if the bad guys have a clue and parked their helos and jets inside hangars, then you need "HE Delay" to punch through the roof and then explode inside to destroy the hangar contents. Remember the 8th Air Force example? Exactly.

Master Gunny Mize moved on to mention the advent of longer-range guns and extendable artillery rounds. As far back as World War I, both the Germans and Allies designed and built massive cannons that could destroy an entire city block in Paris with only one shot. However, they were so big, you could only fire them once an hour and the giant bastards were confined to the railroads, limiting their deployments. Massive cannons such as this couldn't be used effectively in World War II as Allied airpower could spot and attack them so quickly. The United States wasn't immune to this attitude, as we used the massive 203mm artillery piece in Vietnam that fired a 90-pound shell at precisely one round per minute.

The bigger is better mantra of military artillery came to its ultimate conclusion during the 1950s with several nations, including the United

States, developing land-based artillery that could fire "small" nuclear warheads. The American solution was an 11-inch-wide gun that could fire an 800-pound shell that was nearly 5 feet long, yet was designed to land only 10 kilometers away. I know we started this chapter with the definition of the term "danger close," but having a nuke pop off only ten clicks in front of me is not my idea of a fun time. The cannon was fired only one time and scored with a successful detonation at the Nevada Test Range. Nicknamed "Atomic Annie," it was built at Fort Sill, Oklahoma, home of the U.S. Army's Artillery School and where I attended Scout/Forward Observer School. The original Atomic Annie rests among other historical artillery pieces in the base museum after firing its lone Cold War atomic shell.

"Luckily that didn't last," Mize said sardonically.

Artillery and naval gun rounds themselves started to show dramatic improvement with the development of shells capable of dropping small grenade-sized "bomblets" that would scatter over a large area, which is particularly effective against exposed or very stupid troops. Another effective yet very specialized round is known as a "RAP round," which stands for "rocket-assisted projectile." For example, suppose I'm leading my ANGLICO FCT team along a coastline to cover a raiding party, and I need to fire a 5-inch salvo of shells beyond the 17,500-meter range of the then current Spruance class of destroyers deployed by the U.S. Navy from the 1970s to the '90s. A RAP round will punch the shell out to 23,000 meters and allow me to hit my target, say an advancing line of Soviet-made PT-76 amphibious tanks that are attempting to attack the raid force before they can snatch their prisoner for later interrogation. RAP rounds are very effective, but the Navy doesn't like to play around with them as they need to be pulled from the ship's ammunition magazines by individual request, which means the firing gun mount won't be able to fire missions until my RAP round is loaded and sent down range.

Mize also mentioned the improvement in gun recoil systems to keep artillery pieces aligned and on target, plus hydraulic loaders helping to reduce the workload of artillery crews. Anyone who thinks Army or Marine Corps artillery or mortar crews don't work hard in the field should go online and watch one video of a gun crew in action. They bust their asses and there's the ever-present deadly chance of a round exploding or loose powder catching fire. While western powers and the United States have spent billions of dollars, pound notes, and Deutschmarks to improve the accuracy of artillery, you only need to look at the destruction wrought on the civilian areas during the Chechnya rebellion or the civil war in Syria to learn what indiscriminate bombing or supporting arms will do to even a large city.

The incoming shell sounded just like a war movie.

Shrieking in from a Navy destroyer off the shoreline of San Clemente Island, it impacted to the left of our firing position two or three football fields away. We were surprised but no one panicked (the Marines give you an abnormal sense of fear among other things), and we looked at one of our instructors.

"What was that?" we all asked.

"The round skipped," he replied nonchalantly, not even bothering to look at us.

One of our students had been trying to strike a target around 2,300 meters in front of us and 400 feet below in elevation.

When I tell my friends this story, they're stunned.

"You mean to tell me a live shell exploded near you after skipping twenty-three football fields through the air?" they ask, all wide-eyed.

"You got it. Plus it rose 400 feet in the air. How's that for your hard-earned taxpayer dollars at work?" I reply.

"Wow."

You're damn right wow. And we're also going to need a bigger boat. Naval gunfire is probably most famous for the massive shore bombardments during the early morning invasions of Pacific islands during World War II, and of course D-Day on June 6, 1944. Oddly enough, naval gunfire has a reputation for not being able to effectively attack a massed formation of enemy armor. The tankers always say the best defense against a tank is another tank; however, long before D-Day, the U.S. Navy inflicted a massive pounding on the crack troops of the Hermann Goring Panzer Division as they raced toward the invasion beaches of southern Sicily during Operation Husky in 1943. Even when I went to Naval Gunfire School in Coronado, California, my instructors also reiterated that while naval guns are incredibly powerful, they're not so great against armor. That evening after class I walked a few blocks down the street to the little base library and found the classic work by Rear Admiral Samuel Elliott Morrison, *History of the United States Naval Operations in World War II*. A close friend of President Franklin Delano Roosevelt, Morrison was give a commission as a commander and allowed to take part in naval operations around the globe. He wrote on everything from tactics, ships, victories, and setbacks down to individual sailors performing heroic deeds during those dark days. The work was massive: fifteen volumes published over half a decade.

Morrison explicitly details how the Navy cruisers were alerted of the approach of the German tank division determined to push the Allied landing force back into the shallow Sicilian waters. The weak spot of any amphibious landing is the actual beach area itself. Men and materiel are struck by fire and destroyed, blocking the path of invading troops, and scared troops tend to take cover and bunch together instead of maintaining fighting formations. This is why every World War II movie with an amphibious landing has someone like actor Tom Hanks running around screaming "GET OFF THE BEACH! GET OFF THE BEACH!" He's right; get the hell off the beach and the Germans, namely Field Marshals Erwin Rommel and Albert Kesselring, had quickly figured this out. Hence, the Hermann Goring Division was hell bent for the invasion beaches on the southern coast of Sicily. What they didn't count on was the destroyer USS *Shubrick* and cruiser USS *Boise* dropping hundreds of rounds of naval artillery on top of tanks, which splintered the attack and might have saved the entire landing. As naval guns weren't as accurate as they are today, hundreds of rounds were needed, with light cruiser *Boise* being armed with fifteen 5-inch guns alone. I made photocopies of the relevant passages and showed them to one of my instructors the next day, who was surprised to learn of the successful naval gunfire attack on armored formations. After running dozens of simulations in the classroom and computer trainers, it was time for my classmates and I to shoot for real.

San Clemente Island off the California coast is just beautiful. Isolated, surrounded by the bluest blue of the mighty Pacific Ocean, it also boasted hills that reached hundreds of feet in the air. It was a great place to blow the shit out of stuff.

Part of eight Channel Islands off the shore of Southern California, the islands were used for military training and as an early warning system against the Japanese threat during World War II. Most Americans have heard of Santa Catalina and its gorgeous vacation spots, but there are seven more used by the military or serving as natural parks.

I can't remember what one of our students was firing at, some old tank hulk or Amtrak that had sat rusting in the Pacific sun since the 1960s. Even though no more than three hundred military or civilian personnel live or work on San Clemente, it does have a coastal road like many islands. But right next to the impact zone was a small tributary emptying into the Pacific. And a small tributary requires a small bridge, in this case a trestle bridge that reminded me of train trestles in the Midwest and South. In short, I was praying a student would screw up and blast the shit out of that bridge. What a glorious day that would be! Picture it: a young Marine just out of boot camp, trying to find his boots in the world of the Marine Corps and he takes out a bridge on American soil. I could barely contain myself with desire. How would you like to be a member of that group of Marine and Navy instructors standing at attention in the admiral's office surrounded by thirty years of military mementos from the boss's stellar career, while you're stammering about the sudden new line item in next year's budget? Call me sadistic, but hey, I'm being honest. Alas, most of the students fired well, and the lonely little bridge that could survived another day.

As I've alluded to several times in this book, the effect of naval gunfire from U.S. Navy warships is just brutal. During my time the battleships were pulled out of mothballs, fitted with cruise missiles, and sent back into combat while dozens of destroyers and their rapid-fire, 5-inch guns were only a radio call away.

The fifteen years that have passed since I got out of 4th ANGLICO have focused almost entirely on air strikes and laser-guided bombs such as the JDAM bomb unit that permits a guidance package to be attached to any normal "iron bomb" found in any air component of the U.S. military. And no, I've never referred to a regular gravity-dropped bomb as a "dumb bomb," even though the media insists on using that term. While guided ordnance was always called a smart bomb, I often heard regular bombs called iron bombs, but mainly by their actual designation such as a "Mark 82," a standard 500-pound bomb.

I've asked far and wide and have yet to find a single ANGLICO Marine who called in a naval gunfire mission during the wars in Afghanistan and Iraq. Iraq is the more obvious target with miles of coastline. However, just as the brunt of these two wars has been borne by the Marine Corps and Army, the Navy and Air Force have been in the shadows a bit, except when discussing, you guessed it, dropping guided bombs from aircraft.

However, that doesn't mean naval gunfire is dead or outdated. Far from it, with the U.S. Navy actively testing and firing new laser weapons like something out of a James Bond movie and the new superguns that may fire projectiles more than 80 miles. This reflects the post–Iraq and Afghanistan thinking of the continuing (read that: never-ending) Global War on Terror and the supposed shift of American interests to the Pacific Rim to combat the threat of an increasingly belligerent Communist China.

After his just completed 15 months in Afghanistan, present 4th ANGLICO inspector/instructor Lt. Col. Andrew Kelley is well versed on modern artillery. He echoed Master Gunny Mize's comments on the increased rate of fires, but also noted the accuracy of today's individual rounds, an improvement on the massive barrages of World War I that hardly ever worked.

"The biggest development of recent years is the precision delivery of weapons," Kelley said.

While Americans are well accustomed to seeing laser-guided bombs make direct hits on enemy buildings and moving pickup trucks destroyed with Hellfire missiles, I wondered if the forward observer role was going to be diminished, especially with the advent of the JTAC. Kelley quickly countered that the opposite is occurring, with the increased importance of making a positive "eyes on" identification of the proper target, especially after ten years of fighting terrorists, insurgents, and various other idiots hiding and firing at U.S. troops while parked next to a school or mosque.

"A lot of variables of fire support places more emphasis on the forward observer. Target location is more important than ever. The amount of skills required by an observer has been revolutionized," Kelley said.

Ironically the advanced precision of individual rounds and Americans weapons experts seeking a true first-round strike capability using virtually every form of munitions we have has instead placed more emphasis on the forward observer, as they need more proficiency in target identification and selection. Marine ANGLICO companies have always been accustomed to sending their own Marines to the appropriate school, such as Jump School, Naval Gunfire School, Scout/Forward Observer School, or either parachute rigger or Jumpmaster School, and running their own in-house operation known as ABC training or the ANGLICO basic course. With the advent of JDAM units that can take any standard 500-pound bomb and turn it into a laser-guided precision weapon, each of the military services has gotten into the game of delivering ordnance on enemy targets. One result is the standardization of CAS and the creation of formal schools and annual certifications for forward observers to call in CAS. Personally I feel the influence of the U.S. Air Force getting involved with something that Marine ANGLICO has been doing just fine since the Korean War. I'm not against any military branch (my father was in the Air Force after all), however, we don't need to complicate a process that's 50 years old. Plus with the Department of Defense budget cuts that were enacted during President Obama's second term in office, the annual certification programs are going to be tougher to maintain. Also some Marine officers and planners have suggested creating a separate MOS for the qualified JTACs on the ground. Most of the Marines I spoke to don't feel this is a legitimate path for a young Marine, airman, or soldier, and even the Special Ops community won't be able to create senior staff NCOs in the field as young troops run through two or three combat deployments in one four-year enlistment and then move on into civilian life after their good and faithful service to the country. Kelley said his challenge now is to create as many training scenarios as he can locally or during two-week annual training deployments and then repeat them over and over again like a football team during preseason training camp.

"What we try to do is put them in complex situations and repeat them as much as possible. The difficult thing in an ANGLICO company is also the beauty and challenge of it as you never know what you're going into," Kelley said.

Kelley also said that while Marine ANGLICO might be presently bringing "more to the fight than needed" when FCT teams are attached specifically to the U.S. Army, as they now have their own JTACS or the traditional FAC for the U.S. Air Force, with the current state of the world, ANGLICO teams are most likely going to be in higher demand as U.S. forces are training and serving with more and more foreign units around the world. In August 2015 during the writing of this book, virtually the entire 4th ANGLICO unit traveled to Camp Pendleton to practice every phase of ANGLICO training, including communications, air strikes, artillery, mortars, rappelling and fast roping out of helicopters and the tilt rotor Osprey, while also sending a team to San Clemente Island to call in naval gunfire missions with a U.S. Navy destroyer. It was an ANGLICO paradise. I was jealous and told Lieutenant Colonel Kelley how much I wish I could've gone with them. To further illustrate his point, Kelley told me that just as soon as 4th ANGLICO had come back from Camp Pendleton, they were preparing to send Marines to Germany to help train Georgian troops, also train with Bulgarian military troops, another section was traveling back to California to take part in the U.S. Army's famous National Training Center tank battles in the desert, and another section would be traveling to Romania and yet another deployment to Afghanistan. So much for being a so-called Reserve unit.

"4th ANGLICO will train with six different foreign units in six months. It's the beauty of ANGLICO," Kelley said. "At the end of the day, we're more than just fire support experts."

The future of Marine ANGLICO seems to be more of the same, but faster paced and with more precision weapons. This indeed will require leadership, initiative, and tactical proficiency to be pushed down the chain of command even more so than when I was in 4th ANGLICO. If ANGLICO deploys with the Romanians and they can't talk to anyone on their radios, then we'll take over. If the Georgians haven't a clue about

CAS, then we'll take care of that. Sometimes we just do some hand holding and remind them American forces are nearby to help them.

"From corporal to staff sergeant, they're doing normally what a captain would be doing," Kelley said. "You have to get out of your MOS quickly. We have Motor T guys who can do forward observer/communications better than regular [MOS-trained] guys. Forward observers are now better trained than when I was a second lieutenant in the 1990s. It might be a Third World country that doesn't do well what we did fifty years ago. They might be the entire communications network, close air support, or just offer advice. And that might be a corporal. I need five guys to do something they might not know until they get there."

That was the beauty of my time with 4th ANGLICO. To be honest, it was a lot of fun that so many Marines didn't like us (or flat out hated us sometimes), but we knew what we were capable of and always got the job done. That is the point of chapter 18, the fictional chapter I wrote about a hurricane strike on New Orleans or Miami. Every Marine I spoke to regarding this book took it as a simple statement of fact ("Of course we could have") regarding whether one ANGLICO company could lay an entire radio network over the Crescent City. We do this stuff in training all the time.

"No two ANGLICO detachments are going to be the same. Every single one of those is going to be different and you're going to have to figure it out. You have to be a captain, gunny, sergeant, and corporal all at the same time," Kelley said.

One Marine who is well versed in modern artillery is present-day captain, and former enlisted Marine, Hamid Mortazavi. Mortazavi joined 4th ANGLICO in 1997 when I knew him as a very young, highly spirited lance corporal who frequently was as animated as an action figure in a shoot-'em-up video game. We both deployed to Operation Battle Griffin in Norway in 1999, where he was given the always dreaded "Marco Watch" to keep everyone's favorite crazy Marine, Marco, under control and moving in the right direction. It was like being on fire watch in case a fire breaks out, but with Marco you had to put out fires wherever the crazy bastard walked on God's green Earth (see chapter 14). Advancing through the ranks before and after the terrorist attacks of September

11, 2001, Mortazavi suffered a terrible back injury during a parachute jump in 2002 that eventually required fourteen separate back procedures to keep him in uniform.

"I kind of did the Cuba Gooding thing," he said, referring to the Robert De Niro film *Men of Honor*, where Gooding's character suffered a terrible injury and had to prove to the U.S. Navy dive community that he could still serve to proper standards in uniform. Mortazavi succeeded, got healthy, and returned to duty with 4th ANGLICO.

Before I left 4th ANGLICO in West Palm Beach in November 1999, I had learned of several deployments that we would make to the Bosnia and Kosovo area during the American and NATO interventions of the late 1990s. This was the third or fourth combat assignment I had volunteered for, but I got out around three or four months before these deployments left for the Balkans. Mortazavi was on one of these detachments, and just like everybody who's ever served with any ANGLICO unit since the Korean War, he's got plenty of stories about dealing with foreign troops that have absolutely no idea why Marine ANGLICO has been attached to them. Once they finally got to Kosovo, the detachment leadership, with longtime 4th ANGLICO jumpmaster, ops chief, Gulf War veteran, and master sergeant Iain MacMillan being the senior staff NCO, assembled all of the 4th ANGLICO Marines and asked who could speak Spanish. Mortazavi and three other Marines raised their hands.

"You guys are the new Spanish-speaking team," Top MacMillan told them.

The problem was, they didn't really know what that meant. Mortazavi and his Marines would be attached to some army troops from Argentina, and I'm sure the brainiacs at higher headquarters quickly realized it might be beneficial to have someone with the "Argies" who could talk to American fighter pilots. While it's not widely known in America, I've noticed over the years that nations all around the world send combat troops, usually Special Forces types of some sort, to American or NATO-led military efforts. Just as S/Sgt. Teddy Pernal had El Salvadoran Special Forces troops guard over him when Mother Nature called during one of his four combat deployments, I think many of these nations see these missions as a way to "blood," or baptize through combat, their Special Forces in case of an emergency back home.

Mortazavi then learned that his FCT team and the Argentineans would augment a German tank unit that was monitoring the Kosovo border for smugglers bringing in any sort of contraband, including weapons and even human beings. So, just to make this clear, it was one of those typical "figure it out" moments that Lieutenant Colonel Kelley is so fond of talking about: Mortazavi was in Kosovo to help translate Argentinean Spanish into English for the Germans. Perfectly normal, right? Well for us, it was, and is to this day.

Mortazavi said that the Germans had created an observation post along the Kosovo border and in typical German fashion had named it the "Eagle's Nest." After taking a quick tour of their new operational area, a German lieutenant named Holmann showed the Argentineans and the Marines their berthing areas. Lieutenant Holmann wanted around twenty Argentineans and two Marines in one section and the same amount in another. Mortazavi instantly balked at the proposal, knowing that after accomplishing the mission an ANGLICO team's main priority is to not get separated from each other, especially when we have so many radios and classified encryption gear with us.

"I can't split my team," Mortazavi insisted. It was yet another case of an ANGLICO Marine standing up to someone way past their own rank.

Mortazavi began to explain to Lieutenant Holmann just what Marine ANGLICO teams do for a living, with the young German officer telling him that he had been under the impression that the Marines were merely translators for the Argentineans. For the millionth time a U.S. Marine ANGLICO member went into his regularly used and well-worn sales pitch about all of the capabilities of a four-man team.

"We're not translators although we do speak Spanish. I told him I could get air here in ten minutes. When I told him this, he lit up [with excitement]," he said. "The more successful teams had a leadership team that were good salespeople."

"I need to take you to my company commander," Lieutenant Holmann told Mortazavi.

Holmann took Mortazavi to his company commander, whereupon the same sales pitch from fifteen minutes ago was repeated for the armored commander, who to his great credit instantly understood the wide range of assets that he now had immediate access to. Mortazavi said the company commander "screamed something in German at Holmann," Holmann "screamed something back at his company commander in German," and Marine ANGLICO promptly had a new home all of their own. On the very next day, Mortazavi and his team immediately updated a month-old fire support plan that had been designed but left behind by a Dutch unit. In less than twenty-four hours, Marine ANGLICO had gone from being "translators" to the new fire support sheriff in town.

Mortazavi's new German armored friends were so impressed with their new Marine buddies that they assigned the FCT team its own berthing area to live, plan, sleep, and store all the avalanche of communications gear any ANGLICO team hauls around the globe. Much to Mortazavi's chagrin, it was a type of dayroom that was being used every day by German troops to watch television during off-duty hours. To make things even more embarrassing, in 1999 the Germans had found their troops a brand-spanking-new, high-definition television set that was routinely selling for thousands of dollars back home in the States.

Lieutenant Holmann wasn't going to have any of it. Not for his new jarhead buddies, who were most likely the first U.S. Marines the young officer had ever met. Once again Holmann "screamed something in German" and the enlisted troops all charged out chanting "hut, hut, hut" like a bad war movie. Mortazavi was beside himself.

"Oh, shit! I don't want to be the Marine to kick the Germans out of their own TV room," Mortazavi remembered with alarm even after fifteen years.

Just to make things perfectly clear, the Germans placed a sign on the door of the new ANGLICO berthing area that read: "BLOCKED: U.S. MARINES." Fifteen years after the incident, I could still hear the amazement in Mortazavi's voice as we spoke over the phone while he was on a boating trip with his family in sunny South Florida.

As a gunnery sergeant, Mortazavi deployed to Iraq with a 4th ANGLICO SALT team in 2007, where he learned firsthand that in the world of laser-guided bombs, GPS-guided missiles, and Hellfire missiles being attached to virtually every aircraft in the U.S. inventory, artillery was still just as viable in combat as it's always been if not more so.

"Like any other tool, it has its capabilities and limitations," he said. "It's still an excellent, valuable asset. It's almost an art form."

Possibly artillery's greatest asset is that it is truly an all-weather weapon. The guns can fire in rain, snow, sleet, at night, and, most importantly in the Middle East or Afghanistan, during dust storms that can last for days. While everyone is enamored with laser-guided bombs, and don't get me wrong I'm all for them too with their incredible accuracy, in any type of desert environment, lasers can lose their effectiveness or be rendered useless. People forget or simply don't know that the word *laser* is an acronym for "light amplification by stimulated emission of radiation." Invented in 1960 at Hughes Laboratories, lasers are used all throughout society in eye surgery, industrial cutting techniques, and many other applications. There are new laser weapons being tested by the Pentagon that will be strong enough to shoot down missiles or even large aircraft. However, in the desert the dust and dirt flying through the atmosphere will diffuse the light of a smaller laser, such as a man-packed model used by a FAC or JTAC. In other words, the dust, or snowstorm for that matter, will have the exact opposite effect of a laser. Instead of amplifying and focusing the laser's energy, a desert storm will defeat the "marking the target" aspect of any laser.

Artillery doesn't have this problem, and the infantry or Special Operations teams that need some help, and need it NOW!, know that artillery rounds can be hitting near their position in about two minutes if fired properly. They are far from being just "big guns that fire big bullets," in the words of one of my old history professors, Mortazavi explained the myriad details involved with any artillery mission. I was always on a SALT or FCT team, so in all honesty, I didn't care about what the artillery guys were doing. I knew they worked hard and never got any credit or glory from the American public, but they had a Fire Direction Center that used computers to calculate each and every mission as they sat in a truck with a nice warm heater inside.

Mortazavi explained that each mission is a complex mix of the actual rifling on the barrel of each gun, the battery's altitude (Afghanistan is much higher than the deserts of Iraq with much less air pressure at altitude), the size of the propellant charge that explodes to send the round on its way, the Earth's rotation, and even the wear and tear on the inside of the gun tube itself. These calculations are required for each mission for the six guns of a typical artillery battery. Plus, the gun crews are physically handling up to 100-pound shells up to four times per minute as they blast targets 14 miles away. As I've stated, artillery Marines and soldiers work their asses off and no one ever recognizes their contribution to our nation's defense. Plus, artillery bases are prime targets for any enemy. During the Vietnam War fire bases were regularly attacked by North Vietnamese army and Viet Cong units, with more than one Medal of Honor being earned by fire base personnel.

"They're Marines who want to get rounds down range just as much as the Marines who need it," Mortazavi said.

In 2007 Mortazavi's SALT team was operating and monitoring its FCT teams west of Baghdad and Fallujah near the Lake Habbaniyeh and Ramadi area. For once Mortazavi's team was performing in a true ANGLICO fashion, calling in some CAS missions themselves, monitoring their FCT team's activities, coordinating with the U.S. Army units in the Lake Habbaniyeh area of operations, and calling in one thousand artillery missions on their own for the Iraqi army locked in mortal combat with the local militias. Mortazavi said his SALT team fired around 350 high explosive rounds to support the Iraqis, and the rest were actually illumination rounds fired after sunset to reassure the new and very jumpy Iraqi army recruits.

"Anything that swayed in the night, they wanted illumination," he joked.

While this is a nice little joke at the Iraqis' expense, it proves Mortazavi's point about the enduring power and usefulness of artillery on the modern battlefield. Green allied troops needed help whether real or imagined, and his team was able to instantly respond in the early morning hours within a matter of minutes. With some thoughtful officials in the U.S. military expressing concern about our enemies finding a way to use electronic interference to block laser-guided munitions, artillery won't be leaving the Marine Corps or U.S. Army any time soon.

CHAPTER FOURTEEN

A Marine Not Named Marco

"ARE YOU GOING TO WRITE ABOUT MARCO?"

It was one of the most frequent questions Marines asked me after learning that I was "the one writing the book."

"I think I am. But I'm going to change his name to protect him," I answered.

The Marine in question doesn't carry the name of the famous Italian explorer Marco Polo, but every Marine who served with him and reads this book will have no doubt about who I'm describing. It's like writing "former president with beard and stovepipe hat" and making the massive leap of faith that "Honest Abe" Lincoln is the topic of discussion.

Marco could be as funny as any standup comedian I've ever seen on television, but he was so inherently shy around strangers, he would never go on stage. We begged him to let us take him to a comedy club for amateur night so he could just hop on stage and kill the crowd. We offered to pay for his entire night out; we'd show up in force to support our fellow Marine and all would be great. He had none of it. We pleaded, cajoled, advised, and maybe even questioned his manhood a little bit, but then he would just make fun of you in retaliation, and he always won when it came to jokes. Marco was the type who could really only open up around his friends and took it as his purpose in life to make us laugh.

Marco was crazy to be around and I'm not sure he's not actually crazy, but Marines loved him. For example, he had the rare ability to mimic other people's voices, a skill that many very famous and wealthy actors readily admit that they don't possess. I don't know how many times

Marco snuck up behind me, performed a perfect vocal pattern and inflection of a senior Marine in order to startle me, only for me to turn around to see his big, blond, German-looking ass giggling like a schoolboy in the back row of church. Since he actually liked me, he harassed me on a regular basis even when he was a PFC and I was a Goldwinger sergeant with years of experience by that point. Marco didn't care at all.

Marco eventually did go to Airborne School and gained a wide variety of field experience, because he was so funny and inventive that Marines liked to have him around on deployments simply for his entertainment value. Early on in his time at 4th ANGLICO, Marco was seen as just a typical young rowdy Marine, and while he was incredibly funny and fun to be around, like any other junior Marine, you just gave him assignments and strict orders and he would get things done usually in his assigned section of supply. And funny he was.

He actually had set routines where he would take a fictional character from a television show and place them in a military situation such as them being a member of the Marine Corps or as a prisoner of war in the fictional *Hogan's Heroes* television comedy. During my first deployment to Mountain Warfare School, as we were in our eighteen-month training cycle to deploy to Norway in 1996, Marco went with us. After we boarded the buses from the San Francisco airport and began our climb into the mountains, Marines in the back of the bus just started shouting "Marco! Marco! Do something!" What they wanted was for Marco to launch into one of his comedy routines to make them laugh during the long bus ride. Without hesitation Marco began a little skit as the bumbling deputy sheriff Barney Fife from the old *Andy Griffith Show* as a drill instructor in the Marine Corps.

As anyone who has ever seen even one episode of the *Andy Griffith Show* knows, Barney Fife was so incompetent that he wasn't allowed to keep live ammunition in his service revolver. He always put up a brave, shouting front at least until things got rough; then he wilted like a wax flower in the hot sun. He had been through boot camp like the rest of us, so Marco was well aware of how Marine drill instructors behave and how savage they could be toward their recruits. I sat there and marveled at Marco doing a pitch-perfect imitation of actor Don Knotts in character as Deputy Barney Fife screaming at a new recruit just like the abuse we had all suffered at Parris Island, South Carolina, or at the West Coast boot camp in San Diego, California. Many people think Don Knotts was in the Marine Corps, but that's an urban legend. Knotts was in fact in the U.S. Army during World War II and helped to entertain the troops.

The shtick was that Barney Fife and his high-pitched whining voice was screaming at a new recruit to stand at attention only to quickly learn that the new recruit was the size of a defensive lineman in the NFL. The entire bus, from brand-new Marine privates up to our officers and staff NCOs who had seen combat in the Vietnam War, was laughing along with the shrieking Barney Fife. Then Marco hit the punchline as the fictional monster Marine recruit stands up before the bloviating television character. Instantly folding under the threat of such a large human, Fife could only whimper out a soft: "Gee, you're kind of a big fella aren't ya?"

Hell, even the bus driver was laughing his ass off. I know this description doesn't reflect how funny it was that night as a Greyhound bus loaded with U.S. Marines was driving off into the night, but if in your own mind you can hear the voice of the iconic Don Knotts character instantly switching from hardcore drill instructor to scared little boy, you should get the joke. Other times I've seen him speak one sentence during roll call and make 225 Marines laugh like they're watching Chris Rock Live at the Apollo Theater in Harlem. Marco made it up on the spot and that's why everybody loved him so much.

The final time I deployed to Fort Polk, Louisiana, for the three-week battle at JRTC, Marco went with us. By this time it was common practice to assign a new corporal to the "Marco Watch," which was literally serving as a minder to get him in the right place at the right time. Any type of "watch" in the Marines or Navy involves standing over an area, gear, or even a prisoner to ensure everything is in working order. This is why every open barracks in the military of any size posts a nightly roster for "fire watch" to raise the alarm in case of a fire. You check the roster for your name and time to be on duty (in uniform and possibly armed), and it usually lasts an hour when you're relieved by the next guard. But if you got stuck on Marco Watch, it was a full-time job and Marines frequently became enraged with him due to his incessant fooling around and constant need for snacks and sodas of all types, and he was also a pack rat who would steal the hubcaps off of the general's jeep if he felt like it. Don't think I'm exaggerating, because I'm not.

I think my two favorite Marco stories involve a paper plate and him hijacking the bathroom of a Marine Corps master sergeant with twenty-five years of experience. After the above-mentioned JRTC trip of January 1996, we completed our little war in the freezing Louisiana winter and spent a few days in some Army barracks as we prepped and packed for home. I was in a room with my buddy Kenny McKelton and Gonzo, which was next door to M/Sgt. Ronnie Lee's private room. Lee was a good, old-school country boy who later in life had the guts to crawl through the woods at night to place microphones next to drug smugglers plotting their next drug runs. Well, as it happens at least every twenty-four hours, old Top Lee needed to make a "sitting head call" in his private bathroom. After two or three weeks of eating nothing but MREs, you actually need to have a bowel movement more often than usual as the finely processed food will leave you constipated if you don't. Well, Top Lee didn't want that and was looking forward to his "private time," when he crashed into the immoveable barricade of a man named Marco.

Top Lee walked to his room and didn't think anything about the door to "his" bathroom being closed. It was also locked. In the delicate parlance of the U.S. Marine Corps, someone was in his own personal "shitter." Incredulous, Top Lee pounded on the door.

"Who the hell is in there?" he yelled.

It was Marco. And he wasn't budging.

"It's me, Top. I really have to go," Marco said.

"WELL USE YOUR OWN SHITTER MARCO!" Top Lee shouted through the locked door.

Gonzo, McKelton, and I were in the next room listening to this, half laughing and half in amazement over Marco's hijacking of a very senior Marine's private space. As communications chief of an ANGLICO company, Top Lee was responsible for hundreds of radios, antennas, 400-watt communications Humvees, and plenty of gear I won't talk about the rest of my life due to their classification. I always assumed the comm shack was worth millions of dollars. On top of that Top Lee had an amazing combination of a "we're not leaving until the job is done" attitude regarding standards and his true country boy persona—ultimately he was just a nice guy. That doesn't mean that he let us get away with things. As I've written before, during our inspector general examinations, we were allowed a 10 percent margin of error for our fully loaded embarkation boxes. With Top Lee he brought that ship in to dock with an error rate of only 1 percent on a regular basis. He was just that good, and of course, he deserved his own shitter. Who would deny him this simple pleasure and reward of a quarter of a century of public service? Oh. That's who. Marco.

Now keep in mind this wasn't a brief, two-minute episode of Lee yelling at a very junior Marine to vacate his personal private space. It wasn't so much that Marco argued with Lee; he pleaded and begged his case as if Lee was the one who was nuts for trying to get Marco out of his own bathroom in the first place. Marco was like this the entire time I knew him. One time during a cold-weather hop to a National Guard base in West Virginia around an hour south of Pittsburgh (and yes, we drank some great Iron City beer), we were preparing to go out into the field. I was walking around checking on individual Marines, especially the ones who were new to extreme cold weather training or had minimal experience. By this time Marco was actually a pretty good operator in the snow. But since it was Marco, I stopped by just to see what the hell he was up to, which was usually no good. As stated, he was a pack rat who carried a truckload of crap with him no matter where we went, and no matter how much we tried to stop him. Even if we threw his crap in the trash, an hour later someone would look out the window and see Marco's legs sticking out of the dumpster as he was trying to retrieve the stuff we just threw out.

As most of us did, Marco had made a list of all of the gear our commanders needed us to take, plus his own personal gear and whatever the instructor staff had issued to us. He had his paperwork in a Ziploc bag, which is nothing out of the ordinary. However, this is Marco we're talking about. He didn't write his checklist on a waterproof notepad like I used or even on a piece of hard plastic with indelible ink that I've seen plenty of Marines use. Marco had opted instead to write his checklist on a paper plate you would use in a backyard barbecue. And of course to keep it safe and sound, he had it in a 1-gallon Ziploc bag. I thought it was hilarious and tried to take a look at it, but he held it behind his back like an embarrassed little kid, which in a way Marco actually was.

This is the type of near religious fervor that Top Lee was up against. Lee walked into our room with a look on his face like he'd just seen Casper the Friendly Ghost having a cup of coffee.

"I can't believe it. I'm a Marine Corps master sergeant and I can't use my own shitter," Top Lee said in amazement.

After nearly a full half hour of the Top Lee/Marco "Great Shitter Standoff of 1996," Marco gallantly announced, through the closed door mind you, that he was going to make his grand departure. Unbeknownst to Master Sergeant Lee, who walked into his own room with a look of relief on his face, Marco had brought probably two dozen magazines, base newspapers, and a bunch of other junk with him into the bathroom. And there was one other thing Lee did not see coming.

"JESUS CHRIST HE'S NAKED!"

Top Lee shot out of his own room like a surprised church elder on Sunday morning.

Indeed he was. I can still see it today as Marco walked out of Top Lee's private room naked from blond head to the tips of his toes, his arms fully loaded with his uniform, Gore-Tex jacket, combat boots, socks, thermal underwear, and of course every magazine he'd been able to get his hands on. I think he was a lance corporal at the time.

Marco did truly live in his own world. I remember one of our active duty inspector/instructors, a lieutenant colonel who had been in command of Second Force Recon, the Special Ops Marine unit that usually performs hostage rescue missions for a Marine expeditionary force. In other words he was an extremely competent officer whom I liked very much. After returning from Operation Battle Griffin in 1999, we traveled south down Interstate 95 from Camp Lejeune in North Carolina back to the reserve center in West Palm Beach. We stopped to eat at some small restaurant and this particular lieutenant colonel sat down for dinner with myself and Gunnery Sergeant Henry, everyone's favorite Norwegian moose killer. Inevitably the topic of Marco came up and this lieutenant colonel told us a story about how he had asked Marco why he had the wrong type of tire in the bed of his small pickup truck. Trucks and cars made by either General Motors or Ford at the time either had five or four bolts to hold a tire to the vehicle. He pointed this out to Marco and asked him why he had the wrong tire. Marco looked at him like he had just asked the dumbest question in American history.

"I use that as a way to keep all this stuff from flying out of my truck," Marco replied as if he was talking to a small child.

Gunny Henry and I just chuckled and nodded our heads in understanding as we had been putting up with Marco's antics for the last several years. However, there was a price. As Marco's time with 4th ANGLICO went on and he grew older, quite frankly he never really grew up. Plus he had the attention span of a mosquito with a thousand-dollar-a-day cocaine habit. Obviously during field operations this was going to be a problem.

How he managed to get promoted to corporal is nothing short of a miracle from above. It's a move that will forever show how illogical, mysterious, confounding, and sometimes flat-out stupid promotions could be in the Marine Corps. I was always a hard-luck case when it came to being promoted, but I wasn't like one very fine Marine who was a lance corporal for *six years* before he got fed up and basically went AWOL. I saw one brand-new gunnery sergeant sitting by himself holding his beer after dismissal muttering to himself about the sudden revelation. He had been a staff sergeant for less than two years and HQMC reached down and made him a gunny. But making Marco a corporal? An E-4 in the other branches of the military isn't given much responsibility. In the Marine Corps you're an NCO now and are expected to behave as one. In other words you're not one of the boys and girls now, you're a leader. It's a reflection of your new stature that you now wear the famous red stripe down the side of the trousers of your dress blues and you are allowed to wear a ceremonial sword during color guards, funeral details, or while standing as duty NCO. When I was promoted to corporal (six months late of course), I was quickly brought into the commanding officer's office for a quick ceremony. I walked into the colonel's office with Marines saying, "Hey, Messmore, how's it going?" After I pinned on my new stripes, as I walked back to the comm shack to resume my duties, a young Marine I'd never seen before walked past me and said, "Good morning, Corporal." It happens just that quick. Rank. Respect. Responsibility. Rewards.

The duties were basically everything Marco wasn't.

During the mid-1990s there was a very large war game that included the largest mass tactical airborne jump in decades, possibly even since D-Day. The 82nd Airborne, a few thousand British paratroopers, and selected Marine Corps teams would take part in a massive exercise that covered nearly the entire state of North Carolina. Marco of course wanted to go, as he loved this type of field operation. Little did we all know that this would be the end of the line for him. With the war games in full swing, Marco shook off his minder, pulled one of his disappearing routines, and could not be located. The senior enlisted Marine from 4th ANGLICO was our sergeant major, and being fully aware of Marco's past behavior quite frankly didn't give a crap where Marco was. However, the senior Marine officer involved with the operation got wind of one missing Marine and made it clear in no uncertain terms that the Marines of 4th ANGLICO would stop everything they're doing to locate the wayward Marco. I wasn't on this operation, so I heard a lot of rumor and hearsay after everyone got back, but I was told a two-star general got involved and when that happens other problems get solved or heads are going to roll. I also heard that they finally found Marco hanging out with another unit fast asleep on a standard military-issue green canvas cot. Our sergeant major had reached his limit.

Marco was busted, or reduced a pay grade and rank, from corporal to lance corporal. As he was coming up on the years of service anyway, as far as I know he was basically forced out of the unit. I understood the anger of our sergeant major, an extremely competent Marine and leader whom I served with for years and would gladly sit down with for Thanksgiving dinner. But it still did make me sad to see our crazy comedian leave the unit. But as always in the Marine Corps, the mission comes first and Marines always have to get the mission done. I heard later that he had actually managed to join the Florida National Guard. I wondered if it was true and how well he fared in their system, as I had met many

Marines through the years who had transferred to the Guard because it was so much easier to get promoted than in the Marine Corps.

As a testament to the affection 4th ANGLICO Marines have for Marco, fifteen years after I left the unit, two Marines posted a photograph on our social media page proudly posing with him as if he was a Medal of Honor winner or a famous officer such as Gen. James "Mad Dog" Mattis.

"We've had a Marco sighting," the caption said.

The photograph set off a flurry of comments as no one had seen or heard from our favorite crazy bastard in years. Even for Marine paratroopers, Marco was just flat-out, gorgonzola nuts. As much as he drove me crazy, and he did, I miss the goofball and wish I knew where he was to this day.

CHAPTER FIFTEEN

The L in ANGLICO

IT'S FUNNY THAT AFTER I STARTED WRITING THIS BOOK AND INTER-
viewing my old Marine buddies, and then Marines that were still in
uniform and had served in both Iraq and Afghanistan, I kept hearing the
same stories from my time in the Marines, even though I left the service
fifteen years ago. In addition to the standard complaints about how large,
heavy batteries are such a pain in the ass, and how so many Marines
resent or hate us, another common point was that it was sometimes easier to deal with foreign troops than branches of the American military,
especially the U.S. Army.

As the word *ANGLICO* is an acronym that stands for Air/Naval
Gunfire Liaison Company, it's easy to focus on combat arms and jumping
out of airplanes and other sexy topics. But the letter *L* is just as critical
to the ANGLICO mission as radio communications, which I've already
described as the heart and soul of an ANGLICO unit. Whenever we
deploy with foreign troops, after the initial sales pitch of who we are and
what we do, we quickly become teachers, tutors, and advisers to the troops
we're supporting. This is reflected in the several official Department
of Defense photographs I've included showing ANGLICO Marines
working with Japanese soldiers, French fighter pilots, and British Royal
Marines. Over the decades we have served with troops from Japan, Saudi
Arabia, Iraq, Afghanistan, Norway, Corsica, and Sardinia, and with Prin-
cess Patricia's Canadian Light Infantry, when we ran around on the snow
half naked to prove how tough we were. We even served in an advisory
role with various small island nations in the Caribbean.

Americans have heard frequent horror stories in the U.S. media about interservice rivalry and politics that waste taxpayer money and can sometimes get troops hurt or even killed in combat. You have the case of rushing the Colt-manufactured M-16 into combat in Vietnam when it clearly had problems jamming under rapid fire. It was promptly fixed, but many Vietnam veterans have very bitter memories of refusing to carry the new rifles and even opting to carry an AK-47 made by the Communists. Or you have equipment designed by committee, which is what most people think happened with the F-111, which was supposed to be an advanced fighter-bomber that each service could use. Instead it turned out to be entirely too heavy to operate off of U.S. Navy aircraft carriers and also too heavy to serve as a fighter with the U.S. Air Force. Fortunately once everyone gave up any hope of the F-111 being a fighter, it served as a very competent bomber starting in 1968 and then in the raid on Libya in 1986, before dropping more tonnage of bombs during the Gulf War than any other aircraft. Nicknamed the Aardvark, it also serves with the Royal Australian Air Force and was retired officially in 2010.

That being said, I was always taken aback or sincerely shocked by the complete lack of cooperation between the different services of foreign militaries. The two times I deployed to Norway for Operation Battle Griffin, I was amazed when the Norwegian ground troops would tell us how happy they were that Marine ANGLICO were located with them to call in air strikes as the Norwegian air force virtually refused to provide close air support. I guess like all fighter pilots they wanted to launch deep penetration raids to keep the Russians at bay or had dreams of streaking through the skies seeking Mig fighters to destroy, all the while not helping out their fellow Norwegians on the ground. This is especially frustrating and surprising because the Norwegian air force flew the excellent F-16 Fighting Falcon purchased from the United States and manufactured by General Dynamics.

One of my personal favorite encounters with a member of a foreign military was in 1996 during my first hop to Norway. We were getting organized to deploy out into the field and had all of our tents set up in a small camp with some Marine recon teams. A one-star Marine brigadier general who was about 6-foot-7 was wandering around examining each Marine's personal gear, and he seemed to be enjoying himself. For a general the size of an NFL defensive end, he was actually a pretty nice guy. Also there were foreign troops and officers walking around everywhere. Since we were in a foreign area near the battle's area of operations, I think that saluting officers had been suspended, which is what you do in a combat situation because an enemy sniper will instantly spot who is being saluted and place a high-velocity round into their head. I had just finished breakfast at the chow hall when a foreign officer stopped me to ask me directions. I couldn't read the rank insignia on his shoulders as he was from Sweden, but I assumed he was a pilot of some sort as he was looking for the staff of Marine Air Group 42, which is based just outside of Atlanta, Georgia. We jumped with them on dozens of occasions. They were good pilots and crews and we had a great relationship with them. In Marine Corps slang a Marine air group is referred to by its initials M-A-G, or the word *mag* as if you're referring to the magazine of an automatic weapon or a magazine lying on your coffee table at home. Here's the problem.

This particular Swedish pilot was the exact same height as me, and we were standing face to face in the snow. With his short hair, the beret he wore on his head, his big blond bushy mustache, and of course his thick Swedish accent, the image was crystal clear in my head: Oh my God! It's the Swedish chef from the *Muppets*! Now I don't think I'm a good enough writer to accurately describe the Swedish accent of a man looking for "MAG Forwtee Twooo," but like any American who's ever seen the *Muppets*, and quite frankly who the hell hasn't, all I was thinking was "Bork, Bork, Bork, Bork, Bork!" (Beaker's my favorite, but that's for another book.)

I was in serious trouble and I knew it. Because no matter what the man asked me, I was doing everything in my power not to burst out laughing. This would be bad. Very bad. Commissioned officers in foreign nations are frequently if not usually connected to very powerful families, be it due to wealth, privilege, or a two-hundred-year tradition of serving in their nation's military. For example, in many Arab nations essentially the entire officer corps are blood relatives of the royal family. Saudi Arabia is a prime example of this.

Needless to say, I wasn't too thrilled with the prospect of my mom sitting at home back in Palm Beach County, Florida, only to pick up the local newspaper and read the headline "Local Marine Gets into Fight with Member of Sweden's Royal Family." I don't think it would take her too long to figure out who the idiot was that got into a fistfight with King Carl Gustaf's little brother.

Now don't get me wrong, this particular officer was being perfectly professional, polite, and just flat-out nice. So I certainly didn't want to offend the man by explaining to him that I was doubled over in laughter because he reminded me of a puppet. Again that would be bad. Very bad. I hate to say it, but in a moment of sheer panic, Mr. tough guy gold wing paratrooper pointed at a building and said, "I think it's over there Sir!" Then I took off running through the snowy pines laughing like a madman. And I didn't stop running until I was well away from the chow hall so this Swedish pilot couldn't find the dumb-ass Marine who didn't know what he was talking about. Namely, me.

Foreign militaries didn't always have it so good. Rick Taylor was a communications tech in 4th ANGLICO while I served in the comm shack before being assigned to the line platoons for the second half of my career in West Palm Beach. Rising through the ranks from private and retiring as a warrant officer, Taylor was a firefighter in the civilian world, and like many of the communications technicians we had, he was highly offended by improper procedure of any kind. Taylor once told me a story about deploying to serve with the Spanish military, where he was stationed on a Spanish naval vessel for a few days, and how shocked he was to learn how they treated their enlisted personnel.

When I was traveling by rail through Spain, the particular train I was on was stopping at each station, and I felt like I was in a scene from an American World War II movie as families were sending their teenage sons off to enlist in the army. Little Spanish brothers and sisters were frantically waving goodbye to their older brothers while the mothers wept and the fathers tried to stand tall and proud for the rest of their families. It was a very moving thing to witness. When I spoke to one young man who was in my railcar and spoke a bit of English, he made it perfectly clear: If you're a male, as soon as you turn eighteen, you're out of there and off to boot camp.

In some nations that have drafts, their enlisted ranks are a captive audience and they don't feel the need to treat them particularly well. This is exactly what Taylor saw when he told me that some of the enlisted quarters on the ship had standing water in their berthing areas. At the time Taylor was probably a sergeant and couldn't pull rank on anybody much less on a foreign naval vessel, but that didn't prevent him from essentially freaking out. He told his Spanish counterpart in no uncertain terms that his Marines were not going to billet in such filthy conditions, and if I remember correctly, he even got the Spanish sailors to temporarily improve the living quarters of the enlisted sailors around Taylor and his FCT team. Just as when he saw Marines not using our radios or antennas correctly, Taylor, like any good tech, would flip the hell out and correct everyone on the spot until a senior Marine told him to chill the hell out. On that day with the Spanish navy, he did the same thing to make life a little bit better for the enlisted ranks.

There's yet another aspect of Marine ANGLICO that never seems to go away, and that is the subject of what liaison actually means. To me it's a functional part of our job since by default we work with other military units that aren't the Marine Corps, whether foreign or American. Just before I got out in 1999, the rumors of the active duty ANGLICO companies being deactivated became fact with the abolishment of 1st and 2nd ANGLICO. There were plenty of stories flying around: The current commandant of the Marine Corps hated us, we cost too much money to maintain with all of our airborne gear, we had no political power in Washington, D.C., because we were so small and misunderstood, or they were tired of us strutting around like we owned the joint. 1st and 2nd were supposed to be replaced by units called Marine liaison companies or MLCs. For a couple of years, the Marine Corps had been asking all of its units which Marines had language capabilities of any kind, as they were seeing more work with foreign nations after the end of the Cold War. I thought this made perfect sense, but what did it have to do with us? The Marine liaison companies changed their name to Marine liaison elements and were supposed to work as coordinators and connectors between a

Marine expeditionary force, which is the staff of an entire Marine division, and any neighboring foreign units. Again this is perfectly valid work, but has nothing to do with Marine ANGLICO. We constantly are in contact with the units that we are supporting and we pass relevant information up to higher authorities at the battalion and regimental levels, but we still are the ones who actively call in air strikes, artillery, mortars, and naval gunfire. I saw Marine liaison elements or MLEs and Marine ANGLICO as apples and oranges. Presently Marine commanders are using MLEs to interact with Special Operations command, and that's a great development. But again, what does it have to do with me?

It just goes back to the never-ending confusion and misunderstanding about how to properly use a Marine ANGLICO company or detachment. Worrying over what the entire Special Operations command is doing, planning, or scheming is way over my pay grade and most likely none of my business anyway. But what do I care? Staff planning and liaison work with another division might create a mission for me and my Marines, but then it's up to us to get the job done. And quite frankly if a Marine ANGLICO company is commanded by a lieutenant colonel who during wartime would be interacting with the commander of a U.S. Army division, why bring in another element for liaison when ANGLICO was already there? I saw it then and still do today as reinventing the wheel that Marine ANGLICO got rolling back during the Korean War. I also feel the same way about the advent of the JTAC when FACs and ANGLICO have been working in this capacity for decades. Naval gunfire was hardly used at all during the Iraq and Afghanistan wars, and that function seems to have been deemphasized by the other services—but not in the Marine Corps. With the newer emphasis on the Pacific Ocean and the Chinese projection of power, U.S. Navy destroyers will become more and more important over the next several years. And if you have destroyers, that means naval gunfire, and that means you need naval gunfire spotters. I'm quite sure someone will try to readjust the already-existing naval gunfire fire support efforts that have been around since World War II.

For present generations the term "stormtrooper" instantly conjures images of all-white imperial legions fighting to control the galaxy for

George Lucas's evil emperor and his black-clad henchman, Darth Vader. For older generations such as myself, stormtrooper had a much darker, and very real, meaning.

Stormtroopers were the shock troops of Adolf Hitler's crazed and homicidal Third Reich, which had real plans to conquer the entire world. Most Americans don't know, but I've seen the historical maps of how the Nazis had actually drawn lines over maps of the United States and Central and South America, as if simply waving an evil hand in Berlin would make the world collapse before them.

In reality, *Sturmtruppen* were formed early in World War I as small assault teams to "storm" trench positions before a major attack. Part infiltration specialists and light infantrymen, Weimar-era stormtroopers were armed to the teeth with the first modern machine pistols, entire sacks full of hand grenades, and, near the end of World War I, the world's first submachine guns. In their first large-scale attack during Operation Michel in 1918, as a massive artillery barrage of more than three million shells ceased fire, stormtroopers overwhelmed key points in the Allied line, creating holes for following troops. Literally a *half a million* German soldiers flooded through the gaps torn open by the stormtrooper raiding parties.

As the Nazis rose to power in the 1920s and '30s, many veterans who were stormtroopers from World War I banded together for political power and protection. Many, if not most, gravitated to scheming, scar-faced pedophile Ernst Rohm and his *Sturmabteilung* (Storm Battalion), commonly called the "S.A." Rohm gained massive power in the Third Reich, sending his "brown shirts" to rough up communists, labor party members, teachers, Jews, or anyone else for that matter.

After World War II, stormtroopers were usually grouped together with terms such as "Hitler Youth," "Gestapo," "goose steppers," or the above-mentioned "brown shirts." It was always applied to someone you hated who was "marching in and trying to take over everything," whether a business, personal relationship, or, most likely, a political situation. It was an easy and brutally effective insult that would take the wind out of nearly anyone's sails, as no one wanted to be associated with the Nazis and their murderous behavior. Today, a quick Internet image search results in page after page of photographs of the white-armored stormtroopers from *Star Wars*, which is obviously much more positive than visions of Nazi thugs walking through quaint German towns looking for Jews to beat to the ground.

After this short history of the word "stormtrooper," you can imagine how shocked I was to hear someone describe not only U.S. Marines, but my 4th ANGLICO buddies as stormtroopers. Not surprisingly, the story came from old 1st Sergeant Nicolls of big bust–building fame from our Mountain Warfare training cycle back in '94. I also didn't expect to hear a 1980s story of ANGLICO being stuck in a barn for more than a week, because yet another military unit, American, NATO, or otherwise, didn't have a clue on what to do with ANGLICO.

As I've mentioned several times, there are several recurring themes in Marine ANGLICO: Other Marines either don't know what the hell we do or hate our guts for doing it; the U.S. Army thinks we're Greek or Italian and don't know what the hell we do; giant heavy batteries are the scourge of our daily lives; and almost everyone I've interviewed for the book has a story of being stranded somewhere due to some clueless commander. With the stormtrooper story, we again come back to 1st Sergeant Nicolls on a NATO exercise way back in the 1980s. Assigned to a German armor unit somewhere in Europe, Nicolls and Master Gunnery Sergeant Mize, our coin-flipping Vietnam veteran, were introduced to the regimental commander, a very old-school German colonel.

"Vhat is zis?" Colonel Klink demanded. "I didn't order any stormtroopers!"

And with that the old colonel stomped off never to be seen again. At first I didn't know what Nicolls was talking about. As I wrote about above, to me stormtrooper is *not* a good way to be described, much less by a German.

"Stormtroopers? Who's he talking about? Us? Marines? Stormtroopers?" I asked.

"Yes! We didn't even get a chance to explain what we do," Nicolls told me more than two decades after the event.

"So what did you guys do?" I asked.

"Easy. We found a local farmer's barn, staged all of our gear, and slept there for the next ten days," he said.

During the Cold War, NATO forces (the North Atlantic Treaty Organization formed to counter the Soviet threat to Europe) staged military exercises all the time. Simulated battles took place all over Europe with NATO officials dutifully following along to negotiate with irate farmers, homeowners, and ranchers after a tank or armored vehicle plowed across their farmland or smashed through a fence chasing after the "bad guys." NATO officials routinely took out their checkbooks and cut checks on the spot. It's crazy, but true. But it's also crazy that U.S. Marines were sent from West Palm Beach, Florida, to train on the European mainland, but instead got paid to sleep in a German barn.

Though I keep using my experience from JRTC with the 101st Airborne Division's scouts as a prime example of how to use an ANGLICO FCT team, it was also a last-minute decision. The scouts had no idea what to do with us, but being good scouts, they were quick on their feet and realized that we could watch their backs as they ran around Indian country looking for bad guys. We made our assignment up just as Nicolls had in the '80s; ours was just productive and not a waste of talent.

While present-day staff sergeant Teddy Pernal was making me digital copies of his photographs from four combat tours in Iraq and Afghanistan, I of course peppered him with questions of what, where, and how'd you feel. After all, a writer's job *is* to ask stupid questions. One photo showed him so frustrated at the end of a combat mission that he was walking around without a helmet on while still in the field. Another showed him staring at the rear seat of a Humvee plastered with little pockmarks from the roadside bomb that wounded two Marines, including my old teammate Joe Macantee. Pernal was in the rear seat pointing a squad automatic weapon out the window for security when the bomb went off. Humvees these days have 2-inch-thick armored glass for protection. Pernal had the window rolled down and still wonders why he wasn't hit by shrapnel. The blast pattern can be clearly seen spreading from the road surface up to the roof turret that housed the machine-gunner. It reminded me of the damage you see in World War II photographs, mainly of the old P-47 Thunderbolt fighter-bombers that pilots used to attack ground targets over France and Germany. Countless times the tough-ass Thunderbolts brought our boys home after suffering damage just like Teddy's Humvee.

Now, back to the being "dropped off in some godforsaken place" theme of this chapter. Another picture showed Pernal sitting next to a large cargo plane, broken down with no wings or engines. The surrounding area was strewn with rocks like the surface of Mars and as flat as a pool table. Desolate doesn't begin to describe the scene. The wrecked aircraft was about the size of an American C-130 Hercules, but it was foreign and I asked what the picture showed.

"That was at an abandoned airfield that C-130s use for emergencies. It was about 4 miles from the Iranian border," Pernal told me. "We were there about a week."

"If there's nothing there, why was your team there?" I asked.

"They wanted us to control the incoming and departing aircraft," Pernal said.

I was truly stupefied. Of all of the oddball, last-minute, crazy, and flat-out dumb ideas I've experienced or heard about how to use Marine ANGLICO, this was far and away the most bizarre.

"So, NOW WE'RE AIR TRAFFIC CONTROLLERS?" I virtually yelled at Teddy. "Just because we have big radios and know how to actually talk to a pilot?"

"We were that week," he dryly responded.

Talk about the same old song and dance. Time and again for this book, I held my tongue in order not to put words in Marines' mouths. But I kept hearing about the same types of incidents. Now don't get me wrong, Pernal is a remarkably well-trained and combat-experienced Marine who I'm sure did a banner job, but there's a world of difference between staff officers "staying flexible" and just making shit up. Air traffic control in the middle of the Iraqi desert? If you can see to the horizon, how much ground control does a pilot need? Well gee, Scott, you've never done air traffic control before so how would you know? Exactly! Why put me there?

CHAPTER SIXTEEN

Going Gold and Getting Pinned

I'm not one to say "aghast" too often. But that's how people react when I tell them about getting "pinned" in the Marines. The American Heritage Dictionary defines "aghast" as "being struck by terror or amazement." Yep, that's the word for what happens when they pin on the Gold.

And by "pin on the Gold," I mean just that: The metal wings with quarter-inch spikes are shoved into your chest and reinforced with a swift punch right on top.

After I waited two years to go to Jump School, it took about ten months of the right combination of jumps to reach Goldwinger status over several training sessions. I completed the jump that would make me eligible for Goldwinger status, then finished the required complete cleaning of all gear and weapons and went looking for two other Marines who "went Gold" that same day. In the 1990s, 4th ANGLICO always had a beer bash just after a monthly drill and the Goldwingers would hold a ceremony when warranted. If someone was going to hit me, I wanted a full ceremony.

It goes like this: You're stood up against a wall or tree and the first Marine removes the little shell backs from your wings, shoves the spikes into your left pectoral muscle, and firmly seats it with his best punch. From the first hit, Marines were re-bending my new gold wings due to the force of the punches. We had a wood-frame mock-up of a Marine Corps aircraft complete with cables, doors, and ramps to rehearse each jump. Each "hitter" would pull my wings out of my chest, straighten the quarter-inch posts on an exposed two-by-four that was part of the faux aircraft, and then *whack*, right back where they came from: my chest.

So, your gold wing ceremony recipe is as follows:

Insert wings into chest
Hit wings as hard as you can
Shake hand
Say: "Congrats, you're one of us now"
Next guy: pulls out wings, re-bends on wall, inserts into chest, punch!
Repeat forty or fifty times or as needed until done.
The battering ram
You pin yourself, then hit your own wings with combat helmet ten
    times
Goldwinger song

My ceremony was fun. Painful, but fun. It was a rite of passage into a different part of the Marine Corps. If you wanted to be a jumpmaster and control operations, learn how to pack chutes, or transfer to Force Recon and learn high-altitude jumping, each required being a Goldwinger. The battering ram was especially funny and a complete surprise. One of the jumpmasters put a Kevlar combat helmet on his head and six other Marines picked him up, tipped him over, and lined up to hit my wings with his head. Gunny Walsh moved me into position at the end of the aircraft mock-up and gave me some fatherly advice with a Bud can in his hand.

"Here's a clue: when they ram into your chest, LET GO!" he yelled with a laugh.

Just as promised, they rammed me out of the back door and I went flying. Gunny Todd pinned me once more for good measure and passed me a helmet while he poured some beer on the little holes in my chest. Ten strikes by my own hand and then my mates even sang me a song:

Here's to brother Goldwinger, brother Goldwinger, brother Goldwinger
    Here's to brother Goldwinger who's with us tonight.
    He's happy, he's jolly, he ain't shit by golly,
    Here's to brother Goldwinger who's with us tonight.

So DRINK motherfucker, DRINK motherfucker,
DRINK motherfucker, DRINK!
Here's to brother Goldwinger who's with us tonight!

I never resented anyone who pinned me and never had a Marine who I pinned hold it against me. In fact, it bound us together for even tougher things to come over the next several years, even in peacetime.

Walsh and von Heel hit the hardest. Corp. Kenny von Heel was a lanky Recon Marine who'd come to us after plenty of field time including the Gulf War. His years of patrolling mixed well with ANGLICO's fire support knowledge. GySgt. Mike Walsh was a veteran paratrooper who'd started as a radio technician. Since communications are central to anything ANGLICO did, Walsh was ruthless with young Marines who didn't transmit radio signals properly. Walsh was a very patient, intelligent, and thoughtful teacher of military communications. But once he was done teaching and training, either you did it right or he lit you up like the Fourth of July right in front of your grandma.

Everyone thinks that a muscle-bound guy can hit hard, but that's not always true. If he's not loose, he can only cock his fist back to his shoulder. However, Walsh and von Heel were both tall, thin, and with long arms. When these two cocked back to swing, their right fist started moving out by the airport and hit my chest-implanted gold wings just below the sound barrier.

To show how important the ceremony was to us, von Heel had been busy standing duty as NCO of the day. He actually apologized to me for being late and missing my ceremony.

"I would've given you a solid welcome with my right fist," he told me as he shook my hand.

"Hell, I'm still standing aren't I?" I said.

"Well, in that case, stand right up against this wall," he blurted out with a grin.

He almost made my knees buckle, but he handed me his beer. It was similar to the pledge pin scene in *Animal House* with less beer, but more violence.

Rank didn't protect you. I've hit staff NCOs and officers who outrank the hell out of me. You're an officer? Too bad, you're Airborne now. We jump together, we fight and die together.

"Welcome to the club, sir, BAM! Do you need another beer, Captain?" I would ask.

Don't think I'm exaggerating. I'm not. Not everyone was up to it. I got hit by every rank from lance corporal to major. Snipers, fighter pilots, Recon, scouts, comm guys, Navy corpsmen, Motor T ruffians, and Cobra gunship drivers: Most I liked, a few I didn't, but we were all in it to win it.

Some wore a special white T-shirt that each "hitter" autographed. I didn't need that, but I had what no one could take from me: gold wings, Marines who would always be on my side, and jungle boots laced with parachute cord. But most importantly, going Gold meant you had to be a cut above in everything you did. As one Marine Corps inspector spit out after discovering substandard paperwork during an armory inspection of our M16s and Beretta pistols: "I can't wait to talk to this peckerwood. Goldwinger? If he has time to jump out of planes, he's got time to do paperwork!"

The gunny was right. You had to be better.

I know plenty of you are thinking, who cares about a piece of metal? That's easy: You do. Americans all have their own gold and silver they covet and work toward. Gold is the color of Oscars, Tonys, and Emmys. Silver is the metal of choice for the Lombardi Trophy in football and the Stanley Cup for hockey fans. How many of us *don't* own shiny jewelry or watches given by family and friends or bought as a sign of achievement? We were the same with our pursuit of gold jump wings, and we couldn't just go out and buy them. My buddies and I knew we had a rare opportunity that most Marines simply never get. We weren't about to pass on it.

After all, combat training is a deadly serious affair. Even in peacetime, troops die in accidents. After little sleep over three days, lugging radios in my pack, two parachute jumps, throwing live hand grenades, sleeping on a concrete runway, and then cleaning and turning in weapons and classified gear, getting pinned was the good stuff.

After all of that, someone rolled me off the flatbed of a pickup truck to spend the night at Mom's house in Delray Beach. At the time I was living in Gainesville, writing and taking classes at the University of Florida. The next day I drove 300 miles home and rejoined society with no one the wiser that Marine ANGLICO even existed. To this day my mom knows more about ANGLICO than virtually everyone in the world.

Six years later I reached another long-term professional goal, which was deploying to Norway. Everyone in the U.S. military loves to travel and the Marine Corps has been training with the Norgees since the 1980s, but Norway is still a cherry deployment to go on. The scenery is incredible, it was the first and still only time I made it into the Arctic Circle, which few Americans can claim, but most importantly, the Norwegian people are incredible to us.

I've already written how every American who meets a Norwegian anywhere in the world should adopt them for the day in return for their treatment of U.S. Marines and Navy corpsmen. We had completed our two-week fight with the Germans and Dutch Marines and were enjoying some well-earned liberty with the locals, especially after Major Fernandez had relocated us to the indoor soccer facility in the little village of Bjerkvik. The townsfolk took to us in an instant and we hit the bars, restaurants, and clubs with a vengeance, with Norwegian women, and men, in tow. They all had a million questions about the United States and we had a million more about Norway. Is college really free? Why is gasoline so damn high? What do you mean the Gulf Stream comes up here? What's it like in the summer? I found it hilarious that every Norwegian had one question that was the same: "Why are all of the Marines always hanging out by the water?" they asked with very puzzled looks on their faces.

"Because we're Marines! We come from the water! Don't you remember World War II in the Pacific with all the island fighting?" I'd respond.

This seemed to satisfy them, but they still thought we were all loveable knuckleheads just the same. Now how this fits in with a chapter on gold jump wings, I'll tell you right now. The wings I was pinned with were called your "blood wings" for obvious reasons. For the last six years since my own gold wing ceremony, I owned only one pair of gold wings. I wore them whenever I wore one of my uniforms. They were solid brass, and if I needed to wear my dress blues at the Birthday Ball or a friend's wedding, I took them off, made them shine brilliantly with Brasso, and mounted them according to current uniform regulations. I had no doubt about taking them with me 150 miles inside the Arctic Circle. They were as integral to my service as my military ID or my Parris Island dog tags, which I had swiped from my service record book when an admin clerk wasn't looking.

One crazy night in Bjerkvik, after closing every tiny bar in our new tiny town, we walked to the home of one of our newly found Norgee buddies. I can't mention his name because I haven't seen him since, but to be completely honest, Norwegian can be a nearly impossible language to pronounce on your first exposure. One of our drivers during my 1999 deployment to southern Norway told us flat out the first day to call him by his nickname, "Radar." We thought it had something to do with the iconic American television show, which was obviously shown around the world for years and years. However, he was a decent-looking nineteen-year-old kid who didn't look anything like actor Gary Burghoff, who we all grew up watching and laughing with. But we wanted to be good guests and insisted he tell us his real name. Plus, after kicking commie/terrorist ass in combat, Marines are always about Miss Aretha's R-E-S-P-E-C-T. No way were we going to spend almost three weeks with our new driver and not use the name his parents gave him. Gunny Henry, Macantee, and I pressed him for the big reveal.

"Trust me, you can't pronounce it," Radar flatly told us, which only ignited our jarhead sense of competition.

"Come on, Radar, tell us your name," we said.

Well, Radar was right. His first name, I think, was spelled Radr, and the second letter R had a rolling sound much like Spanish. We failed miserably.

"Radrrrrr," I said.

"No."

"Radarrar."

"No!"

We tried around ten times and took his advice: He was Radar and he wasn't offended at all. Plus, he was a damn good Bobcat Vehicle driver, the tracked little truck that we lived in for two weeks. Now back to the early-morning party in Bjerkvik, which was across the fjord from the fabled port city of Narvik.

Our host was a great guy whose name I couldn't pronounce no matter how much I tried, and he was simply a great party MC. He called his friends, they brought some girls with them, and we started sampling more of the local moonshine until around four in the morning. I was grooving on the local beer called Mack Ul, a pilsner in a pint glass that was my favorite. I was sitting on a couch with Troy Sutton, the corporal who tried to drown himself burning our code books just before Gunny Henry tried to run over the giant moose. Impressed with our host, I told Troy we should give him a gift of some sort, like one of our caps or a unit T-shirt. Usually very level-headed, Sutton hatched the genius plan of pinning him with one of our sets of gold wings.

"ARE YOU NUTS! Pin a foreign national? And a civilian on top of that?" I shouted.

I didn't want to cause a scene, but I quickly pulled some serious "I'm a sergeant and you're not" rank on his ass and that was the end of that crap, or so I thought. It came time for me to use the bathroom, and I handed my pint to Troy to hold, naively believing my hooch-swilling corporal would listen to me. I took my time in the bathroom, admiring the Norwegian wood finish, softly humming the Beatles song for the millionth time, as the beautiful pine was everywhere in Norway. Then I walked out and almost did something in my skivvies that I should've just done in the commode.

Pinned up against the wall was our gracious host with five 4th ANGLICO Marines pounding the hell out of the guy. He was a beefy bastard so it wasn't hurting too badly, and he was happily laughing his ass off. I was speechless. For those of you who don't know, the Marine Corps is a fierce down-to-the-individual organization. If you spot something wrong, you correct it on the spot or make a little plan for later. Woe to the Marine who didn't carry a pen and notebook to show a solution when a superior demands why you didn't "do something in that situation." What this meant for me was, since I was the senior Marine, it was my fault. No debate, no discussion, no football huddle or hugging it out to discuss our feelings. You're a sergeant; take care of it. That's the rule and it applies to every Marine down to the youngest private on fire watch at midnight.

Of course, in my beer-addled state, my logic was thus: "Well, if I'm going to get a court-martial for beating up Norwegian civilians, I might as well deserve it."

So I joined in myself, but it would be done the right way. If something went wrong or we had to take our host to the hospital, it would be all my fault anyway, so what the hell? After blasting Sutton with some choice profanity that I won't write here because my mom is going to read this book, I made my decision. Since I already had decided I wanted to reward our host's inherent Norwegian friendliness and we were already beating him on the chest, I opted for one of my prized possessions. I would give him my blood wings and be the first to give the old smackaroo. I explained to him what blood wings were and how few Marines have them. He was genuinely touched by the gesture, which I acknowledged by punching him hard enough to bend the wings almost in half. We maybe hit him five or six times, but we all had a great time and then really started to party. Not one of the Norwegian women so much as batted an eyelash at this admittedly ridiculous scene, probably because Norwegian women are also subject to the military draft in Norway and serve alongside the men on exercise and during training or natural disasters.

The party broke up around 5:00 A.M. and we walked back to our favorite indoor soccer field and flopped into our sleeping bags. We had all of our radios, weapons, and field gear packed up, ready to go, and under 24-hour guard so we didn't need to be up early the next morning. Today, getting "pinned" is strictly verboten in the Marine Corps and pinning a foreign civilian is inconceivable. I haven't seen any of these Marines since I got out in '99 and haven't contacted the man we pinned since 1996. I'm quite certain he still has my blood wings and maybe he'll be told about this book. After all, when I first signed up for Facebook, a Norwegian girl from my first Operation Battle Griffin found me and emailed for a while.

I wonder if she remembers that early-morning gold wing "ceremony." But then again, Norwegian women could be an entire chapter of their own. Bright, smart, pretty, and not afraid to defend their own nation, they give American women a run for their money.

And ANGLICO Marines always wonder why so many people think we're crazy!

CHAPTER SEVENTEEN

Motor T

THE ENTIRE TWELVE YEARS I SPENT IN 4TH ANGLICO IN WEST Palm Beach, Motor T (Marine slang for Motor Transport) was run by M/Sgt. Joe Vicente and his right-hand man, GySgt. Otis Henry, the moose-murdering driver from Battle Griffin '96 inside the Norwegian Arctic Circle. A Vietnam veteran whom I found very easy going as long as you acted right, Vicente held an iron grip on his Marines. Invariably two things happened during our final formation on any drill weekend: Motor T always, and I mean always, showed up last, but they marched in formation better than any other group. Tight, well-disciplined, no-nonsense, and ready to go. Me and my buddies in Comm could drill just fine, but we never stopped talking or getting yelled at by Gunny Walsh so we weren't too sharp. Too clever for our own good I guess.

In a normal Marine battalion, Motor T would be part of headquarters platoon, but again we weren't normal. We had so many vehicles—5-ton trucks, Chevy SUVs painted camo, white vans used for airport runs, and about fifty Humvees parked out back—and they all needed to be cared for, which is why 4th ANGLICO's Motor T section was so large. Since Comm and Motor T were right next to each other, we knew how hard they worked. In fact, I always felt Motor T was the hardest-working, knuckle-busting group we had. Until you've lent a hand changing the tire of a 5-ton truck, you haven't handled a wrench before my friend. It's called a 5-ton because that's how much it can carry, even on a dirt road in a Third World country. On a highway these beasts can hit 65 for 300 miles on each tank of diesel. Each tire was nearly 5 feet tall and was so heavy it wouldn't stand up straight on its own. Plus, the tire rim was in two parts, so you had to use a crowbar to rip off the old tire that was literally fused to the rim due to high pressure. I helped "bust tires" for a day and I couldn't believe how hard it was. I gladly went back to Comm and played with the radios and classified crpyto gear so I could feel like a fuzzy-headed James Bond again.

In the late 1990s the Motor T I&I was Sgt. Travis Smith, a North Carolina boy who loved NASCAR and fixing broken stuff. Smitty was responsible for one of the most original ideas I ever saw at 4th ANGLICO. Many times active-duty Marines would arrive in West Palm Beach expecting three years of easy duty on South Florida beaches. They quickly learned that 4th ANGLICO deployed Marines around the country and even the world almost every month. One benefit: We didn't have time to play little mind games that veterans complain about and cite as a primary reason for leaving the service. At 4th ANGLICO we had operations to go on, young Marines to teach, and a crap-ton of materiel, weapons, gear, and classified communications gear to get ready and maintain.

Country boy Smitty spotted this in a heartbeat. One too many times he saw Humvees come back from an operation worn out, broken, or sometimes just wrecked. Again, back to the "we're not normal" thing. When we supported the Army or a foreign military unit, the Marine driving the Humvees wasn't a Motor T guy. We weren't on base to get expert help, the operation was at fever pitch, and the Army didn't care one way or another. The driver was a scout/forward observer like myself, a radio operator, or, worse still, one of our officers who was used to flying F-18s and couldn't restrain himself.

"Hey, if I can land on a carrier, I can drive this damn thing . . ."

WHAM!

"What was that story about landing on the USS *Nimitz*, Captain?"

On active duty, getting a Humvee license was a two-day class driving around a huge parking lot on a huge base like Camp Lejeune. Smitty didn't have that luxury, so he went to his boss and asked for enough money to take five or so Marines from every section in 4th ANGLICO, drive out in the Florida muck, and spend two entire weeks teaching and torturing his new charges. I've seen the pictures. Smitty would drive a

Hummer into the black muck, spin the tires, and yank the steering wheel
left and right until the vehicle was buried up to the hood.

"OK, Carty, you're up! Get it out, and if you break it, you pay for it."

Then Smitty would go sit under a tree and watch while the drivers
ignored everything he taught them and worked themselves half to death
under the August sun of South Florida. But if you broke something,
Smitty made you pay. It just wasn't necessarily with cash. Humvees, for
a combat vehicle, have these terrible, screw-on, plastic fan blades to cool
the radiator, which are located at the front of the engine compartment, so
if you drive through water, it hits the blades immediately. Since Congress
awarded the Hummer fan contract to some campaign donor's idiot little
brother, the flimsy plastic blades snapped right off. When the Humvee
students drove into Smitty's swamp, it was readily apparent who listened
to the Great Smitherini and who didn't: They slammed into the 5-foot-
deep, pitch-black Florida muck and swamp water and promptly snapped
off each plastic blade. One: In the Marine Corps you're paying for this.
Two: At Smitty's Swampland of Humvee Mud and Mayhem, he made
you pay with a bit more creativity.

You, young and stupid Marine, are changing the fan yourself and
then running half-inch rope through the center hole of the busted fan
and wearing that around your neck for the rest of the school, which
means you spend nearly two weeks in the South Florida sun with the fan
belt albatross of stupidity chafing the back of your neck. Or in this case
the entire busted engine fan assembly hanging from a half-inch rope,
minus the plastic fan blades of course. Guess we should've paid attention
in class, huh?

By this time I had moved back to South Florida from Gainesville
and was a staff writer at a Broward County newspaper. For some reason I
stopped by the unit and was walking to the Comm section to say howdy,
when a Marine named Michael Bourre from our section stopped cleaning the black muck from his Hummer and ran over to say hello to me.
There he was in all of his broken-fan, giant necklace glory and I thought
he'd lost his mind.

"What the hell are you doing, Bourre?" I asked in one of the more
confused moments in my life.

"Sergeant Smith makes us wear these if we hit the water too fast," he said with a smile. "Plus, I have to pay for it."

He told me the same story I just told you with the look of a child who's telling the "other" parent why they've spent their day locked in the garage for being such a colossal pain in the ass.

"So Smitty taught you not to drive like that?"

"Yes, Sergeant," Bourre said.

"Smitty even showed you first?"

"Yes, Sergeant."

"And you still did it anyway?"

"Yes, Sergeant."

"And for two weeks you wore that busted pig around your neck all the time?" I asked.

"Yes, Sergeant Messmore," he said.

I was thrilled.

I immediately tracked Smitty down and asked him how he'd come up with such a brilliant idea. You see, Marines love the idea of "you gotta pay" if you screw up. It can be really bad if you're a bad Marine (losing rank, a fine, another Marine beating your ass after work) or just hijinks meant to hammer home a lesson. I immediately tracked down the awesome Sergeant Smith and congratulated him on his great training methods, but also his attitude adjustment techniques, i.e., the fan belt albatross.

"How'd you come up with that? That's awesome!" I practically yelled at Smitty.

"Yeah, a few never listen, so I gotta reinforce it somehow. After that they never do it again," he said with a smile.

Smitty really did thrash his new drivers. A couple of communications Marines had run to Walgreen's to develop film and showed me pictures of Humvees buried up to the hood, Marines driving through water with the brackish fluid literally just below their chins, and a few of them actually dodging small fish swimming through the cab of the Humvee.

Here's the thing about *all* Marine Corps vehicles: Each one has an exhaust stack that reaches 60 inches above the ground. It looks like an old wooden stovepipe and allows our vehicles to drive through 5 feet of water with ease. Even fully loaded 5-tons can do this. It was one of the most frustrating things to watch television coverage of the Hurricane Katrina aftermath in New Orleans, when I knew perfectly well that 5-ton trucks and Humvees could drive in that flood water to bring in aid and take out survivors.

However, you can't just crash into even 3 feet of water and not expect to suffer damage, or worse lose control of the vehicle. Think of how many times you've watched the news and learned of a death during a flood somewhere in America. A lot of the time, some redneck tried to blast through some water in his truck, lost control, and drowned. Slow down, and I mean 3 miles an hour or less, keep your eyes open, both hands on the wheel, and you'll get through it. Or, just find another damn route. It's yet another little lesson that every time we take on Mother Nature, she tends to hand our ass to us on a silver platter. The following year I saw firsthand the fruits of Smitty's two-week drivers' school of death and destruction.

I had signed up for another detachment being deployed to JRTC, which the Army had relocated from Fort Chaffee, Arkansas, to Fort Polk, deep in the pine woods of northern Louisiana. We were given the usual assignment of providing naval gunfire support to a battalion of the Florida National Guard. It was June and hotter than hell with dust from tanks, Bradley Fighting Vehicles, 5-tons, Hummers, and even helicopters kicking up clouds of the stuff. I was designated as the team chief of an FCT team that would support a Guard company that would protect the battalion's main supply route or MSR. The main supply route is just that: the main route that carries the majority of the beans, bullets, and Band-Aids needed to keep any armed force on the move. It's also one hell of a target, so bad guys love to blow the shit out of MSRs. Think of all the IED attacks on U.S. and allied forces in Iraq. Exactly.

I found our host Florida Guard infantry company and reported to the first sergeant, a red-haired career man who quickly grasped what an ANGLICO team could do if properly employed. They were a Florida Guard infantry company from the Orlando area who nicknamed themselves the "Nasty Dogs." They had stenciled 10-inch "ND" logos on all of their vehicles and every other damn thing they owned, obviously in violation of Army regulations. They didn't give a damn and my team loved the crap out of it.

Since the first sergeant had bright red hair, his radio call sign was obviously "Red Dog" and his captain's call sign was naturally "Big Dog." Red Dog introduced me to Big Dog, who actually listened to what I had to say for once and promptly told me: "For the next two weeks, unless I'm sleeping or taking a shit, every time I turn around I expect to see your face," he said.

"Roger that, Skipper," I replied with a big grin.

This was a man who got Marine ANGLICO. I had used my converting 5-inch guns to artillery millimeters trick ("Twenty rounds a minute? Are you shittin' me?") and it worked like a charm. It worked so well that Red Dog unknowingly gave me the best compliment another service member ever gave this Marine.

JRTC is a massive, high-tech game of laser tag. Two-inch sensors called MILES gear are attached to everything. And I mean everything: me, you, the colonel, jet fighters, wandering sheep, helicopter gunships, and tanks, just everything. I never saw a service dog at Fort Polk, but I'm sure little Sparky would've been wired up too. The reason is, instead of shouting "you missed me" like a bunch of fourth graders playing cowboys and Indians, if someone's laser-tipped M-16 rifle hit you, the beepers went off and you were a combat casualty.

At JRTC each player in "the box," the 40-kilometer area where the battle rages for two weeks, carries a small envelope containing a "casualty card." When you got hit, the referees would grab your card, open it, and pronounce your "wound." It could be superficial, ugly, or killed in action, KIA. The U.S. Army did a good job of determining the usual ratios of wounded, missing, and killed during major combat operations. It's a fine job of using statistics to show the reality of the world and not what you want it to be. Unfortunately, defense contracting reared its ugly head.

As long as I've been associated with the military, American citizens have always complained, bitched, or flat out yelled at me for all the wasted spending at the Pentagon. Honestly folks, when a billion or two dollars are on the line, do you really believe big business, Congress, and everyone's greedy relative *doesn't* get involved? Here's the point: The casualty card brown paper envelopes were so poorly made, i.e., almost as thin as plastic wrapping for leftover food, all you had to do was bend the envelope and you could plainly read what would happen if you got "shot." We'd compare them and even trade them like baseball cards.

"Hey, I got shot in the ass!"

"Uh-oh, I'm a head wound!"

"Crap, I'm KIA no matter what I do. Why bother busting my ass?"

The best card of all was the RTD: return to duty. Even if you get caught in the open with an F-16 dropping a 2,000-pound bomb on your forehead, you walk away scot-free. No matter how many atom bombs land on your crotch, alligators bite your head off, or Andre the Giant chucks you off the Cliffs of Insanity, you get a free pass. Yep, a combat Get Out of Jail card and collect two hundred dollars to boot. It was another Army attempt to bring as much chaos to the situation, which is the hallmark of all combat. Chaos, the unknown, and what the hell do we do now?

Which brings us back to Red Dog, the Nasty Dog's crimson first sergeant. While I was preparing my team for the battle, Red Dog took receipt of roughly 230 casualty cards from the battle referees. After learning the power and glory of Marine ANGLICO, Red Dog proceeds to eyeball each card, bend it into the light (Hallelujah!) searching out the golden Willy Wonka RTD cards. He found them. I don't know how many, but the Red Dog knew where they were going.

Big Dog got one, you *know* Red Dog got his RTD, probably the three platoon commanders and a machine-gunner or two, and then he had four left.

"Here ANGLICO. Use them wisely," he told me.

"Yes, Red Dog," I said, already replacing his rank with his radio call sign.

Now understand this: Red Dog gave four U.S. Marines whom he met yesterday four golden tickets versus his own troops. I guess he felt our use of firepower could keep his boys alive when things got hot. As I said: It's still the best compliment I've gotten from another service member.

My driver was a young lance corporal named Eugene Baggett who everyone called "Deej." As team chief, a job that was supposed to be held by a captain and not a sergeant, I had to keep track of three battalions' schemes of maneuver, the locations of their units, and whom I could fire naval gunfire over. If I saw OPFOR troops trying to exploit the seam between two battalions, there is no way an Army lieutenant colonel is going to give clearance to some unknown jarhead on the radio trying to call in twenty rounds of high explosive from a Navy destroyer. It was a trying three weeks with denial after denial from battalion. Deej had taken Smitty's two-week Swampland mud bath and drove our comm truck like I'd never seen before.

Since we weren't firing NGF missions, we became the company commander's private bodyguards and fed intelligence to the SALT team and Division Cell. With our powerful MRC-138 comm Humvee, we could talk to anyone. Enemy Hind helicopter gunship streaking overhead? Blast off a message to higher-ups with the direction of flight. It was more of a Recon function, but what the hell? We always did the job at hand, which is why we trained in so many different topics back home in West Palm Beach.

One morning Big Dog asked us to ride shotgun security for some transportation soldiers who were running a mission to retrieve a wrecked Humvee. Three Army Hummers blasted off with us in fourth place armed and ready to shoot. We drove into a forested area with dozens of felled trees the size of small telephone poles. I've seen plenty of U.S. troops—way too many actually—with the attitude of "hey I didn't pay for it, I don't care if it breaks." It's a horrible, immoral, and unprofessional attitude you don't see as much in the Marine Corps. After all, we all pay taxes don't we? *You* own the vehicle! Why break it? This was a group of guys who had such an attitude. These guys, not our awesome Nasty Dogs I'll mind you, blasted over the fallen trees like they were driving in the Baja 1,000 with a $100,000 trophy truck dirt racer. Well, they weren't. I never thought you could break a Humvee without some sort of gunfire involved, but these guys were just more dedicated I guess. Instead of having one Hummer to retrieve, now we have two more: one with a broken axle and one with a busted drive shaft.

"How the hell do you break the axle of a Hummer?" I shouted at everyone within earshot.

They were embarrassed and wouldn't even look our way, as I put out my team on security, which is what Big Dog had asked me. I was furious, but mainly I was in a state of disbelief. I wasn't expecting to see a 60-ton

M1 Abrams battle tank flying across the pine tree tops, but that would've freaked me out too. But there were no such shenanigans with my driver. The man, the myth, the legend: the Deej.

Deej did precisely what Smitty taught him: This isn't a race. You're on your own, calm down and get it done. It's still one of the roughest rides I've ever been on. Rolling over multiple telephone pole–sized logs turned our comm truck into a bunking bronco. Everything that wasn't tied or bolted down, including us, was suspended in midair like the inside of an Apollo space module. I had slammed my Kevlar helmet on the center console in disgust. I can still see the vision of my 4-pound helmet suspended in midair after being launched after each vertical bounce. Deej kept focused on his 1-mile-an-hour road race and everything worked out great. The Army broke their Hummers; we didn't. The Great Smitherini had struck again.

CHAPTER EIGHTEEN

Code Name: Karen

AUGUST 13, 1998

Everything was a go. No one had ever expected to pick up a mission like this. For years every Marine and Navy corpsman in 4th ANGLICO had focused on becoming proficient in fire missions for artillery, naval gunfire, and calling in jet fighters or helicopter gunships to destroy enemy troops and weapons, most of which were designed and built in the former Soviet Union.

Then Hurricane Karen wasted the Big Easy and most of the shoreline towns of the Gulf states. Washington, D.C., hadn't had the brains to even consider using a full ANGLICO company after the disaster of Hurricane Andrew cutting through South Florida like a chainsaw in 1992. Taylor had always been disgusted about sitting around listening to news reports of looting, burning, and zero communications after Andrew.

"We could have blanketed the entire area with a radio network and kept Tallahassee and Washington informed with status reports from all the major areas of Dade County," Taylor thought to himself.

Is there rioting in downtown Miami? An FCT team posted on top of the old 50-story Centrust Building could observe the city for miles using high-powered, German-made Steiner binoculars to spot any unrest or smoking buildings. Handheld lasers could tell the exact range to the danger area. It would've been a snap: You could see rioters or a burning building through your binoculars and shoot a laser to a building next to it. With GPS and maps of the city, all you had to do was take a compass heading to the "target," draw a line from your position on your map showing the distance from the laser shot,

214

and "ta daa": There's your problem area. The city map would show it right at your fingertips: the Dade County Court House on Flagler Avenue. Of course! Criminals are trying to get their thug buddies out of the joint. Or burn their records, or whatever! Get someone over there!

Since we could have placed a heavy FCT team with up to twelve Marines to rotate shifts, our communications ability would've been enormous.

Look to the north and the American Airlines Arena has a large and growing crowd, but there's no rioting. Look to the east; there's no looting at Bayside and no smoke is rising from fires at South Beach in the distance. Look to the south and the skyscraper banks that line Brickell Avenue all seem to be ok. Probably because they hired former military to guard the big banks, but who cares? They're getting it done, aren't they? Looking west, it's a bit too far to see details from the Orange Bowl, but there's no rising smoke in that area. So far, so good. It's hotter than hell, but no hotter than any other South Florida summer.

What this obviously fictitious section is meant to illustrate is the capabilities of Marine ANGLICO and how simple it would be to shift gears to a non-combat scenario. We trained constantly on our communications gear: in the field, at night, in the rain, in the searing heat of South Florida, and freezing our butts off in Norway, Fort Drum near Syracuse, New York, or the Sierra Nevada of Mountain Warfare School in California.

The Hurricane Andrew incident is real and pisses me off to this day after nearly twenty-five years. I was living, writing, and working in Gainesville, Florida, 300 miles from the Reserve Center in West Palm Beach, and from time to time my car broke down. Of course, when you're in the Reserves, when your car breaks, it's right before drill weekend. I think it's in the Constitution between Freedom of Speech and the Right to Bear Arms, because it happens every time. I called in with enough prior warning to reschedule my drill time. The Marine Corps has a great policy in recognition of how far its Reserve Marines travel to drill each month and how dedicated they are. If you are excused by the proper person (in my case, my sergeant major), then you were fine and got proper credit and pay as long as you came in to serve within the 30 days before next drill. While I was on the phone, I asked if we were going south to help out in Miami. We weren't. I couldn't believe how dumb this decision, or lack thereof, was.

Here we were, 40 miles from, at the time, the worst natural disaster in U.S. history with two hundred U.S. Marines who are constantly trained to send message traffic and keep others informed of the present situation. An ANGLICO company has dozens if not hundreds of radios that cover the UHF, FM, HF, and VHF spectrum of radio frequencies and the newer models all have an internal SATCOM function. The mission, and Marines, can switch tasks in an instant. Sitting in Iraq with three pickup trucks full of terrorist idiots speeding down the road toward a United Nations checkpoint? Get on your HF radio and call in a fire mission to wipe them out in the blink of an eye. Are you a lone lance corporal sitting on a 50-story resort hotel rooftop in downtown New Orleans in 2005 and spot a large group of ugly sorts walking south on St. Charles Avenue toward the Garden District? Pick up the handset for the FM radio to alert the local authorities and order the PFC next to you to use the HF radio to alert the SALT team, which will instantly relay the message to the Division Cell at Camp Shelby around 100 miles away. Obviously, the Division Cell is sitting in a very large room or tent with at least one representative from FEMA, Homeland Security, the FBI, DEA, Customs, each branch of the U.S. military, the Pentagon, White House, and maybe even the governor of Louisiana. Remember the story I told about the OPFOR C-130 full of paratroopers flying directly over my FCT team's position at JRTC in '95? As soon as I sent that report over the HF net, everyone in my chain of command knew a paratroop attack was going down in real time. If the Division Cell really has their crap together, they wouldn't need a report from the SALT team, as they would be listening to each FCT team's transmission twenty-four hours a day. There is no excuse, then or now, for the way the government handled Hurricane Andrew, and the complete lack of information coming out of New Orleans after Hurricane Katrina, and the media also has a large share of the blame.

In short, this is what I want: ANGLICO FCT teams with up to twelve Marines for three eight-hour shifts stationed on selected roof-tops of very tall civilian buildings with clear views of any disaster area, especially the downtown business district, airports, and any officially designated refugee/evacuee centers. Second, battalion-level SALT teams should be placed to monitor all of its assigned FCT teams and relay information to higher headquarters to include the commanding general, governor's office, and also the civilian leadership in Washington, D.C., be it the Pentagon, White House, or both. Not only is this entirely feasible, it was possible in the 1970s. Retired first sergeant and wild man Parks Nicolls put me in my place when I told him my best radio shot was with a PRC 104 high frequency radio. On paper a 104 has a 300-mile range and that's when it's tested under optimum conditions. I performed one solitary radio check from Fort Benning, Georgia, 750 miles back to West Palm Beach, Florida. Nicolls countered with a story from the 1980s when he built a long-range antenna to make a radio check with MacDill Air Force Base in Tampa, Florida, from Sardinia. You know, the little island off the coast of Italy? Radio waves do funny things, bouncing off the ionosphere and thermal gradients, but a 6,000-mile radio shot is unreal and SATCOM had not even reached the field yet back then.

Ideally, the federal government would already have a signed agreement with the owners of the tall or critical buildings our FCT teams would occupy. It isn't too hard to determine which sections of the country are disaster prone and what type of calamity you'll be facing when you get there. Lake effect snow doesn't hit Florida; that's Chicago, Cleveland, and Buffalo. Hurricanes don't bother Tornado Alley too often, and raging fires or mudslides mostly go after California, not New England and its nor'easters.

My thinking for a mission to New Orleans would be as follows. I would be leading eleven other scout/forward observers and radio operators into a situation with minimal threat of violence as we would be very elevated, and if I can avoid it, I'd rather not be spotted. Panic-stricken refugees would never cease trying to get our attention, and we couldn't communicate in any way with them, which would only serve to anger them about any rescue efforts. In short, angry, hungry, thirsty refugees are primed to start a riot.

If we're lucky and the Feds found a building with a heliport, the pilot could place my team right on target. The first four Marines charge down the ramp of the helicopter, move off the heli pad, drop their backpacks, and perform an armed sweep of the rooftop. Who knows who might be up there? Looters can be ingenious in how they gain access to homes and buildings. If we find any, kick them downstairs, and let the police scoop them up after they've had a fun time walking down fifty flights of stairs.

The second four Marines, including myself, exit the helicopter, run off the pad, and immediately turn on our radio equipment to make contact with higher-ups and send our first status report. The last four Marines will remove the crapload of gear we brought to live in our sun-baked island in the sun for the next week.

The presently outdated high-frequency radio that I operated for twelve years, the PRC 104, was a true man-packed system, as all of our radios were. That means that they could operate on batteries only and already had an amplifier to boost the radio signal. When you turned a 104 on, it spent sixty seconds tuning to the radio frequency you had punched in. During this one-minute tuning process, it made a steady pinging sound in the handset that could be heard by anyone who was monitoring that frequency. This would be a good sound to the Division Cell 100 miles away in Camp Shelby. They know what time my team is going to insert, as they created the plan and all of the timelines. If I'm set to land at dawn, which the Louisiana Department of Wildlife and Fisheries lists at 5:37 A.M. on your typical September 1st morning, then within five minutes the Division Cell is expecting to hear all three of my 104 sets start pinging away. To them that means "he's there, he's down, the security team has already run their sweep, he's setting up comm, and the last group is unloading the helicopter." And the Marines I served with, such as Gunny Walsh, would be staring at their watches fully expecting me to start speaking at sixty-one seconds. The pinging stops and I start.

"Lightning one-one, Lightning one-one, this is Lightning one-three, radio check, over," I would call.

"One-three, this is One-one. I read you Lima Charlie. What is your status, over?"

Lima Charlie is Marine radio slang for "loud and clear." Most people think that's just military jargon, but it isn't. It's two separate issues. If you and your buddy are back at base testing radios, usually you'll stand a couple of hundred feet away and send silly little messages back and forth. If a radio is malfunctioning, say you can only hear every third word, but the signal is very loud because your friend is just across the way, then he's "loud but broken." If he's too far away or his battery is dying (usually the case) but you can understand him, then he's "weak but readable." Radio keywords are essential because they save valuable time on a radio network. A large net could have dozens of people trying to speak at the same time, and in combat, getting shot at just makes things worse. Think of the wasted time if I transmitted that I'm fine, Johnson's fine, Rodriguez is fine, etc., on down the line and then listed all of our equipment. Unless I drop all of our food off the side of the building, it's a given that the MREs are doing just fine snuggled in their cardboard boxes. Meanwhile, other teams are trying to check in at the same time.

Just like a quarterback shouting out play calls at the line of scrimmage, one word can mean a lot. During my time at 4th ANGLICO, for some reason we had a preference for American automakers while other units preferred colors. If I transmit just one word to describe a situation, I won't be tying up the radio net with too much traffic. It takes a ton of practice, just like the NFL, but it can be just that simple. After the helicopter lifts off, I send my second message:

"Lightning one-one, this is one-three, Buick moving on to Ford, how copy."

"One-three, I copy Buick and Ford. Out."

Buick: We're here with all the gear and all OK. Ford: we're establishing security, setting up all the radio nets, conducting proper radio checks with our SALT and other teams, and then setting up the tarps and ponchos for protection from the sun. Two words and everyone's on the same sheet of music. It's a thing of beauty.

And what a pile of gear we would bring if it was up to me. Each Marine would have full combat equipment with an M-16 rifle with six magazines of live ammunition. I would also bring at least one M-16 with an M203 grenade launcher slung underneath the barrel, not to fire high-explosive rounds, but to fire tear gas grenades at any rioters threatening us plus star shell rounds for nighttime illumination. Smoke rounds would be helpful to direct helicopters to rescue landing zones in the immediate area of our building.

For twelve Marines spending seven days on any post requires quite a bit of food and water. At three meals per day, that's 252 meals in twenty-one cases weighing 12 pounds per case. At least seventeen 5-gallon jerry cans full of water would be needed for a minimum of 1 gallon of water per Marine for each day, and most likely would require resupply around day five. Anyone who's ever been through a hurricane can well attest that the days just after the storm have gorgeous blue skies, but it's hotter than Hades outside. With water and MREs alone weighing nearly 1,000 pounds and very bulky, I would split them between two wooden pallets; one pallet could easily handle the weight, but they would probably be stacked too high for safety on only one pallet. Twenty-one cardboard boxes of our MREs with our long-range antennas placed on top would work fine after the aircrew attached the nets to the pallet.

After all, the antennas are two of the main reasons we would be frying like eggs on top of a New Orleans hotel. As described in the communications chapters, antennas that don't move too often have a very nasty habit of being seriously blown the hell up after the enemy pinpoints your location. But we're not moving for seven days, and there's no enemy, so it's going to be great to use two separate 30-foot antennas 50 stories in the air. However, another heavy item we'll need are sandbags, just like in the World War II movies. Out in the field, troops can set up their tents, ponchos, or even antennas with metal stakes just like your family uses when you go camping. On top of a resort, that won't be happening. I don't think your typical billionaire is going to be too happy when he turns on the evening news to monitor the rescue effort he's proud to be a part of, only to see a dozen U.S. Marines swinging sledgehammers as they drive metal stakes into the roof of his beloved Crescent City pleasure palace.

With two portable antennas sporting four guy wires each, and some type of anchoring device needed to secure each Marine's poncho to cover their sleep area, I'd call that around fifty sandbags weighing 25 pounds apiece. Also, if we had them, I would insist on old-school fold-out cots for my Marines to sleep on. I slept in and on some strange surfaces during my time with the Marine Corps, including on the ground inside the Arctic Circle and on the concrete airport runway in Fort Begging, Georgia. But a full week sleeping on concrete won't cut it. Throw in one embarkation box with around one hundred batteries and I think I'm looking at three wooden pallets fully loaded plus each Marine's combat gear and mountain rucksack weighing in at 65 pounds. It's a lot, but once we insert, we ain't leaving.

Now it might seem odd that American troops are strictly forbidden from interacting with hurt or suffering citizens in situations like these, but keep in mind why ANGLICO would be there: observation, reporting, and relaying critical information. Living in South Florida for so long, I've been through countless hurricanes. Trust me, people freak the hell out. The worst cases are people who have never been through the process. They don't prepare, they act like a real tough guy, but after the storm they have a look of severe shock, muttering, "I had no idea it would be that bad, I was actually scared." No kidding moron; I tried to warn you. I *did* warn you. If these folks spot U.S. troops, they're naturally going to run straight for them, even if it's only to welcome them and thank them for help. However, if I'm calming you down, playing with your seriously cute little kids, and getting hugs from the entire neighborhood, then I can't be sending radio traffic on my 400-watt radio truck, now can I? Exactly.

Sgt. John Taylor was a very senior sergeant with nearly ten years of service from California to Norway, the swamps and crawdads of "Loosiana" to the sub-zero white snow of upstate New York, closer to Canada than Syracuse. Taylor was used to his ANGLICO company breaking itself apart and putting it back together to fit whatever the hell mission the Fourth Marine Division headquarters decided to hand off to us. Ironically, Fourth MarDiv HQ was in New Orleans, which had just been pounded, punched, and flooded by Hurricane Karen. No one was even positive if the HQ was in operation, so we got our orders and just planned on our own as we have always done.

Every team was going in heavy. More ammo, more radios, more Marines, more slash wire, full-size 292 and 2259 antennas, boxes and boxes of MREs that would most likely be shoved out of helicopters by crew chiefs during resupply, every laser we had in the armory, and, most important, entire pallets groaning under the weight of 5-gallon jerry cans full of water. With no need to be on the move, the rooftop OPs would be like World War I artillery spotters with heavy, long-range binoculars mounted on tripods. Made in Germany by Steiner, they could see forever and Taylor marveled at their quality and the fact that someone in Washington actually let HQMC buy such a pricey piece of gear. Everyone knew we might be stuck on top of a skyscraper with no sun protection for a week.

Oh well, it can't be any hotter than South Florida after our hurricanes, Taylor thought. The assembly hall at 4th ANGLICO was full, but very quiet. Each Marine was running scenarios through their fuzzy little heads. Would we take fire? Would I actually have to shoot an American citizen? The rednecks always talk about shooting looters, but it's different when it actually happens. Would the higher-ups forget we're on top of some damn building like the time in Norway when they kept leaving us off flight manifests going back to the States?

Due to the severity of the situation, only the most senior and experienced Marines were assigned to the mission. Officers and staff NCOs had been pushed "upstairs" to the Division level and to lead the SALT teams that would monitor and control the FCT teams stationed atop each building. With so many government agencies involved, we would need Lieutenant Colonel Keith to stand up for us, keep the communications flowing to whoever needed it, and ensure we were looked after.

"ATTENTION ON DECK!" Sergeant Major Mize shouted.

The assembly hall went silent as we all sprang to attention and Keith walked to the front, standing before a large map of New Orleans. Man, this gig is actually going to happen, went through the mind of each Marine.

"We've all seen the news and we all know the situation," Keith started. "Other than the obviously weird fact that some of you will be spending up to seven days on top of a luxury hotel that usually charges four hundred dollars per night, nothing should come up that you haven't been trained for or performed a thousand times. In fact, all of you have been selected for your experience regardless of rank. Johnson over there is the most junior corporal we have, but he's a wiz-bang radio operator if I've ever seen one. We're putting his ass on the tallest building we can find so Washington can't complain about not getting any good scoop on what's happening in the Crescent City. Sergeant Taylor, he's going with you."

"Aye, aye, sir," Taylor responded.

It was great news and a great relief. Johnson was an awesome radio operator who tinkered with radios and field expedient antennas to get maximum range out of each radio. If you ever had to chastise him, it was that he couldn't keep his hands off of them when they were set up correctly. Keith used a white board to list each team, their assignments, and the avalanche of gear we were taking.

Lieutenant Colonel Keith and Sergeant Major Mize would lead the Division Cell (call sign Lightning 11) at Camp Shelby, a Mississippi National Guard base just up Interstate 59, around 100 miles from downtown New Orleans. It was a huge training base that had prepped several units for deployments to Iraq and Afghanistan. Shelby was the perfect location to organize the rescue effort and the right place for an ANGLICO commander. SALT Alpha would be led by Major Fernandez (call sign Lightning 12) and control FCT teams 1, 2, and 3, with call signs Lightning 13, 14, and 15, respectively. SALT Bravo would be led by Major Merrill (call sign Lightning 16) and would run FCT teams 4, 5, and 6, with call signs of Lightning 17, 18, and 19.

Each team was much larger than Taylor had ever seen or heard of. Normally a SALT team was attached to a battalion command and led by a senior captain who was a Marine pilot to coordinate air strikes with the Army or foreign troops. On paper around ten radio operators would man the radios to keep him informed of each FCT team's actions and whereabouts. Taylor always found working at the SALT to be just like the old expression that combat is endless boredom interrupted by five minutes of abject terror. You could pull a midnight shift, struggling to stay awake due to eight hours of zero activity. But as soon as the boss sticks his head in the tent or Humvee for a quick update, all hell breaks loose and you get your ass chewed out for not keeping him "in the loop."

On paper an ANGLICO FCT team was led by a marine captain with a staff sergeant as team chief. Four enlisted Marines were trained as scout/forward observers or field radio operators. Everyone was cross trained to perform everyone else's job, which is why ANGLICO units never have a second thought regarding placing a junior rank to lead an FCT team. After Hurricane Karen one of those Marines was John Taylor.

As he looked at the whiteboard behind Lieutenant Colonel Keith, Taylor was pleased. This detachment was loaded with more talent than he had ever seen. If a Marine was young, he was smart, energetic, and easy to work with and most likely a cop or firefighter "in the World." The older Marines with more rank had been around the block, and the world, dozens of times, with some going back to ground combat in Vietnam. I love it when a plan comes together, as they said on The A Team *television show that Taylor watched as a kid.*

Lieutenant Colonel Keith told us the plan.

Somebody at the Pentagon got smart and sent a fighter reconnaissance plane over New Orleans taking real-time photography at low levels, but also infrared images to show just exactly where the floodwaters were located. As the SALT teams would be set up on the ground on the edges of the city, we needed to be certain of each dry spot. As the world knows now, New Orleans is a shallow fish bowl. With Hurricane Karen moving north and losing her strength over the American Midwest, the floodwaters should stay where they are and not threaten any SALT team location. Regardless, twenty-four-hour shifts and basic security would be just as critical as in combat.

"All right Marines, here we go. 4th ANGLICO's goal is to create a basic radio network that covers the entire city of New Orleans. As you can see on your maps, Armstrong International is only 12 miles as the crow flies to the convention center, which is gaining stranded residents by the hundreds, if not thousands. You FCT team leaders are there to observe, report what you see, relay messages from other ANGLICO teams to higher headquarters, and respond to any request from myself or your SALT commanders. You are not in the business of riot control, shooting at looters or criminals, or air traffic control. Some of you FCT teams will be 50 stories or more in the air. That's 500 feet minimum. It's really nice of you to try and give all of your food to a starving resident, but I can assure you that an MRE dropping to street level from 50 damn stories is going to kill anyone who tries to catch it. You will be frustrated seeing all of the carnage beneath you. But the best thing you can do for these people is to keep higher headquarters informed about what exactly is going on below you. Making accurate and timely reports will allow rescue units to respond to the proper location and not fly around looking for trouble."

It was great to see someone finally got it right. Hell, not even during the Gulf War in 1991 did the Pentagon activate all of 4th ANGLICO. They took one platoon and the rest of us sat around for six months playing "pack your bags, don't pack your bags yet. It drove Taylor nuts and especially hurt his mom.

Not now. Two SALT teams would run three FCT teams each while the rest of the company helped run the Division Cell and stand by to insert when needed. The colonel continued.

"We will all fly on four C-130 aircraft from Marine Air Group 42 directly to Camp Shelby, Mississippi. Sergeant Major Mize and myself will establish the Division Cell and link up with the Louisiana and Mississippi National Guard. Now look at your maps Marines. SALT Alpha will be inserted by two CH-53s at the riverside tip of Algiers Point. Find Jackson Square in the French Quarter, look southeast almost directly across the Mississippi River, and there it is. It's perfect for a SALT. It's a grassy spot about the size of a football field away from rioters or panicky residents, so we won't need to fight off well-meaning people trying to electrocute themselves on our comm gear. A follow-on lift will have the 53s bring in our MRC-138 radio trucks slung load under the bird.

"The Marines of each SALT will be on the first 53 to insert, with the second bird carrying the bulk of the heavy gear and enough provisions for a seven-day mission. Now, for our rooftop observation points. Each location has been approved by Washington and the owners have signed agreements granting rights for observation purposes only, with the U.S. government paying for any damage. I don't need to remind you to leave this place in better shape than when we found it, as that's what we always do anyway. OK.

"Sergeant Taylor's Lightning one-three will be on top of the 63-story Crescent City Resort Hotel just east of the Superdome. It's less than 300 meters from the stadium so you should be able to count people's front teeth with the Steiners we're bringing. Plus, it should provide full view toward the convention center and over the southern part of the city.

"Staff Sergeant Gonzalez's Lightning one-four will be on top of the Louisiana State Supreme Court building right in the French Quarter. The Quarter is an internationally known cultural landmark and Washington is demanding to know of any foolishness going on ASAP. It's right across from K-Paul's famous restaurant, and down the way from Antoine's, but you won't be eating any shrimp etouffee on this trip, boys.

"Lightning one-five led by Gunny Lorenzo will be on top of the Post Building right next to Harrah's Casino. Gunny, you'll have an easy 'eyes on target' of the entire convention center area just as Lightning 13 will be keeping

an eye on the Superdome. For now, everything seems to be calm at the conven-
tion center but there's just a ton of people on site and it could blow up at any
moment. You'll probably want to have two Marines with binoculars staring
right at it at all times. I would suggest two-hour shifts, but it's your team, so
have at it.

"Now, Marines, look to the north shore of the city along Lake Pontchar-
train. See the triangular airport? That's the New Orleans Lakefront Airport
and it's been in operation since the 1930s. Since the recon flight showed some
water buildup in the center of the airport and covering the eastern runways,
Major Merrill's SALT Bravo, Lightning 16, will establish their site, here, east
of the entire airport on the breakwater of the South Shore Harbor Marina.
I'm sure the sailboats and yachts of the marina are scattered about like my
son's Tonka trucks, but that spit of land is 600 meters long and more than
100 meters wide. It's another perfect spot for a SALT team and can monitor
the teams on the north side of the city. SALT Bravo will insert using the same
methods as SALT Alpha.

"The three FCT teams inserting on the southern shore of Lake Pontchar-
train just might end up acting as relay or retransmission sites due to the levee
breaks. The Ninth Ward and the University of New Orleans campus are basi-
cally lakes filled with muddy water. The levees built along the south shore of
Lake Pontchartrain seem to have kept the shoreline, your future observation
posts, dry. But the levees are also keeping the floodwaters in the neighborhoods
just south of the lake. Infrared from the photo recon run is showing some sec-
tions with water as high as 9 feet. As more forces penetrate the city, boat teams
can use our radio network to transmit or relay message traffic back to Camp
Shelby and the command authority. Gunny Duce's Lightning one-seven will
insert at Breakwater Park, another marina with a breakwater three football
fields long and 100 meters wide. Anyone visiting any of the marinas is either
there to gawk at rich people's wrecked boats or rich people checking on their
boats. Either way, they should go about with their sightseeing or planning
their insurance claims, so you should be well away from any crowd problems.

"Captain Macantee's FCT team, Lightning one-nine, will insert on the
west side of the Pontchartrain Causeway at a 200-by-200-meter grassy area
located just in front of the Pontchartrain Center, where they hold conventions
and such. Look along the shoreline all the way west of the city just before where

the marsh line starts. See it? There shouldn't be any floodwaters in these areas as fighter recon has shown the bulk of the floodwaters stopped abruptly at the 17th Street Canal, around 7 miles east of Armstrong International.

"Lightning one-eight led by Captain Martin have been cleared to operate inside the fence line of Armstrong International. This is where the L in ANGLICO comes from folks: liaison. I need to know the operational level of the airport, any mishaps, crashes, fuel spills, crazy people running around on the runways, the types and numbers of military units as they arrive, and for God's sake keep an eye on the Russians when they land their cargo aircraft. This won't be easy for you Marines with Team one-eight. Jet aircraft and helicopters taking off and landing twenty-four hours a day won't be good for your sleep habits, but hey, we all get the assignments we get. Captain Macantee, I expect you to act as a mini-SALT to assist Martin's team with their message traffic. As the airport comes back on line, the number of radio signals, microwave traffic, and radar waves will probably play havoc with one-eight's radios.

"And let me make this perfectly clear to all of you," Lieutenant Colonel Keith intoned. "Every human being has the right of self-defense, especially you and where you're about to go. But the Rules of Engagement (ROE) are very simple for this operation: You are only allowed to defend yourself or prevent a deadly scenario directly in front of you. You're not there to chase, arrest, or shoot looters. Your job is to tell us so we can send the cops to do it for you. Any questions? Good. Now, let's get back to preparing our gear."

This is but one fictional scenario, and I'm sure my old ANGLICO buddies would have a field day tearing it apart and showing me every little fault with my genius plan. But remember back to the weeks after Hurricane Katrina when *zero* information was getting either in or out of New Orleans. The steps outlined in this chapter would have been far superior to anything that happened in 2005, and yes, my fellow Marines and I could accomplish this very handily. Of course, more FCT teams would be fed into the city as the ground situation improved due to heavier units arriving with more capable communications systems. But two of these six teams would be in a great position to observe two of the worst areas after Katrina: the Superdome and the Convention Center. This isn't to knock the other services at all. The Navy Seabees are great no matter what they do. The Air Force has Combat Control Teams (CCT), some of the most highly trained troops in the military who the American public also knows nothing about. CCT teams are fully qualified to jump in with Army Rangers, Recon, Delta, or a SEAL team and set up a temporary airstrip. Furthermore, they are all fully certified FAA air traffic controllers. I thought of CCT often after Katrina struck the mainland. ANGLICO could have laid a radio net over the city, and CCT could have brought in their mobile radar sets to set up shop at Armstrong International and the Lakefront Airport. If either airport had serious damage to their runways, the Seabees or U.S. Air Force Red Horse Squadrons could repair them in short order. Plus, look at your favorite satellite mapping service online and check out the northwest corner of the Superdome complex. See that giant H painted on the ground? That's an 80-by-80-foot helicopter landing pad that has been run by the City of New Orleans since the late 1990s. Place a CCT trooper right there to control military traffic and more aid could have gotten to those suffering people. Of course, if you plan correctly, they could talk to us in an emergency. Other than the loss of life and property, the other great tragedy of Hurricane Katrina was how much aid the U.S. military could have provided with existing units.

Now, for all of you skeptics out there, I can hear you complaining already.

"But Scott, these things are just not that simple. Trust me, I'm a lawyer. I know these things."

Well, actually counselor, you don't. We've had fifteen years since September 11th to plan, arrange, coordinate, and rehearse this scenario. Yes, the federal government would need to reach out to perhaps a dozen owners of high-rise office buildings, hotels, resorts, and government buildings, and yes, it would probably take a few years to sign a deal. I made up the names of the buildings in the New Orleans scenario, except for the one public building, the courthouse. But go online and look at satellite maps of New Orleans and you can see for yourself the high number of buildings that could be used by troops to keep an eye on the city and relay critical data to Camp Shelby, Baton Rouge, the Pentagon, and even the White House. Very high buildings sit right next to the Superdome and the Convention Center, and if you also research a flood map of the disaster, you'll easily see that both areas were bone dry, just like the French Quarter. In other words a quick report the day after Hurricane Katrina struck would have alerted the authorities to this fact and a helicopter-based rescue effort could have been started. The technology and troops have been in place for decades, and I served with one such unit for a dozen years.

Now being a political science major and huge fan of the U.S. Constitution, the greatest government document ever written, I can assure civil libertarians, the American Civil Liberties Union (ACLU), and various anti-government types or conspiracy nuts, that this plan would in no way threaten American liberties. The Posse Comitatus Act of 1878, which strictly prohibits federal troops from being used as law enforcement personnel, doesn't apply. While ANGLICO Marines are without question federal troops, who are they going to arrest from the top of a 50-story skyscraper? They won't be intruding on any Americans, because everything they observe will be in full public view and we've never had any spy tech or eavesdropping capability anyway. Also, information on the locations of potential observation points, helicopter ports, or city parks is all in the public domain anyway. A simple web search would suffice, especially for aviation as pilots need up-to-date data for flight operations. Local police and the Louisiana National Guard, as long as the Guard is under state (the governor's) command and control, will be making any necessary arrests.

For all of you conspiracy lovers out there who are going to scream "Government takeover!" or "Bill Clinton caused Pearl Harbor!," fewer than two hundred Marines are not going to be able to take over a flooded city still occupied by tens of thousands of shell-shocked citizens. One week on station, observe, send radio traffic as needed, and then go home. There is no threat to civil liberties here. Besides, after all the fightin' and fussin' over government use of troops during the Katrina rescue operation, eventually nearly fifty thousand troops were deployed throughout the entire Gulf region from Pascagoula, Mississippi, west to Baton Rouge. (And no, I didn't vote for Clinton, but I know he didn't cause Pearl Harbor either. Let's focus a bit folks.)

The fictional start to this chapter about using an FCT team in downtown Miami is a bit more true to life than you think. I won't mention the current name of the building as I don't know the folks who own it now, but up until around 1987 the Centrust Building was a shining beacon in Miami. Built with three receding sections, the building would be lit with white light that shined straight up into the night sky. Boat captains sailing in from the Bahamas actually used it as a lighthouse for navigation. During the Christmas holidays it would shine with red and green plus huge ornaments to celebrate the season. Then the boss of the Centrust Bank was charged with nearly seventy counts of fraud and various other criminal acts. Well, it ain't called the Centrust Building any more as you can imagine.

But a beautiful building it remains. It's still right in the middle of the city. Best of all it still has a helicopter landing pad right on the roof. See where I'm going? Even if the heliport is no longer in use, a chopper could hover in the open space and Marines could fast rope to the rooftop. A fast rope is a 4-inch-thick rope that is just like the old sliding poles in firehouses. With practice you can place twenty-five, combat-loaded Marines on the ground, a ship at sail, or a rooftop in less than three minutes. Plus, the pad would be a perfect spot for resupply missions. I can only imagine the incredible view of Biscayne Bay, the Miami skyline, cruise ship row, Star Island, and South Beach across the water. However, my FCT team could report on everything we see and send an instant message to higher headquarters. We held communications exercises for *years* practicing this exact type of mission. Granted we wouldn't be calling in F-18 Hornets to bomb selected targets in the city (I am a Dolphin fan after all), but we could direct medevac or supply missions to the right areas.

Many political, civic, and business leaders have never served a second in the military and are flat-out ignorant of the U.S. military's capabilities. They failed New Orleans after Hurricane Katrina, and that was nearly fifteen years after Hurricane Andrew, and they botched the response to that storm too. This is the same crowd responsible for the 2008 economic collapse and two Middle Eastern wars with no end in sight.

Lawyers can't do it. MBAs can't do it. The U.S. military can.

CHAPTER NINETEEN

One Mission of Many

DURING THE SUMMER OF 2012, 4TH ANGLICO MARINES SET UP their targeting equipment, radios, and of course weapons on top of an unknown rocky hill overlooking one of the hundreds of nondescript villages located throughout the Iraqi and Afghan combat zones. This is one of my favorite methods of employing any Marine ANGLICO team. If a Marine ANGLICO FCT team is not going out on its own or tagging along next to a company commander from the Army or a foreign unit, one of the best ways to use them is to place them on overwatch. While an infantry platoon or company or some type of Special Operations team hits a designated target with a very specific objective such as capturing a single individual or even rescuing hostages or captured prisoners of war, ANGLICO has your back covered the entire time.

In a sense it's an old mission with new high-tech gear that I never envisioned when I served from 1987 to 1999. Most Americans don't know how many different nations sent combat troops or some type of material aid during our combat time in Iraq and Afghanistan. The former Soviet territory and now independent nation of Georgia sent ground troops who served with Marine ANGLICO under combat conditions, and even tiny El Salvador sent some of its Special Forces to help out. After Great Britain and Canada, perhaps America's most long-term and staunch ally is Australia. Going back to the dark days after Pearl Harbor, Australia has stood and fought with America, including the Vietnam War as they saw the communist expansion as a direct threat to their way of life and future. Plus, Aussie troops are tough as hell, operate very well, and love to drink, cuss, and have fun just like us Yanks.

Jumpmaster, JTAC, and four-combat tour veteran S/Sgt. Teddy Pernal told me about how Australian Special Forces were busy searching for various "high-value targets," in Pentagon speak, individuals who were still on the run from Saddam Hussein's murderous reign, high-ranking Al Qaeda terrorists, or sometimes just newly created criminals taking advantage of the chaos of any war zone. Just like Delta and Task Force 160 dragging Hussein out of his rat hole in Iraq, Special Forces of many nations friendly to America were also searching for suspects all over the two combat zones. Pernal said a portion of Marine ANGLICO was detailed to support the Aussie Special Forces on a regular basis, which is when this particular summertime 2012 mission came down from higher headquarters.

"They would find these high-priority targets and helo insert behind some mountain. ANGLICO would go with some snipers and Recon, Aussie Special Forces and set up on a mountaintop throughout the night," Pernal told me in the West Palm Beach Reserve conference room three years later. "In the morning the Aussie assault force would helo into the village and take over the village."

This is a method of insertion that seeks to surprise an enemy force by landing troops anywhere from 3 to 6 kilometers from a target so the enemy can't hear the helicopters. As loud as modern military helicopters are, their sound signatures fade rather quickly, especially with hills, valleys, and particularly mountains between your attacking force and the enemy. (In an earlier chapter this is why my FCT team and the 101st Airborne scouts were moving 6 kilometers in front of the friendly lines.)

Pernal explained that the ANGLICO FCT team, snipers, and Recon bubbas would set up on a hilltop throughout the night. At dawn, or just before daybreak as I would prefer, the Aussie Special Forces team would use helicopters to assault directly into the village on their hunt for their assigned high-value target. Pernal said that these types of mission weren't the dedicated "kill mission" so often portrayed in the media, especially since the death of Osama bin Laden. In my own words, not Pernal's, if you can capture a guy for extensive interrogation, that's great, but if he puts up a fight, then he's going to get put down. After all, it's not like any high-value target is going to be wandering around in the desert or the local shopping mall all by themselves.

"A lot of these guys are surrounded by guards and you take fire as soon as you land," Pernal related. "Most of the helo inserts, the helicopters were being shot at with RPGs, small arms fire, machine gun fire, so they'd make contact before they would even land. They'd get off the helicopter shooting."

Any type of assault force from any nation on any mission would be glad and thankful to have a team covering their backs while also occupying the high ground.

"I'd say the most success I've had with foreign nations is old-school rock drills. I've literally taken flat stones and put them on the ground and said, 'This is me, this is you.' I then explain how I want things to happen or how it'll fit in with what they want to happen. Nine times out of ten that wins them over. I'm not saying it's elementary, because sometimes you're sitting down with full-bird colonels from other countries. They like to see that because they get a visual concept that defeats the language barrier. If you put me on the ground with you, I'll get you some 'bang.' But if you put us in the sky somewhere, it will be a lot better for us."

One photograph in this book shows a reclining Pernal studying reconnaissance photographs held down with stones. While this might be a simple map study for his own team, over the decades thousands of ANGLICO Marines have performed this ritual for foreign commanders, and as Pernal already stated, it usually works like a charm. Also in the photograph is one of my favorite pieces of gear: the air panel. As I wrote in the Marine Speak chapter, American units have used air panels since World War II to identify themselves as "friendlies" to overhead attacking aircraft. Basically it means bomb the other guy and not me.

"The ANGLICO name carries a lot of weight in the air community. The ground guys still don't know what we do," Pernal said. "They get used to our call signs very quickly. They see our call sign come across and they know 'hey, this guy means business.'"

These photographs of one of the countless missions run by Special Operations units throughout Iraq and Afghanistan are excellent examples of how to use an ANGLICO FCT team. Laid out among the rocky boul-ders of a nameless hilltop, Marines are operating laser range finders in case CAS is needed, another is on a SATCOM radio to communicate with the rear or higher headquarters, and someone gets stuck schlepping the portable UAV (unmanned aerial vehicle or drone) that can be assembled on-site and thrown into the air by hand. This particular model is called a Puma, and its onboard cameras and sensors are effective for looking over a ridge line to see and attack enemy forces; however, it is louder than the newer models of UAVs. Pernal said that while a Puma can make a bit more noise, you just have to know how to use it, such as tracking a moving target in a pickup truck and the driver can hear the UAV over the sound of the traveling vehicle. And with modern weaponry it's a done deal: If I can see you, I can hit you. If I can hit you, I can kill you. I'm sure it's got to be a pain in the ass to carry a small airplane around in your backpack in the Afghan mountains, but to have the capability to control your own little bird and peek over the next ridge line is something I never envisioned the entire time I was in the Marine Corps.

But the real point of this small chapter on one of the countless mis-sions against high-priority targets is to show what Marine ANGLICO really excels at. Foreign units and U.S. Army infantry companies need to understand that a Marine ANGLICO FCT team is a well-integrated, multiple-threat team that has been trained in calling in air strikes, naval gunfire, mortars, artillery, and even AC-130 Spectre gunships plus year after year of endless communications exercises. In other words we're not here to walk on point for your infantrymen. We're not here as an extra working party to clean out your latrines that you should have taken care of two days ago anyway. Also, while any group of Marines will never hesitate to pull the trigger when necessary, an FCT team is not an extra squad for you to maneuver around the enemy unless it's an emergency. We're here to help, but how we help is by bringing in a hailstorm of American-made steel upon the enemy. And we can't do that if you don't know what we do.

Personally if I was on this mission, and possibly the photographs don't show the entire layout of this emplacement overlooking the small Afghan village, as a team chief I would have my best Marines prepared to call in artillery or CAS aircraft, and one Marine monitoring the command radio network for coordination. Obviously each Marine would have his own radio, which is why ANGLICO carries around so much gear and the heavy and hated batteries that accompany our lives no matter where we go. Whichever group was going to assault the village in the valley below, their mission priority and tactics would obviously have to take precedence. However, for a raid of any type, I would place the target directly in front of me at the twelve o'clock position or on a compass at 0 degrees. I would then coordinate with the assaulting commander to establish set boundaries to my right and my left that he and his troops were simply not allowed to cross. This could be that the assault force needs to stay within the range from ten o'clock on the left to two o'clock on the right (or on a compass this might be from 310 degrees on the left to 50 degrees on the right). This would be part of my own personal dog-and-pony show detailing what Marine ANGLICO does and proving to the raid force commander that anything or anyone outside of those parameters would be quickly wiped out if they are identified as hostile targets.

This is what communication and coordination is all about, and it is a constant process in the military. If a raid force has successfully captured their prisoner and his bodyguards are starting to make a run for it, since my team is on an elevated position with very powerful German-made Steiner binoculars, we can send the radio operator an urgent message about "ten to fifteen enemy fighters armed with AK-47s and RPGs escaping to the West." With so many civilians in the area in any section of Iraq or Afghanistan, we're not just going to call in jet aircraft and bomb the living hell out of everything until we have a positive ID on who's trying to escape. Needless to say a group of men running like hell in the right direction carrying automatic weapons and rocket-propelled grenades is not going to be too hard to spot for me and my team. This is one of my favorite uses of a Marine ANGLICO team, as the raid force commander can concentrate on his assigned mission and not have to pursue any enemy, and can start his extraction from the area with his new prisoner.

I know for a combat story this little chapter is a little sparse on details, cool military jargon, or even the exact location. However, this is part of the bread and butter of what Marine ANGLICO does, and far from being an exceptional story, it is a completely normal example of what we are capable of getting done. Over the course of writing this book, I mentioned to plenty of ANGLICO Marines my fictional chapter about Hurricane Karen and how our company alone, 4th ANGLICO, could easily have placed a radio network over the entire city of New Orleans after Hurricane Katrina or even Miami after Hurricane Andrew. In every case each Marine quickly agreed, as if I was making the most obvious statement in the world, and to this day they, and I, are still confused why Washington, D.C., did not let us help in Dade County or the Big Easy.

The next chapter will show in great detail what only four U.S. Marines and coordinated airpower can really do.

CHAPTER TWENTY

We're Coming to Get
Lightning Two-Two

AMERICAN MILITARY HISTORY HAS PLENTY OF EXAMPLES OF INDIVIDUAL troops fighting and surviving against impossible odds that are frequently made into books and Hollywood movies. Sgt. Alvin York shot more than one hundred German soldiers in World War I, earning his Medal of Honor, and is still regarded as a hero a century after that terrible war. World War II, due to its global reach and six-year duration, had plenty of heroic deeds that defied the odds. In the European Theater infantry lieutenant Audie Murphy sent his surviving platoon members to the rear while he held off roughly two hundred Nazi troops with machine-gun fire and calling in artillery shells. In the Pacific War, during the early dark days of the American campaign in the Solomon Islands, fighter pilot and Navy hero Butch O'Hare shot down seven Japanese planes in one engagement, which is why the Chicago airport bears his name to this day. Marine fighter pilots such as Jeffrey Leblanc and Carl Smith flew stubby Grumman F4F Wildcats and shot down five enemy planes or more during one mission to earn their Medals of Honor. On the island of Guadalcanal infantry Marines such as Manila John Basilone fought off hundreds of assaulting Japanese soldiers singlehandedly.

During my time with 4th ANGLICO, the closest I came to witnessing this type of effort and dedication involved the week-long saga of my friend Chip Hanke's FCT team on Operation Battle Griffin in 1996. Assigned to support a Norwegian infantry company, Hanke and his teammates, my old friends Joe Macantee, who would go on to earn a Purple Heart in Iraq, and Jose Jimenez, were given the radio call sign of "Lightning 22." They proceeded to break nearly every rule of CAS, blew the living crap out of every opposing force that came near them by controlling literally hundreds of air strikes in only three days, and earned a fearsome reputation that reached all the way to the Norwegian Royal Palace and the ears of King Carl Gustaf. In fact, just before the end of "the war" in Norway, fed up Dutch Marines sent around two hundred troops up the mountain that Lightning 22 was positioned on. That's two hundred troops versus four U.S. Marines.

Now *that* is being a pain in the ass, my friends.

During our nearly two-year training cycle to prepare for our deployment to Operation Battle Griffin in 1996, after attending Mountain Warfare School in the snow and huge redwoods of the Sierra Nevada in California, 1st Platoon under the command of Major Fernandez traveled to Fort Drum, New York, about an hour outside of the basketball-crazed town of Syracuse. As I've written before, our instructors for this final exercise that everybody needed to pass satisfactorily in order to get their ticket punched to go to Norway were the expert Arctic warfare teachers from the 25th Marines.

For an entire week hundreds of Marines from around the country jammed into the Fort Drum base movie theater, an old-school venue complete with wooden stage and giant screen to show movies to troops and their families on the weekends. The instructors from the 25th Marines along with exchange officers from the British Royal Marines and the Dutch Marines taught us everything they knew about how to survive and fight in temperatures that were not supposed to rise above freezing even during the warmest part of the day. One Dutch Marine went over every piece of clothing and boots that we had been issued prior to arriving at Fort Drum. It might sound odd that someone's job in the military is to be an expert on clothing, but the Gore-Tex clothing system that the U.S. military issues its troops is nothing short of miraculous if you're serving on the ground.

Even for a studly Marine like Chip Hanke who had operated in the field for years, including being decorated in combat for his actions during the Gulf War, Fort Drum wasn't going to be a happy adventure for one very specific reason. This would be the first time that Chip had ever seen snow. It didn't help that the area went through one of its worst storms in years while we were out in the field. Chip is his usual blunt self when describing his feelings about Fort Drum.

"I hated the cold," he said flatly.

The final test of our training that each Marine had to successfully make it through in order to make the magic carpet ride to Norway, and of course hang out with all those nice Norwegian girls underneath the neon-glowing cloud formations of the aurora borealis, was simply called survival night. And it means just that. The instructors were going to take our tents and stows away from us, and we had to use all of the techniques, tricks, and tactics that we had been covering for nearly three weeks and be alive the next morning. At this point it's pretty cut and dried: If you quit, you failed and didn't get to meet any Norwegian women. If you are alive and well with all your fingers and toes, then get ready to have the time of your life marveling at the fjords and breathtaking mountains covered with miles of pine trees that all seem to reach a hundred feet into the sky.

For the millionth time during my stretch with 4th ANGLICO, we broke apart our detachment in preparation for survival night. Major Fernandez wisely took a quick inventory of who was the most experienced in extreme cold weather environments and placed them in charge of each little survival hot team regardless of what their actual rank was. For example, a lieutenant and staff sergeant who had served on the West Coast and spent years training in the desert and deploying to Panama, undergoing jungle training and making deployments to the islands of the Western Pacific, would have to set aside their rank and pride and let a sergeant or even possibly a corporal with three or four cold-weather deployments run the ship just for this night. It was a great testament to the Marines of 4th ANGLICO, and one of the reasons I stayed for twelve years straight: Not one high-ranking Marine even batted an eyelash at this instant field reorganization. While Chip Hanke had only seen snow for the first time fewer than three weeks prior to his first winter survival night, he was widely experienced and respected, and a decorated combat veteran. In fact, his tent team had two or three lance corporals with even less winter training than he did, so he was the one in charge.

I can't remember what type of survival structure Hanke built. There are a lot of different types of survival shelters that you can build in case you find yourself stuck out in the wilderness during an emergency. One type of very effective shelter is a simple lean-to with the opening facing a small fence constructed of wooden sticks with a fire placed in between the lean-to and the little wall. The small fence made of sticks is designed to reflect the heat of the fire back into the lean-to. For some reason people lost in the woods always try to build a little survival hut that looks like a pup tent. It's not too hard to understand why a pup tent shape works fine for millions of little American boys and girls camping out with the Boy Scouts and Girl Scouts or even just spending a cool fall night out in the backyard at Grandma and Grandpa's house. The problem, and you can see it time and again on these so-called reality television shows that put people out in the wilderness and expect them to survive a week with a pocketknife, a sheet of plastic, and a bag of marshmallows, is that every time someone tries to make one of these pup tent structures made out of wood and underbrush, they are simply too big for long-term survival.

To survive in the cold, your body needs to generate its own heat, whether internally through the digestion of food or drinking hot wets as discussed earlier, or externally through a heat source such as indoor heating or an outdoor fire. Two immediate problems with the pup tent–style structures are (1) they don't have an opening in the roof that allows you to build a tiny fire inside the structure and (2) they always have too much empty space because people are too concerned with comfort; and without a heat source all that space will quickly cool to the same temperature outside of your survival hut and make you miserable or possibly even kill you. On the survival night in Fort Drum, one of the Marines listening to his Walkman while hanging out in his sleeping bag said a radio station in Syracuse was reporting the temperature was going to drop to 25 degrees below zero. We were a full hour north of Syracuse and out in the field far away from the steam-driven heat of any old American military base. It was probably a full 10 degrees colder where we were located as we watched a couple of five-ton trucks cart off our tents and cooking stoves. One of the tent teams was very busy building this huge survival shelter that would accommodate someone 6 feet tall standing up in the middle of it. As the night wore on and the temperature started to drop dramatically, Major Fernandez could clearly see that they wouldn't have time to finish and there was no way they were going to be able to keep the large structure warm. He directly ordered them to select another type of survival hut. By that time it wasn't a hard choice as nearly everybody else was done and snuggly tucked into their sleeping bags while this team was still under construction.

I was with my good buddy Jim Carty and Major Fernandez, who selected a small, low-to-the-ground triangle structure to build based on his multiple trips to Mountain Warfare School in California. When I mean small, I mean small. Each side of the three-sided little hooch was the exact length of each Marine after they zipped up inside their sleeping bag. We placed our packs and gear outside of the structure and laid our M-16s next to us, and placed chocolate bars, bread, and mix for late-night hot wets inside of our sleeping bags. In the center of this triangle was another small triangle, where we built a very small fire that we were going to take turns stoking with small twigs for the entire night to keep us warm. This is why you don't want a structure that's too tall, because you're simply wasting energy heating the peak of a pup tent when you are lying on the cold ground. The triangle hooch that Major Fernandez built was so low to the ground that when I was arranging all my gear and my sleeping bag, when I tried to work on my hands and knees, I couldn't fully extend my arms because the logs of our roof were tightly pressed against my back. It was small, it was tight, and we had a small fire to keep us warm. But just like everything in extreme cold weather, you have to keep your head and stay awake when it's your turn on fire watch to keep the home fires burning. And let me tell you, if you think it's easy to conduct Marine Corps training all day long, build your own survival hut when you know it's going to be 25 degrees below zero, and then lie horizontal inside of a sleeping bag at three o'clock in the morning without falling asleep, you are a clinically delusional human being who needs to spend some time with Dr. Melfi from *The Sopranos*.

Chip Hanke and his little band of Arctic warriors had built a good enough survival hooch to where they could have a fire of their own for warmth, but that didn't make them feel any better. One key to a survival night fire that Major Fernandez taught Carty and myself was to build a small fire and feed it with small sticks one by one, much like the American Indian tribes would do. I have a feeling that Hanke ran out of fuel and started to have doubts whether he would make it through the night without jumping in the warming tent, which would disqualify him for the trip to Norway. One of the Arctic instructors warned Hanke and his team about staying out in the field for the entire night.

"I had a huge fire. I was so miserably cold. I don't care dude. Don't pass me! I'll go sit in the desert," Hanke told the instructor.

Well Hanke and his team did manage to struggle through our survival night to see the dawn of a new day, although one of his Marines stayed up the entire night relocating from one fire to another to keep himself warm. We razzed this Marine pretty hard for not going to sleep, but he didn't care as he had survived the cold, hadn't he? However, the Arctic instructors were rather pissed off at him, as the point of the entire survival night was to employ what you learned and prove you could get some sleep time in such a harsh situation. I'm proud of the fact that I had started the night in my sleeping bag with only the bottoms of my polypropylene long underwear on my body and then put on my top and ate some food with a hot wet when it was my turn to wake up and man the fire watch of our little fire that could. For someone who had lived in Palm Beach County for so long, I was turning into a very competent Arctic warrior.

Fourteen months later all of us were 150 miles inside the Arctic Circle. Even on a peacetime exercise we would have to employ everything the Marine Corps had taught us about mountain warfare plus living and fighting in extreme cold weather.

While I ended up driving around in the communications Humvee that Gunny Henry and I used to try to kill a Norwegian moose with, Hanke's team embarked on a saga that's still a little hard for me to believe, even though I was on the same operation. It started out with the same old ANGLICO song and dance, teaching an infantry company commander about what Marine ANGLICO does and how effective we can be. For Battle Griffin that would mainly be CAS provided by American jet fighters and helicopter gunships. There were plenty of artillery batteries in the area, but with the typical Norwegian mountain running anywhere from a 25- to 45-degree angle, artillery shells couldn't reach the back side of a mountain if enemy troops were placed there. Aircraft obviously could attack them from any angle, and since the Norwegian Air Force wasn't too fond of supporting the ground troops, American airpower actually served Norwegian ground troops more so than their own countrymen.

Even though I've had limited contact with Hanke since I got out of 4th ANGLICO, when I interviewed him for this book, he instantly began talking about the same topics that every other ANGLICO Marine has faced for decades. For Hanke's unit, call sign Lightning Two-Two, Battle Griffin '96 began with a decided whimper instead of a very loud bang from the sound of incoming F-18 Hornets or a Cobra gunship. CAS missions are controlled and assigned to an area of operations by the direct air support center or DASC, who was known on this operation by his radio call sign of "Chieftain." Well, apparently Chieftain was either a former Recon Marine or merely someone who was enraptured with their hardcore reputation. Now I've known hundreds if not thousands of Recon Marines, and they're all great. However, while CAS is one of the many tasks that Recon is capable of performing, it's not central to what they do. For example, Recon Marines are trained to insert behind enemy lines, patrol to a road intersection, and use a very specialized piece of gear that measures and tests the composition of a dirt road and how much of a weight can be carried by that road whether by military truck, light armor, or heavy tanks. For example, during the Gulf War, if central command wanted to know if the Iraqi army could send some of their tanks to a certain area, Recon was inserted and measured the weight-bearing capacity of that road. They then sent a report stating whether a modern 50-ton battle tank could traverse the area. Consequently, the general could determine precisely where to place his own heavy tanks to combat an enemy force and not spread his forces too thin.

So the Recon-loving Chieftain was sending virtually all available air assets to Recon's area of operations and not providing any aircraft at all for Hanke and his Lightning 22 buddies. This went on for days. I can't even imagine the frustration of going through the motions of explaining the ANGLICO mission to a foreign officer who accepts what you tell him, only to sit there for two or three days not being able to help the units you were tasked with supporting. But even a Marine with Hanke's depth of experience couldn't have imagined just how bad it was about to get.

"I remember the Norwegian commander saying, 'I need air assets now,'" Hanke remembered. "The man in charge was pissed. Then he stopped feeding us and stopped giving us gas."

I've heard a lot of crazy stories about dealing with the Army and foreign troops, so many that there's no way they would fit into one book. But I was stunned when Hanke told me that someone stopped giving them food and fuel due to a situation that was beyond their control. ANGLICO Marines consider it normal to be left behind or forgotten after a military exercise; it's just part of what our crazy little life includes. However, having a host unit cut off your food was a shocker. The Norwegian infantry company commander simply abandoned Lightning 22. So instead of using all of our high-speed radio and digital communications gear, or applying our years of training in independent operations and jumping out of planes, Lightning 22 was reduced to huddling in the back of a combat vehicle and actually started rationing their food to survive. Hell, even at Fort Drum during survival night, none of us were short of food. Even the multiple times I trained with the Army at JRTC, I knew I would be so busy that I could only afford the time to eat one MRE per day, but that didn't mean I wasn't being issued my rations. I received all of my MREs; I just couldn't get to them.

While they were rationing food and trying to stay warm, the Marines of Lightning 22 grew increasingly frustrated as they watched entire flights of F-18 Hornets bypass their position on their way to attack targets somewhere else in the battle zone. They were emplaced on the front side of a snow- and ice-covered mountain and received no small amount of attention from the opposing force made up of Dutch Marines and German army units that were training outside of German soil for the first time since World War II. The opposing forces were scouting their position and harassing the Norwegian infantry units as they rode snow-mobiles up the side of the mountain. One night while every member of Lightning 22 was clustered in the back of their vehicle hungry, cold, and seriously pissed off at the general situation, a soldier of the opposing force abruptly opened up the rear door and demanded that they surrender. Macantee quickly and expertly grabbed the barrel of the soldier's rifle so he couldn't point it at any member of Lightning 22. Hanke and his teammates were in such a rotten mood that they refused to surrender; they also even refused to fight and just told the guy to piss off. Which amazingly, he did.

"We almost beat his ass," Hanke remembered years later.

The Marines of Lightning 22 were out of patience and out of gas, lit-erally. After the second and third day of being ignored by the Norwegians and watching Marine Corps F-18 Hornets fly over their position time after time, Joe Macantee looked up and proposed a very radical solution.

"We can call them," Mac said.

"I know," Hanke replied.

Macantee pressed the issue and was even more direct. "We can get on the guard net and grab them," Mac said.

What Macantee was suggesting was abandoning the entire Marine Corps procedure for calling in CAS missions. These were strict procedures that we practiced in training thousands of times each year and performed live at Camp Lejeune or the Avon Park bombing range in central Florida on the west side of Lake Okeechobee. On any military radio the "guard net" was the network of frequencies that were monitored in case someone was having an extreme, usually life-threatening emergency. The guard net was "in the clear," which meant that the radio message wouldn't be encrypted or scrambled and anyone listening to the frequency, including the enemy, could hear everything that you were saying. Hanke was reluc-tant at first, but he was just as fed up as the rest of the team including the team leader, a former enlisted Marine who had risen through the ranks to become a major. When Hanke asked his team chief about the possibility of getting into so much trouble that it might ruin all of their careers, the usu-ally extremely friendly and easygoing major had a quick and curt response.

"Screw that shit! I ain't getting into trouble," he said to Lightning 22.

And with that quick piece of Marine leadership, Lightning 22 basically went off the reservation.

Hanke picked up the handset of a PRC-110 UHF radio and began the ridiculous task of transmitting over an open frequency in an attempt to reroute military aircraft to change their attack runs. This is not supposed to be possible. And by not possible I mean as in two plus two is not supposed to equal anything but four.

"Multiple targets in area! Do you want to play?" Hanke yelled over the guard net.

Hanke made radio call after radio call. Hey you! We're here! We have targets! All for you! No dice. Section after section of F-18 Hornets flew by, most likely to support the Recon Marines that Chieftain was madly in love with. Hanke made more transmissions until he thought he would go crazy. Just think of the situation that the Marines of Lightning 22 were in. You've spent years in an organization that eats, breathes, and even sleeps over its commitment to duty, country, helping your fellow Marines, and doing the dirty work no one else has the desire or guts to do. Don't think I'm joking: If you leave for the day and don't empty the small, green, government-issue trash can *and* you can't even replace the paper-thin plastic trash bag, then you're screwing over your fellow Marine. This is no exaggeration. You will be roundly rebuked by your section chief or platoon sergeant for letting your brothers and sisters down. With that being said, how would you like to stand on the side of a frozen mountain 150 miles inside the Arctic Circle watching thirty-million-dollar attack aircraft fly overhead time and time again? Hanke was beside himself with anger and frustration, but he kept yelling over the open guard net. Lo and behold, it worked.

"All of a sudden, one F-18 banked and came back," Hanke said.

It was Hammer 11.

And he was ready to play.

This is not supposed to be possible. There are prearranged code words to have CAS missions aborted and rerouted to other targets. In World War II both the Nazis and Japanese employed thousands of decoy tactics, even including repairing and repainting captured B-17 Flying Fortresses that would join formations and open fire on them. It became so frequent that toward the end of World War II, American bomber crews would open fire with their .50-caliber machine guns on any plane that tried to join their formation.

But something in Chip Hanke's radio transmissions got to the F-18 pilot with the call sign Hammer 11. Maybe it was the desperation, the tone of Chip's voice, or that the voice was so "American" that Hammer 11 decided to take a quick look. He was flying almost 500 knots after all, so it wouldn't take much time to turn around and recon an area as long as he stayed safe. Before sending any requests for CAS, Hanke needed the pilot to trust him.

"Just do a flyby and tell me what you see," Hanke told Hammer 11.

"Lightning 22, they're all over," Hammer responded.

"Clear our perimeter and then take our targets," Hanke told him.

Hammer 11 and his wingman quickly declared "bingo" on the radio, meaning they were getting low on fuel and needed to return to base. The Norwegians were starting to have faith in Marine ANGLICO and American airpower after Hammer 11 took out some immediate threats. Then in yet another act of "The Eternal Sales Job," Hanke asked Hammer 11 if he would do a flyby for the Norwegians. We frequently asked for flybys or a "Kodak pass" during training, and if they have enough fuel, pilots are usually thrilled to comply with a high-speed pass lower than anything you would see at a Super Bowl or the Indy 500. Hammer 11 apparently took Hanke's request as a personal challenge and screamed in low from east to west just above the ground.

"He must have been 100 feet off the deck," Hanke said, still marveling at the sight more than fifteen years later.

Hammer 11's wingman, always referred to in CAS terms as "Dash 2," also accepted the challenge and opted to beat out his flight leader. He even gave the Marines of Lightning 22 a little heads up over the radio net.

"Hey Lightning 22! Look behind you!" Dash 2 shouted.

Hanke, Jimenez, and Macantee spotted the second F-18 far below them as he sped off the water of the fjord and started to climb up to their position.

"He was literally just hugging the side of the mountain. I was staring right at him. I could see his face mask," Hanke said.

Dash 2 stood his F-18 Hornet on its tail and took off to rejoin Hammer 11, who had some reassuring words after days of frustration for Lightning 22.

"Stay warm boys. We'll be back," Hammer 11 radioed.

And came they did. First it was more Marine Corps F-18s. Then the British flew in with their Harrier jump jets, which can drop a bomb inside of an office trash can when flown by the right pilot. Then Marine Corps Super Cobras came in, which is when Hanke performed his human body method of marking the target that I wrote about previously. Afterward, Hanke told me he felt bad and unprofessional for telling the Cobra pilot that he was the one "wearing faggy purple glasses," but the heat of battle is a real phenomenon even during peacetime.

"He just looked at me and shook his head," Hanke told me.

Hell, it's my favorite story about Chip. Plus it worked, so who cares what a snotty pilot thinks? Go hit the damn target!

During the next three days, Lightning 22 selected and called in an astounding six hundred CAS missions and basically stopped the entire exercise in its tracks in the immediate area of their position. But after three days of doing nothing and then three straight days of calling in more air strikes than I've ever heard throughout my entire career in the Marine Corps, Lightning 22 simply burned out and decided to return to the rear area for a little bit of rest, but mainly to resupply with fuel, water, and food. As they were looking forward to getting back to the rear to warm up, a pilot made one more earsplitting flyby directly over their heads.

"You could hear our teeth chattering over the radio," Hanke said. "He was so low he almost popped our eardrums. He almost hit our 10-foot whip antenna."

After their completely improvised and unauthorized grab of supersonic jet fighters out of the sky to attack opposing force positions, Hanke and Lightning 22 were sure they were in trouble. However, they quickly learned they were actually gaining a bit of a rock star reputation for the incredible job they had done. U.S. Marines and staff officers began coming up to them to find out if they were the team that was almost single-handedly kicking the crap out of the opposing force.

"People came up to us and asked 'are you Lightning 22?,'" Hanke said.

"Maaaybe," was Hanke's suspicious answer.

They quickly found out that not only were they not in trouble, everyone was thrilled with their behavior, and in fact, the king of Norway had already been scheduled to land by helicopter near their position and give them a personal royal thank-you.

"It was like a fun day at an amusement park," Hanke said.

After being shunned and literally cut off by the Norwegian infantry company commander when they couldn't get any air assets, now the Norwegian soldiers were thrilled with Lightning 22, showering them with compliments and even presents. The Norwegians gave the Marines of Lightning 22 locally made liquor, the much-coveted field knives used by Norwegian troops, and even animal skins covered with thick fur. It was a complete turnaround. Always being fully aware of how Marine ANGLICO troops literally had to advertise what their capabilities were, Hanke told me that every time Lightning 22 called in a CAS mission, they asked the pilots for a quick flyby not only to impress the Norwegians, but mainly to impress upon them ANGLICO's full capabilities.

However, Operation Battle Griffin '96 was not over. Lightning 22 was promptly refitted and refueled and sent back up to the same ice-covered mountain to work their special brand of CAS magic for the rest of the operation. Lightning 22 found a good position on the front side of the mountain that offered a beautiful view of the valley and the jet black waters of the fjord below them. Things were calm until night fell, when something truly amazing happened, something I have difficulty believing that any military would do except for the fact that my old friend Chip Hanke told the story to me. In the dark, and during a military force-on-force operation, the opposing forces ran a convoy with the lights blazing in the dark along a road on the valley floor. How anybody could do this even in a peacetime operation is something I can't comprehend. Behaving like this in front of a Marine ANGLICO FCT team is nothing short of suicidal. If the opposing Dutch Marines were really tired of playing war, then the Marines of Lightning 22 were going to happily put them out of their misery.

Lightning 22 wiped out the entire convoy. Since it was a peacetime exercise complete with umpires and referees deciding who's alive and who's dead, the convoy was required to sit out of the game for several hours to force their commanders to deal with the loss and of course their incredible stupidity. While this might sound silly to people in the civilian world, during training with thousands of troops out in the field trying to practice and learn, if a unit gets destroyed, you can't just send them home. Just like at JRTC in Fort Polk, Louisiana, it takes a ton of money, time, and effort to get troops to the training areas in the first place, and they simply need to get a vigorous workout. However, this particular convoy yet again displayed both their lack of military discipline and their extreme suicidal tendencies by hitting the road again, with their lights on, again.

"So we wiped them out again," Hanke remembered. "It was like we were untouchable. It was back-to-back-to-back air [strikes] until midnight."

With the Norwegian infantry soldiers completely on board with Lightning 22 and thoroughly enjoying the aerial acrobatics of the best the U.S. military could provide, Norwegian soldiers basically stopped fighting and came out of their bunkers and combat vehicles to simply watch the show that was right in front of them.

"It was like a grandstand behind us," Hanke said. "Everyone just knew us. They knew our call sign. I thought 'this is weird dude,' it's like we were hunted."

In another questionable move by the opposing forces, they launched boats across the fjord in attempts to get to the other side and assault up the mountain where their host infantry unit was located. Hanke said the pilots arriving on station had a field day with the easily spotted small boats on the fjord and proceeded to destroy the attacking force. F-18 Hornets were attacking so low that the ground effects of the aircraft and the jet engines were clearly visible.

"You could see the water turning because they were so low. They were in heaven," Hanke said.

One pilot who really enjoyed his workday and earned his paycheck was Lightning 22's old friend and original supporter, the indomitable Hammer 11.

"Hammer 11 was always a wild guy. Dash 2 would always take off after hitting a target. This guy [Hammer 11] would stay and do aerobatics to show the Norwegians," Hanke said.

On the final day of the exercise, the opposing forces had had enough of Lightning 22 and sent two infantry companies, roughly two hundred soldiers according to Hanke, to take out the Marines. Hanke said the peak of the mountain behind them was too rough for a rear assault, and a flanking maneuver the opposing forces tried was broken up just as every other action within eyesight of Lightning 22. Battle Griffin '96 finally came to an end, but before Lightning 22 came off the mountain, a pristine white helicopter landed near their position and out stepped the king of Norway. Hanke said that obviously the Norwegians were all crapping in their pants with their head of state appearing out of the sky. Though Americans typically see royal families from other nations as mere puppets or figureheads that have no power, almost all the Norwegian citizens I spoke to were in favor of their monarchy and liked their present king and queen, although they weren't too keen on some of the royal children who were more interested in having a good time than affairs of state. What most Americans don't understand is that while an elected prime minister is the head of government, the head of state is actually whoever is the sitting monarch at the time. In 1996 it was King Carl Gustaf, and even he was told about the incredible job of a little group of U.S. Marines with the call sign of Lightning 22. Hanke said the Norwegian king was friendly and walked down the line shaking hands with troops from many nations who had performed so well preparing to help defend his nation and countrymen.

"He said, 'you guys did an awesome job.' It was an honor, but it was an honor to show what Marine ANGLICO can do," Hanke said.

Finally done with their job of calling in hundreds of air strikes during Battle Griffin, the Lightning 22 team chief Major Vorpe took his Marines into town for some serious R&R, and while enjoying some fine Norwegian Pilsner beer in a local pub, another Marine called out to a warrant officer who was drinking in the same bar. It was Chieftain, the guy who had sent virtually all available CAS to Recon's area of operations and stiffed Lightning 22 for three or four days. Hanke used his characteristic blunt nature to confront the Marine Corps warrant officer, who outranked him by several pay grades.

"No offense, sir, but you treated us like shit," Hanke told him. "His face just dropped."

Major Vorpe cussed Chieftain out and left him sitting by himself. Lightning 22 never did get a full explanation of why they had such a difficult time requesting any closer support and were forced to hijack passing aircraft by hailing them on the radio. Chieftain's unprofessional behavior notwithstanding, after serving time in three separate combat zones, Hanke's service with Lightning 22 is always going to stay with him, and is a great example of what Marine ANGLICO is capable of if properly supported. It's also a perfect example of how ANGLICO resorts to simply making things up to get the job done.

After not speaking with him for a long time, it was great to learn that Chip Hanke was the same old jarhead I served with for so many years. I asked him how many ribbons he'd been awarded for all of his service. Though he served in Iraq early in the war (a tour he left for only two days after the birth of his son), Hanke told me that he never got his campaign medals for his combat service in that theater. He started ticking off all of the combat tours, peacetime operations, and even drug interdiction missions throughout the Caribbean area during the 1990s. In an age of excessive ego and twenty-four-hour media coverage, Chip Hanke is the kind of guy who wasn't even positive how many ribbons he had: an incredibly tough guy with a successful military career, but humble nonetheless. But he had no doubt about the numbers regarding the truly astounding exploits of Lightning 22 during Operation Battle Griffin '96: six hundred missions in three and a half days. It was simply astounding, and that's how you get introduced to the king.

"It all turned out great. It was one of the highlights of my time in the Marine Corps," Hanke said.

CHAPTER TWENTY-ONE

The ANGLICO Marine Who Never Was

PEOPLE LIKE TO ASK FRANK CANADA ABOUT FEAR.

Namely, was he scared while he was in combat during the first Gulf War that began after Saddam Hussein invaded and occupied Kuwait? Like many combat veterans, Canada tells people that there is always so much activity preparing in training for combat that you don't have time to think or worry about being scared. Even during peacetime there is so much activity out in the field, but if you have any time off for anything, you usually grab something to eat and find the nearest secluded spot where you can grab some shut-eye, because you don't know when you might get the chance again. For Canada any apprehension or fear disappeared after the first round being fired out of the 25mm chain gun he was operating from a U.S. Army Bradley Fighting Vehicle.

"I don't know what it is, but after that first round I never heard another explosion again," he told me.

By chance when I spoke to Canada on the phone from his home in central Florida, it was exactly twenty-five years to the day since Hussein invaded Kuwait. Canada had joined the Marine Corps in 1978 and served as an infantryman before being assigned to the prestigious Marine barracks at 8th and I in Washington, D.C., which is the home of the commandant of the Marine Corps, the official battle colors of the Marine Corps, the famous Silent Drill Team, and even the official bulldog mascot, who is always named "Chesty" after the most decorated Marine of all time, Lewis "Chesty" Puller. Canada was initially assigned to the headquarters company performing security background checks for

Marines who were due to be assigned to either the White House, the State Department, or HMX-1, the helicopter squadron that flew the president and his family via helicopter from place to place. Being a highly motivated individual, Canada approached the Marine in charge of the companies that marched during official state ceremonies and asked if he could join the marching platoons. I've been to 8th and I and the two hundred or so Marines who perform in parades are almost uniform in height. Canada is 5'8", so he wasn't considered for the marching platoons when he first reached his new post. However, he was a Marine in good standing and was accepted, although he was placed all the way in the back row due to his height. One of the highlights of his time in the Marine Corps was when Canada had just joined the marching company and took part in President Reagan's inauguration in 1981. It isn't too hard to show his friends where he was located in a photograph of the event. "Whenever I see the picture I look at the rear of the column and I can find out exactly where I am," he said with a laugh.

Short jokes aside, Frank Canada is one of the few Americans who has marched in a presidential inauguration. Ten years later, instead of the glitz and glamour of Washington, D.C., in full celebration, Canada found himself staring at a beat-up secondhand Bradley Fighting Vehicle that his team (Firepower Control Team 10) had been given so they could keep up with the scouts of the 2nd Armored Division for the attack on the Iraqi army. Canada had joined 4th ANGLICO about the same time I did in 1987 and gone to Jump School and Naval Gunfire School; however, he oddly wasn't sent to Artillery School and had to learn it from other Marines at our unit in West Palm Beach.

From August 2, 1990, through the entire fall, the days were vivid and sharp as our unit prepared for war. Rumors were flying around like seagulls at the beach, and we struggled to find out which ones were true. We were all struggling with school, jobs, family, and our own personal feelings about what we all considered to be an impending major battle in the desert that would most likely include some type of chemical warfare. I was almost constantly on the road as I was working for a small traffic engineering firm, driving all over Florida measuring traffic volumes and parking data. After one trip I stopped by my mom's house for a visit or possibly a Sunday dinner, and she promptly told me that 4th ANGLICO had called. I immediately knew why: They were looking for volunteers for combat. In one of the more dramatic and emotional moments in my life, I called back to learn from then GySgt. Mike Walsh that in fact 4th ANGLICO was looking for volunteers first before they simply started assigning people. I made this phone call with my mother standing right next to me. My mom could read my face and tell exactly what was going on. Walsh told me that we were preparing to fight entire Iraqi armored divisions in strict Soviet-style battle formations. It would be a big fight, but we had little doubt that we would blow the living shit out of a system we had trained for years to defeat.

I took some time to think about it and mull it over, and eventually I did toss my camouflaged hat in the ring to go to the Gulf as did most of my Marine buddies—because that's just what Marines do. We volunteer when others don't want to do. The leadership of 4th ANGLICO convened a meeting and ran through the entire roster of Marines who met two criteria: Each Marine had to have attended a formal MOS school such as Naval Gunfire School, Scout/Forward Observer School for artillery, or Communication School to be a field radio operator. Plus, each chosen Marine had to have attended Airborne School, as no one knew what our assignments in the Gulf could be. We could easily be assigned to either the 82nd or 101st Airborne Divisions, or some general in the Army after learning about all of our capabilities would simply make a snap decision to parachute us somewhere out in the middle of nowhere to monitor Iraqi movements. Looking back on the Gulf War, it would not have been such a bad assignment to use most ANGLICO teams for just that purpose. If we're far enough down in Indian country, basically anything we saw would be the bad guys and we could destroy them; and if things got too hot, you could have just extracted us by helicopter. Piece of cake. Canada said he fully expected to be assigned to the 82nd Airborne and possibly even parachute directly into Baghdad for the fight of his life.

After initially being assigned to a British armored division, FCT 10 was finally assigned to the scouts of the 2nd Armored Division, a group of soldiers Canada grew to have an enormous amount of respect for because of how well they took care of Canada and his teammates. However, the armored soldiers who had spent years training in 60-ton M-1 Abrams main battle tanks and 25-ton Bradley Fighting Vehicles that fired TOW (tube launched, optically sited, wire guided) antitank missiles and 25mm cannons weren't impressed with the canvas-covered Humvees that FCT 10 drove up in. "You can't have Humvees out here!" the astonished tankers told them, more than slightly alarmed.

"We don't have any tanks. We're ANGLICO," Frank responded.

"We'll find you one," came the answer.

Canada and his teammates assumed the Army would most likely produce an older model armored personnel carrier such as the Vietnam War–era M-113, which resembled a giant metal shoebox on metal tracks. Canada also assumed that the Army would help a brother out and provide a qualified school-trained driver for the personnel carrier. He was wrong on both counts. The tanker boys from the 2nd Armored Division had indeed scoured the entire division and found the most beat-up, broken-down Bradley they could, which obviously no one else wanted to ride into battle. Of course this was the one assigned to the newly attached Marines. Canada couldn't believe his eyes. Even the Marines who had never trained with a Bradley Fighting Vehicle could tell this particular vehicle was a junkyard dog. While ANGLICO Marines are completely accustomed to being flung into new situations where they have to find new ways to get the job done, this was a different situation entirely. Canada said that the Army sent its Bradley gunners to a school that lasts for months, yet he was being asked to learn how to operate the vehicle in a matter of weeks before jumping off into combat. Kenny von Heel, the former Recon Marine who almost buckled my knees when he hit me during my gold wing ceremony, was given the task of being the driver for this 25-ton monster that he had never even sat in before. FCT 10 started taking dawn-to-dusk classes reading Army field manuals and being instructed by other soldiers of the U.S. Army as they all got ready to cross the sand berm into Iraq. The more they learned about their Bradley, the more Canada, von Heel, and their teammates discovered all of the equipment that their very own special Bradley was missing. It was now even more obvious that their Bradley was the black sheep of the entire 2nd Armored Division. Fortunately, two things happened. One, the ANGLICO Marines of FCT 10 remembered the time-honored tradition of the U.S. Marines stealing things from the U.S. Army. Two, they learned the whereabouts of the division motor pool, which was loaded with vehicles of all sorts being repaired or maintained. In the shifting sands of the Saudi Arabian desert, the midnight supply depot was open for business. "We would steal gun sights, everything," Canada remembered.

After several nocturnal visits to the 2nd Armored Division's motor pool, Canada and his teammates were feeling pretty good about their Bradley Fighting Vehicle. After all, they didn't have much choice, and they were doing the best they could to get ready to ride along with the division's scouts to fix and locate the Iraqi armored forces. Right about this time a Humvee rolled up to their position with a sign fixed to the front window of the vehicle with the words "God Squad" written on it. The Humvee was driven by two chaplains in the U.S. Army, and they were moving around the area tending to their fuzzy-headed flock of soldiers and now a random group of Marines. Canada greeted the two chaplains and asked the obvious question, if one of them could bless their vehicle for the trials and tribulations in their future. The chaplains had obviously spent quite some time around U.S. armored divisions as they took one look at FCT 10's armored steed and made a very quick decision.

"Son, this Bradley is in such bad shape it doesn't need a blessing, it needs an exorcism," the chaplain told Canada.

Thanks for the heartwarming vote of confidence, Padre. In yet another on-the-fly innovation for FCT 10, since Canada was a firefighter and paramedic in the civilian world, someone waved their magic wand and made him the team's designated medical person, though that job is usually given to a U.S. Navy corpsman. In an amazing coincidence for those who know their military history, when Canada and another actual Navy corpsman went to their battalion's medical aid station to gather medicines and medical supplies for combat wounds, he quickly noticed the unique name of the Asian-American U.S. Army major. The major's last name was Yamamoto, and he spelled it the exact same way as the famous Japanese admiral who planned and led the attack on Pearl Harbor on December 7, 1941. Canada, being a history buff like most U.S. Marines, minded his manners and observed proper military respect, but also politely asked the good major if he was related. As it turns out, the major was Admiral Yamamoto's grandson, and had quite the good sense of humor about it.

"It's okay, I'm on your side now," Major Yamamoto said with a smile.

It couldn't get much stranger for the Marines of FCT 10. They're about to drive and fight in an armored vehicle that was loaded with stolen parts, they had yet to perform any of their normal ANGLICO mission, and now their medical supplies had been issued to them by a man connected to one of the most significant dates in American history.

The 2nd Armored Division's scouts were in a formation of six Bradley Fighting Vehicles, and FCT 10 would be a seventh vehicle moving along to call in any needed air strikes or artillery, or so Canada and his teammates thought. While their Bradley was fully loaded and capable of firing its machine guns and 25mm gun, they were still focused on their traditional ANGLICO mission of supporting the U.S. Army or foreign troops with Navy and Marine Corps assets.

"It wasn't our intent to engage anyone. We were just preparing to shoot for safety [to defend themselves]," Canada said.

Well as anyone who's ever served in any military around the world knows, what really rules the day is Murphy's Law. Whatever can go wrong, will go wrong at the worst possible moment. For FCT 10 that meant that as soon as the scouts were preparing to jump off and go search for Iraqi tank formations, one of the scout's Bradleys promptly broke down and Team 10 was quickly brought up to serve as the scout platoon leader's wingman, as Bradleys fight in pairs much like jet fighters do.

While ANGLICO Marines are very familiar with the culture and some of the rhythms of how the U.S. Army operates, outside of the small Marine Corps tank battalions, we are hardly experts at tank warfare or how to deploy them properly, as our main job is to destroy them when on the enemy's side. As the ground war started, Canada told me that the scouts he and Team 10 were attached to were roughly fifteen minutes driving time in front of the main line of M1 battle tanks. Canada marveled at the site of the Bradley vehicles, including his own, charging across the desert just like the cavalry back in the Wild West or in a John Wayne movie. The scouts quickly found the Iraqis and blew past them just as quick. "The scouts went in first and were taking fire from behind," Canada said.

The scouts disengaged and returned to the main battle line so the M1 main battle tanks could take over the fight and severely maul any Iraqi units they came across. Discussing his lack of recognition of gunfire and explosions after firing the first rounds of his life, Canada still marvels that he climbed out of his Bradley and sat next to the turret as the M1 battle tanks destroyed the Iraqi tanks one by one like in a war movie. Back on the move again, it was time for some serious engagement with the enemy after Canada's only weeks-long crash course on being a gunner for a Bradley Fighting Vehicle. Canada said at the time, a normal load of ammunition for a 25mm gun was three hundred rounds with 230 rounds of high-explosive shells and seventy armor-piercing rounds. Army intelligence working with Special Operations teams and Recon teams that had penetrated Iraq before the ground war started had learned just how much armor they were facing. Therefore the ratio was reversed with 230 rounds of armor-piercing shells and seventy high-explosive shells. This would serve Canada and his teammates very well when they opened fire on enemy personnel carriers. The high number of armor-piercing shells would penetrate the armor of the Soviet-made vehicles, and the ensuing high-explosive rounds would detonate inside the vehicle destroying it and killing the crew.

After virtually no training on how to operate or fire a 25mm gun, Canada performed so well that the U.S. Army nominated him for a Bronze Star with a combat V for valor device that was eventually approved by HQMC. After his gunnery crash course, Canada destroyed two BTR-70 armored personnel carriers, an older-model T 55 main battle tank, one solitary Iraqi soldier, and the unfortunate crew of idiots who were completely convinced they could run an American blockade of armored vehicles by riding through it in a Chevrolet. Yes, you read that correctly. Chevy versus Bradley. This is a contest that will always end badly for you. Canada's army scout compadres had taught him a weak spot on the BTRs: the seam where the small turret meets the body of the armored vehicle. However, this required a shot from the side. A shot on the front wouldn't penetrate the BTR's armor as frontal armor is always the heaviest and strongest. Canada eventually figured out that his rounds were hitting the target, as the armor-piercing rounds were indeed slicing through the weak spot and disappearing inside the vehicle, whereas when the steel tips or high-explosive rounds hit, he could see them ricochet off the side of the BTR. "In most cases it would stop, start to smoke and then erupt in a fireball," Canada said.

FCT 10 also had their share of close calls. The original laser designating device the Marine Corps had brought was the very large and cumbersome MULE that I've discussed in this book already. It had a huge carrying case with it and reportedly cost a quarter of a million dollars. It was a pain in the ass to carry around whether in its casing or not. Canada said they had to strap the entire apparatus on the outside of the Bradley, because the confines of any armored personnel carrier are just too small. Needless to say, the MULE was riddled by Iraqi machine-gun fire and declared a combat loss. Another time a tank round, fired from somewhere friendly or otherwise, passed so close over the top of Canada's Bradley that the incredible velocity of the cannon round sucked dirt off the floor of the Bradley out of the top of the open hatch. That should give you an idea of just how powerful modern weaponry actually is.

Near the end of hostilities, two of Canada's Marines dismounted their Bradley and ran out front to search and neutralize a small bunker complex. They quickly went out of sight and were gone too long, so Canada was sent out to find them. Running along the sand with his M-16, to his shock, anger, and most likely horror, Canada discovered that the ammunition magazine had fallen out. Since he shifted to wearing the standard tanker's jumpsuit (which looks just like a flight suit), he wasn't wearing his normal deuce gear, meaning he had no ammunition except for one solitary round chambered in his M-16. There he was: in the middle of the war of his generation loaded with exactly one bullet like Barney Fife in the old *Andy Griffith Show*. After twenty-five years and a career as a firefighter, Canada can joke about the crazed situation he was in.

"I decided I would shoot exactly one guy or be the one Marine who surrendered," he told me with a laugh.

Canada finished out the remainder of the very short ground war capturing and collecting Iraqi prisoners of war. Canada couldn't help but wonder how effective the Allied blockade efforts or air attacks on supply columns had been as every Iraqi he came across was wearing brand new camouflage uniforms and smoking fresh packs of cigarettes. Canada would receive another commendation, a Marine Corps Meritorious Mast, for teaming up with a Navy corpsman to perform medical triage on twenty-two wounded or starving Iraqi prisoners of war. As far as all the high-speed, low-drag ANGLICO, airborne-all-the-way, bad-ass stuff that he was trained for?

"We did nothing with the ANGLICO thing," he flatly said.

But he still ended up with a Bronze Star.

In one final crazy act of Frank Canada's wartime experience, one day's mail call brought a pleasant and pretty message from home. Canada said mail was very slow getting to the desert, usually around six weeks late. Throughout the Gulf War ordinary Americans were encouraged to send mail to our troops in the desert. Troops in the Gulf were given literally tons of mail from school kids and every kind of perfect stranger. During one mail call the designated mailman said one letter contained a picture of a girl. Even though Marines share everything with each other, including secrets we don't tell anyone else, Canada promptly pulled rank as the senior sergeant and took possession of said letter. The photograph showed a pretty blonde girl from Florida wearing a nice sweater and holding a can of beer. Canada had his priorities straight.

"To be honest, all I could think of was how great it would be to have a nice cold beer right now," he said.

Well, Canada didn't get his beer, but he did get a new pen pal in the name of one Suzanne Elizabeth Birch. They wrote to each other for the rest of the conflict. They wrote each other when Canada returned home to central Florida. Letters led to phone calls. Phone calls led to more phone calls. More phone calls led to a first date, then more dates, and they've been married for twenty-two years. If people ask who first introduced them, Canada has a quick answer:

"That's easy. I tell them Saddam Hussein did!" he said with a laugh.

And that might be the most ANGLICO story of them all.